62

D0848812

HAMMETT: A LIFE AT THE EDGE

BY WILLIAM F. NOLAN

BIOGRAPHIES

JOHN FITCH: ADVENTURE ON WHEELS (1959)
BARNEY OLDFIELD (1961)
PHIL HILL: YANKEE CHAMPION (1962)
JOHN HUSTON: KING REBEL (1965)

CRITICAL/BIBLIOGRAPHICAL STUDIES

DASHIELL HAMMETT: A CASEBOOK (1969)
HEMINGWAY: LAST DAYS OF THE LION (1974)
THE RAY BRADBURY COMPANION (1975)

COLLECTED PROFILES

MEN OF THUNDER (1964)
SINNERS AND SUPERMEN (1965)
CARNIVAL OF SPEED (1973)

NOVELS

LOGAN'S RUN (1967)
LOGAN'S WORLD (1977)
LOGAN'S SEARCH (1980)

HAMMETT
A LIFE AT THE EDGE

BY

WILLIAM F. NOLAN

CONGDON & WEED, INC.
NEW YORK

Copyright © 1983 by William F. Nolan

Library of Congress Cataloging in Publication Data

Nolan, William F., 1928–
Hammett: a life at the edge.

Bibliography: p.
Includes index.
1. Hammett, Dashiell, 1894–1961—Biography.
2. Novelists, American—20th century—Biography.
I. Title.
PS3515.A4347Z794 1983 813'.52 [B] 83-1798
ISBN 0-86553-081-5
ISBN 0-312-92281-7 (St. Martin's Press)

Published by Congdon & Weed, Inc.
298 Fifth Avenue, New York, N.Y. 10001

Distributed by St. Martin's Press
175 Fifth Avenue, New York, N.Y. 10010

Published simultaneously in Canada by Thomas Nelson & Sons Limited
81 Curlew Drive, Don Mills, Ontario M3A 2R1

A list of photo credits appears on page 266.

All Rights Reserved
Printed in the United States of America by The Haddon Craftsmen
Designed by Irving Perkins
First Edition

To the memory of my friend
and co-founder of
the Dashiell Hammett Society of San Francisco,
M. J. "Jack" KAPLAN—
a good man
and
a tough Pinkerton

He lived life at the edge, because he saw himself as a man who possessed no future. . . . Hammett had no expectation of being alive much beyond Thursday.

—NUNNALLY JOHNSON

CONTENTS

x

PREFACE

Samuel Dashiell Hammett, the internationally famous author of *The Maltese Falcon,* was a zealously private man, and during his lifetime very little was publicly revealed about him. At his death, in 1961, he was still being described as "the mystery man of mystery fiction."

The enigma persists, despite a remarkable renaissance of interest in Hammett's life and works. His classic novels and stories are continually reprinted in a wide variety of editions around the world, and the man himself has become a popularized myth-figure in novels and films, on television and in published memoirs. Yet the question continues to arise from this mirror-maze of images: who was the real Dashiell Hammett? Was he the tortured alcoholic of the film *Julia,* as portrayed by Jason Robards? Was he the tough, avenging writer-turned-detective of the Joe Gores novel *Hammett* and of the movie that Francis Ford Coppola made of it? Was he the burned-out, ravaged Marxist intellectual revealed in Lillian Hellman's trio of best-selling memoirs, *An Unfinished Woman, Pentimento,* and *Scoundrel Time*? Was he the patient, world-weary manhunter, deftly played by James Coburn in the television miniseries "The Dain Curse"? Was he the stalwart, implacable upholder of the Writer's Code, as presented in the KQED documentary "The Case of Dashiell Hammett"?

Richard Layman's extremely valuable 1981 biography, *Shadow Man,* was a scholarly compilation of data, especially regarding Hammett's career. My approach is far more personal. I have attempted to bring Hammett, the man as well as the writer, out of the shadows, to render him in full dimension for the reader. Through his letters, interviews, memoirs, and public statements, and through the memories of those who knew him best, Hammett speaks often and at length in these pages.

This biography is backed by fifteen years of research, dating from early 1967, when I began gathering material for my study *Dashiell Hammett: A Casebook* (published in 1969). That modest volume, slim in size and content, was the first book-length treatment of Hammett and his work. Although it contained biographical elements, it was primarily bibliographical. Its purpose was to serve as a basic reference on Hammett's writings. I was gratified by the book's critical reception—and by the Edgar Allan Poe Special Award it won in 1970 from the Mystery Writers of America. It was meant to be a starting point in Hammett research, and it achieved its aim. As critic Philip Durham stated: "Writers who take up the fascinating life and letters of Dashiell Hammett will have to begin with this book."

Some did. *Casebook* happily inspired further Hammett research, particularly by William Godshalk, Joe Gores, David Fechheimer, Hugh Eames, Peter Wolfe, and Richard Layman. Together they unearthed a great deal of important new material.

But I was not satisfied with my book. I had not told the complex life story of the man himself. I kept gathering material, talking to those who had known Hammett, updating my files, following leads, issuing new checklists to supplement the data from *Casebook*, writing magazine and newspaper articles on Hammett, learning more about him each year.

In 1976 I spoke on Dashiell Hammett's film career at the Hammett Conference, sponsored by the University of California at Berkeley. In 1977 I was a guide for the Hammett Walk through San Francisco to locations significant in his life and his writing. And, in October of that same year, at a dinner in the Maltese Falcon Room of John's Grill on Ellis Street, the

late Jack Kaplan and I founded the Dashiell Hammett Society
of San Francisco.

The more I learned, the more vividly I realized that Hammett was a man of startling contrasts and contradictions. Gentle and patient with the callow young soldiers he served with
during the Second World War, he could be abrupt and savagely cutting with literary bores and other pretentious people. A restless romantic (one Los Angeles columnist called
him a "Hollywood Dream Prince") with a strong sexual drive,
he pursued countless women, yet was serious with two: his
wife, Josephine, and his longtime companion, lover, and
friend, Lillian Hellman. (An interview with the late Mrs. Hammett is reflected in this book.)

Dash Hammett cut a striking figure: tall, sword-slim in a
dark, double-breasted suit, wearing a soft roll-brim felt hat,
shoes shined to a high gloss, display handkerchief folded
casually into an upper coat pocket. One is struck by the intense, arresting eyes, the trim mustache, the patrician nose,
the gray-white, deeply waved hair, the lean-fingered gambler's hands, the aura of confidence and resolve, of elegance
and style. Hammett retained his striking appearance into late
middle age—but in the closing years of his life his face reflected sadness, frustration, and, finally, a sick and lasting
exhaustion.

Moving in the theatrical circles of Hollywood and New
York, he was a hard-drinking, inveterate partygoer, yet he
remained essentially aloof, retaining his fierce sense of inde-
pendence. Few of his gaudy "show biz" companions knew
much about the real man with whom they reveled.

During most of his life Hammett rebelled against what he
felt was a corrupt political system in America, yet he volunteered for service in both world wars. His firm integrity led,
finally, to a federal prison sentence in 1951, which he served
as resolutely as he had served his three-year stint in the storm-
blasted Aleutians during World War II.

Hammett's code of honor was deep and steadfast; when he
gave his word, he kept it. Throughout his roller-coaster life

of wealth and poverty, of immense highs and desperate lows, he played no one's game but his own.

Here, then, is the man himself, in all his contradictions— from his birth in Maryland in 1894 to his death in New York in 1961. Beyond myth and legend, revealed in his faults and virtues, his successes and his failures, here is the man behind the black mask.

Here is Samuel Dashiell Hammett.

William F. Nolan

HAMMETT: A LIFE AT THE EDGE

1

THE BEGINNING OF THE HUNT

*Being shot at . . . is one thing you never get to
like.*

—HAMMETT

EARLY IN 1934, at the height of his career, with his fifth novel, *The Thin Man,* newly published, Dashiell Hammett was asked by a reporter for the secret of his success.

Hammett shrugged. "I was a detective," he replied, "so I wrote about detectives. Everything came from that."

Although he was an avid reader of mystery stories as a boy, having discovered the joys of the West Lexington Library in Baltimore at an early age, there is no evidence that Hammett ever dreamed of becoming a professional detective. Police work did not run in his blood.

The Hammetts established themselves in southern Maryland, on the banks of the Patuxent River, in the beginning of the nineteenth century. Dashiell Hammett's great-grandfather, Samuel B. Hammett, operated a two-story log trading post which also functioned as a post office. The store prospered and, by 1827, a 200-acre farm had been added to the family holdings. The area was then known as Hammettville.

Dashiell Hammett's father, Richard Thomas Hammett, was born there in 1860. The store was later sold, but the farm, with its three-story white frame farmhouse, was retained. Assembled in part with wooden pegs, the house was something of a local curiosity. In 1892 Richard took his new bride, Annie Bond, to live there, and within four years they had three

3

children. Their first child was a girl, Aronica Rebecca, called Reba. Samuel Dashiell came next, and then another son, Richard Thomas Jr.

Hammett wrote of his birth in a brief autobiographical sketch for *Black Mask* in 1924. "I was born in Maryland, St. Mary's County, between the Potomac and Patuxent rivers, on May 27, 1894," he stated. "Our family background was Scottish and French. The family name on my mother's side was originally 'De Chiell' with the accent on the second syllable."

Hammett's mother was proud of her French ancestors and looked down on the Hammetts. She was an upright, aloof woman, so dignified that some in the family referred to her as "Lady." She spoke contemptuously of what she called "male carousing," and had no patience whatever with the drinking habits of the Hammett men. Her health was precarious, and she fought intermittent bouts with tuberculosis, the disease that Hammett would inherit and combat for a large part of his life. She felt closer to Samuel than to her other children, and he received her warmest attention. In one thing they stood opposed. Baptized a Roman Catholic, Hammett disliked religion and seldom attended mass. Many years later, Lillian Hellman called him "a bitter ex-Catholic."

Young Samuel, however ("I was always Sam or Samuel. Nobody called me Dashiell or Dash until I began to write"), did not get along well with his father, who served as the local justice of the peace and was rigid and severe. In researching this period of Hammett's life, novelist Joe Gores found that Samuel *did* enjoy duck hunting with his father in the salt marsh country along Chesapeake Bay. Young Samuel used a "four-ten single shot," which was almost too big for the boy.

When Samuel was six, the family was disrupted. Although he had long been a Democrat, Richard Hammett decided that he might have a better chance at running for state office if he sought Republican financial support. It was an unwise decision. The town's reaction to his sudden switch was hostile. As one local resident remembered the incident: "A lot of people got riled up over it. They ran him out of the county more or less on a rail." Branded a turncoat, Richard Hammett sold the farm and moved the family to Philadelphia. Richard's political duplicity shamed young Samuel, widening the gap between father and son.

Money became scarce for the Hammetts in Philadelphia, and young Hammett, at seven, borrowed a bicycle from a neighborhood boy and managed to earn a few pennies each afternoon with his own paper route. The family was soon uprooted again in a second move, to Baltimore in 1901, where the elder Hammett found work as a clerk. They settled into a middle-class three-story red brick house at 212 North Stricker Street.

As the family maverick, young Samuel grew up tall and bony and stubbornly independent. At ten, unable to afford cigarettes, he and an older pal resorted to stealing them. ("We'd swipe Old Mills, because they were stronger than Piedmonts, and then we'd hide out in the basement to smoke them.") When Hammett's father found out about the thefts, he became enraged and threatened to send the boy to an orphan asylum unless he mended his "wild ways." Hammett's brother, Richard, was in much stronger fatherly favor, and the two boys almost never got along; even as adults, there was always tension between them. But he was fond of Reba, his sister, and he maintained this affection over the years, never losing touch with her.

Despite an outer show of piety, with church attendance each Sunday, Richard Thomas Hammett was a brazen and ceaseless womanizer. A big man, at six-three, weighing 200 pounds, with snow-white hair, he wore his clothes with flair and could turn on the charm. His pursuit of women occasioned bitter family quarrels. Young Samuel considered his father a hypocrite and always sided with his mother during these shouted confrontations.

A Baltimore neighbor and boyhood pal of Hammett's, Fred Worden, recalled that young Hammett was "a fiend for books . . . he introduced me to the pleasant business of reading books borrowed from the Pratt Library branch then at

Hollins and Calhoun streets. Sam and I favored swashbuck-
lers and mysteries." Hammett's mother respected intelligence, and she bragged about the number of library books
Samuel read each week. This obsession with books, however,
presented a problem. Samuel would often read all night, and
when his mother came in to call him for school in the morning, it was almost impossible to wake him. Thus he was often
tardy, and began to have trouble at school. In 1908 his father
became ill and could no longer work. Samuel, then fourteen,
left the Baltimore Polytechnic Institute to take a job as messenger for the Baltimore and Ohio Railroad. His formal
schooling had ended. Now he would learn from life itself.

Many of the lessons were harsh ones. Over the next seven
years, into his young manhood, Hammett got a knockabout
education as a freight clerk, a stevedore, a timekeeper in a
machine shop, a yardman, a cannery worker, a junior clerk in
an advertising agency, and as a nail-machine operator in a box
factory. "I was an unsatisfactory and unsatisfied employee,"
he wrote in *Black Mask*, "constantly moving from one job to
another. Usually, I was fired."

He was easily bored by routine, and refused to conform. He
recalled one job for which he arrived late each day for a week.
Finally, his angry employer told him he was through. Seeing
the logic in this, Hammett had no objection. On his way out,
he was stopped by the employer. "Give me your word it won't
happen again, and I'll let you stay." Hammett smiled and
shook his head. No, he couldn't give his word; he would not
lie to keep a job. And he walked.

At twenty, in 1914, already emulating his father in the pursuit of women, Hammett contracted gonorrhea. And in this
same period he was also, as he later put it, "discovering the
joys of a bottle." Sex and hard drinking, along with his passion for reading, were permanent addictions.

During 1915 Hammett obtained work with a firm of Baltimore brokers, Poe & Davies, adding up stock market transac-
tions from a ticker tape. "I had a lot of trouble with figures,"

he wrote later, "and could seldom get the same total twice."
Again he was fired.

Checking the help-wanted columns in the local papers, he
encountered an enigmatic ad that drew his attention: it failed
to specify the type of job involved. Applicants must have
"wide work experience" and be free to travel. Travel where?
For *what*? Intrigued, Hammett responded to the ad—and
found himself at the Baltimore offices of Pinkerton's National
Detective Agency.* The agency, it turned out, often hired
men with "variegated" backgrounds, and the fact that Hammett's career had been so erratic actually counted in his favor
with them. They wanted young men, they said, who could
respond to all situations.

The agency always referred to its detectives as "operatives"; its founder, Allan Pinkerton, felt that the term reflected the no-nonsense aspects of the job. Pinkerton disliked
the term "private eye," although it was derived directly from
his agency trademark, a drawing of a wide-awake eye, accompanied by the slogan "We Never Sleep."

When young Sam Hammett became a Pinkerton operative
in 1915, at a starting salary of $21 a month, the agency had
been functioning for over six decades, and was operating out
of twenty offices across the nation. Its history was wild and
colorful. Pinkerton ops had trailed outlaws across the bad-
lands of the Wild West, infiltrated Confederate lines in the
service of Abraham Lincoln, pursued lawbreakers into the
jungles of Central America (a fact that doubtless inspired
Hammett's first *Black Mask* crime tale), policed boxing matches, traced stolen gold, and assisted law enforcement officers
throughout the land. Published statistics indicated that, in
just fifteen years, they had "apprehended over a thousand
forgers, burglars, sneak thieves and hold-up men."

Born in 1819 in Glasgow, Scotland, Allan Pinkerton was a

---

*The Baltimore Branch of Pinkerton's was located in the Continental Building—
clearly the source of Hammett's fictional Continental Detective Agency.

large-nosed, hard-muscled Scotsman who emigrated to
America as a young man and settled in Chicago to ply his
trade of barrelmaking. As a hobby, he engaged in "amateur
crook catching," and soon gained a reputation for ap-
prehending wrongdoers. In the late 1840s the mayor of Chicago appointed him the city's first police detective. By 1850,
he had resigned to establish his own agency and hired nine
men to be his first official Pinkerton operatives. He trained
them himself, under his dictum: "It is held by the agency that
the ends, being for the accomplishment of justice, justify the
means used."

One historian has observed: "If it was impossible for Pinkerton to secure justice except by kidnapping, he and his men
would kidnap." Pinkerton's own handbook avowed the expe-
dient approach: "It frequently becomes necessary for the Detective, when brought in contact with Criminals, to pretend to
be a Criminal . . . and assume the garb of crime. To act
[effectively] he has, at times, to depart from the strict line of
truth, and resort to deception."

Biographer James D. Horan detailed Pinkerton's methods
of training his ops: "He taught them the art of 'shadowing,'
of disguise, and of playing a role. His office often resembled
the backstage of a theater with Pinkerton demonstrating to an
operative ready for assignment how to act like a 'greenhorn'
just off the boat, a bartender, a horsecar conductor, or gambler. He kept a large closet in his private office filled with
various disguises."

Nor was Pinkerton himself afraid to "mix it up" with badmen, often riding shotgun on stages, or foiling bank holdups.
Possessing a "venom and fury that numbed lawbreakers," he
earned headlines for his capture of Frank Reno, the elusive
train robber. In 1908 he issued a wanted poster on Harry
Longbaugh, "the Sundance Kid," for train robbery and rus-
tling. In chasing badmen across rough country, he became an
expert horseman—and a surviving photo shows the bearded
and resolute Pinkerton astride a tall stallion in Civil War days.

Although they differed in physique, Hammett and Pinkerton shared an essential ability to endure on-the-job hardships, including physical abuse from criminals. Slender but wiry, Hammett was over six feet tall and possessed surprising strength. However, for detective work, a sharp brain was even more important. Hammett won his first promotion by tracking down a stolen carnival Ferris wheel. As he later explained: "It was simple. I used deductive logic. You don't steal something that big for your back yard. I knew it had to be at another carnival." Patiently, he ran down local carnivals with Ferris wheels until he found one for which the carny boss had no proof of ownership. Simple.

The operative responsible for Hammett's detective training was James Wright, a squat, street-tough little bullet of a man, already a legend in Pinkerton circles for his daring and expertise. He was then the assistant manager of the Baltimore office, which was an important link in the Pinkerton chain, since there was no other branch office farther south. From Baltimore, agents ranged across several states.

Jimmy Wright—who later served as Hammett's model for the Continental Op—was rough on his men, but played what Hammett termed "a straight game." He taught young Hammett the basic code of the agency: Never cheat your client. Never break a law that violates your integrity. Stay anonymous. (All written case reports were unsigned, and were filed by the detective's number only.) Never take physical risks unless absolutely necessary. And, above all, be objective; never become emotionally involved with the client or anyone else connected with a case.

This code became fixed in Hammett's mind. It not only served him as a working detective, but it gave him a set of personal rules that shaped his actions and thoughts throughout the remainder of his life. And, of course, it provided the thematic core of his fiction. It was this code that Sam Spade and the Continental Op lived by.

Now, for the first time in his life, Sam Hammett was happy

with a job. On call twenty-four hours a day ("We Never Sleep"), he enjoyed being a Pink; his boredom vanished. The profession demanded wit, patience, adaptability, and nerve. Each case was different; each day offered fresh adventure. Yet his new profession also had its bizarre side.

"Detective work is often ridiculous," Hammett pointed out. "An operative I knew was looking for pickpockets at the Havre de Grace race track—and had his wallet lifted! . . . I was once falsely accused of perjury—and had to perjure myself to escape arrest. On another occasion I was shadowing a man who got lost in the country; I had to step forward and direct him back to the city. Then there was the police chief in the South who gave me a detailed description of a suspect, complete even to the mole on his neck, but neglected to mention that the man had only one arm."

Foul weather had once helped him win a conviction. He was transporting a prisoner from a ranch in Gilt Edge to Lewistown, Montana, in winter, when his car broke down. The prisoner, who had stubbornly declared his innocence, had been captured without a coat, and wore thin coveralls. Hammett was warmly dressed. As they sat through the long, frosted night awaiting help, the man got colder and more miserable by the hour. "At dawn," said Hammett, "his morale was so low he made a full confession."

False identity was often required of a Pinkerton agent. In Oregon, Hammett introduced himself as the secretary of the Civic Purity League, hoping to obtain information on a suspect. The information did not turn up, but before he could make his exit he was cornered by a dedicated woman purist who subjected him to a long discourse on the erotic effects of cigarettes on young ladies.

Another case required him to spend three months in a hospital as a patient—in conversational pursuit of a suspect in the adjoining bed. And, in yet another guise, he worked with a stool pigeon to obtain case data, playing the role of a fellow crook. There were times when an operative's false identity could be *too* convincing. Hammett recalled "a detective who disguised himself so thoroughly as a crook that the first policeman he met took him into custody."

In a 1930s interview Hammett remembered the night a loaded gun was tossed into his lap. "Happened in Detroit. I was sitting over a beer with a tough little mug in a speakeasy, when a fight started across the room. 'Hold this, pal,' he said, tossing his .45 Colt into my lap. 'I wanna get inta that fight!' Luckily, the .45 didn't go off." Hammett told the same interviewer about another "particularly rough" experience with the agency. "We were sent to this house to arrest a gang who'd been stealing dynamite. Once we were inside, the whole gang attacked us and our men were being knocked around. Things got hot." Caught up in the battle, Hammett didn't feel the knife wound in his right calf until he looked down "to see this guy whittling away at my leg." He managed to subdue his assailant, but carried a leg scar for the rest of his life. Lillian Hellman noted "the bad cut on his legs and an indentation in his head from being scrappy with criminals."

Hammett worked as a Pinkerton across several states, and despite his conspicuous height and shock of prematurely light hair, he earned a reputation with the agency as an "ace shadow man." Surveillance was one of the jobs for which Pinkertons were most often hired, and Hammett's ability was highly valued by the agency. In Washington, D.C., he once shadowed a subject he described as a "boring fat man thought to be a German secret agent." Hammett used him as the model for Casper Gutman, the rotund villain in *The Maltese Falcon.*

The art of shadowing, claimed Hammett, was relatively simple. There were four rules: keep behind the subject; never attempt to hide; act naturally, no matter the situation; never meet the subject's eye.

"Barring bad breaks," he continued, "the only thing that can make you lose contact is over-anxiety on your part. Even a clever criminal may be shadowed for weeks without suspecting it. I knew one operative who shadowed a wily old forger for more than three months without arousing his suspicion.

I myself tailed a fellow for six weeks, riding trains and making half a dozen small towns with him. You don't worry about a suspect's face. Tricks of carriage, ways of wearing clothes, general outline, individual mannerisms—all as seen from the rear—are much more important to the shadow man than faces."

Many years later, to his writer friend S. J. Perelman, Hammett related one of his most amusing "shadow" cases, involving a jewel salesman suspected of being a thief. His name was Finsterwald, and Hammett was hired to follow him until his guilt could be established. Finsterwald set off on an extended sales trip, with Hammett right behind him all the way—first by train to Philadelphia, then more train trips, to Hagerstown, Richmond, Raleigh, Knoxville, Macon, and, finally, to Savannah.

"I kept him within my sight all the way," Hammett said. "We were in this park in Savannah—with him sitting on one bench and me on the other next to it, reading a newspaper. I got interested in a certain news story and, next thing I know, Finsterwald is hovering over me, asking if we'd ever met before. He thought I looked familiar. I said nope, we'd never met."

The suspected thief came over and sat down next to Hammett, engaging him in conversation. He suggested they find a bar and "have a few beers." Hammett said okay.

"After about five bottles of beer, Finsterwald was getting loaded," said Hammett. "He began treating me like an old buddy. He asked if I'd like to make some easy money, and I said sure, what did he have in mind." Finsterwald proposed a scheme in which they would share equally in the profits of a jewel theft. He would stash the stolen gems in a Miami railway checkroom, then mail the claim ticket to Hammett, who would contact a fence, collect the money, then meet Finsterwald in Altoona for the split. "I agreed, and we drank on it to seal the bargain."

When Finsterwald took a train to Miami, Hammett alerted the Florida police. The thief was arrested and jailed. "Old

Finsterwald was a very confused guy," Hammett said. "I'd say that poor bird must have spent the next couple of years scratching his head and saying to himself, 'Jeez, it was foolproof! How the hell did they catch on?' "

Hammett became quite knowledgeable in matters of criminal lore:

- "The pickpocket has no status in the world of crime. Pocket picking is the easiest to master of all criminal trades. Anyone who is not crippled can become adept in a day."

- "Of all the men embezzling from their employers with whom I had contact, I can't remember a dozen who drank or had any of the vices in which bonding companies are so interested."

- "Of all nationalities, the Greek is the most difficult to convict. He simply denies everything, no matter how conclusive the proof may be—and nothing so impresses a jury as a bare statement of fact, regardless of the statement's inherent improbability or obvious absurdity in the face of overwhelming contrary evidence."

- "House burglary is probably the poorest paid trade in the criminal world. I have never known anyone to make a living at it. But few criminals of any class are self-supporting unless they toil at something legit between times. Most of them live on their women."

- "The value of fingerprints is overrated. Even when the criminal makes no attempt to efface the prints of his fingers, and leaves them all over the scene, the chances are about one in ten of finding a print that is sufficiently clear to be of any value."

- "That the lawbreaker is invariably apprehended is probably the least challenged of myths. The files of every detective bureau bulge with the records of unsolved mysteries and uncaught criminals."

During the summer of 1917, on assignment for Pinkerton's, Hammett became involved in a shocking event that left him angry and embittered. He was one of several operatives hired as strikebreakers against the I.W.W. (International Workers of the World) by the Anaconda Copper Company in Butte, Montana. It was then common practice to use Pinkerton operatives in this capacity. They were known as "union busters," and were quite effective in the role.

"I had no political conscience back in '17," Hammett later said. "I was just doing a job, and if our clients were rotten it didn't concern me. They hired us to break up a union strike, so we went out there to do that."

Hammett discovered that one man in particular was causing major trouble for the mining company. His name was Frank Little, a labor union organizer known as "the hobo agitator." Little, who had lost an eye, was part Indian and possessed a warrior's tenacity and courage; he would not be bluffed or scared off. Union members supported him enthusiastically as he raved and shouted against the injustices at the mines.

"That's when an officer of Anaconda Copper offered me five thousand dollars to kill him," Hammett said. The offer shocked him, and he made it clear he wanted no part of any such deal. The company turned to other methods. Soon thereafter, in the dead of night, Little was seized by vigilantes and lynched at a railroad crossing with three other men.

Hammett was stunned and sickened by these blatant murders—and Lillian Hellman came to believe that this was the key that opened his mind to what he saw as the corruption of the system. The assassination of Frank Little, in August of 1917, helped lay the groundwork for Hammett's shift to radical politics in the thirties.

Three months prior to this grim event, the United States had declared war on Germany, and Hammett began to envision himself at the front in combat against his country's enemies. In late June of 1918 he resigned from Pinkerton's to enlist in the army—but instead of being shipped overseas, into combat, he was assigned to the Motor Ambulance Company of Camp Mead, Maryland, as a transport driver. Disheartened and frustrated, Hammett tried to make the best of his situation, but he was never comfortable behind the wheel of the awkward, top-heavy ambulance he'd been assigned to drive. While he was transporting some patients from the hospital, his ambulance struck a rock in the roadway, overturned, and dumped the startled patients into the dirt. This accident, for which he took full blame, was traumatic; he swore he would never drive again. And there is no evidence that, once he was out of the service, he ever did.

An epidemic of Spanish influenza was ravaging U.S. military camps in 1918, and Hammett fell victim to it in early October, spending three weeks in a field hospital. By April of the following year, he had been promoted to sergeant, but his health was now a problem. In late May of 1919, two days after his twenty-fifth birthday, Hammett was back in the hospital. The doctors discovered that his lungs had been damaged by the attack of influenza and that he now suffered from tuberculosis. Discharge papers were prepared, and Hammett left the army, sick and weakened, weighing only 140 pounds. Needing rest, he returned to live in the family house in Baltimore. He fought with his father and was eager to establish a separate residence.

He gave up cigarettes and regained strength, then signed on again with Pinkerton's, at a salary of $105 per month. But he was soon back in the hospital and, by December, was declared to be fifty percent disabled. He was granted a pension of $40 per month.

Released from the hospital, he again resumed detective work for Pinkerton, and sought a new post. In May of 1920 he was informed of a job opening at the Spokane branch. With his weight back up to 155, he felt strong enough to accept the transfer.

Working out of Spokane as home base, Hammett ranged the western states for Pinkerton. He trapped a smooth-talking forger in Pasco, Washington; he rejected an offer to enter the narcotics trade from a pusher in San Diego; he ran down a window-smashing jewel thief in Stockton; he studied the art of faked prints with Wesley Turner, of the Spokane police identification bureau; he brought in a tough railroad track worker in Montana; he tracked a fugitive swindler in Seattle; he arrested an Indian for murder in Arizona. . . . The game was afoot, and he was savoring what writer/detective Joe Gores has described as "the special joys of manhunting, the dangerous sport of beating the criminal who is trying to beat you."

Each case was new, each case offered its special challenge. One of them, according to Hammett, dealt with gambler Nicky Arnstein. Nick was a dapper gentleman who wore monogrammed twill-silk pajamas, kept seven toothbrushes in his bathroom, and owned a stable of racing thoroughbreds. In 1915 he was convicted on a swindling charge and sentenced to Sing Sing for two years. Out of prison, he became the second husband of comedienne Fanny Brice. By 1920, Nick was again in trouble with the law, named as the mastermind of a plot to steal five million dollars in securities from Wall Street brokers. A newspaper account stated: "Detectives seek Arnstein, known to police as a member of the notorious Gondorf band . . . who fleeced scores of men in this city for sums aggregating upward of one million dollars."

Many years later, drinking with columnist Leonard Lyons at the Stork Club in New York, Hammett noticed Fanny Brice sitting at a nearby table. He began to chuckle quietly to himself. Lyons asked him what was so amusing.

"It's about Fanny," Hammett said. "We're pals now, so I don't want her to know what I'm going to tell you."

Lyons agreed to keep silent.

"She was married to Nick Arnstein back in '20," said Hammett. "I was on the case for Pinkerton, and tailed her for weeks hoping she'd lead us to Nick. But he finally turned himself in."

"And she never knew you were shadowing her?"

"Nope, she never did. I was a pretty fair sleuth in those days."

Detective work eventually took its toll on Hammett, and by November of 1920, only six months after he'd left Baltimore, he was again bedded with lung trouble, at Cushman Hospital

in Tacoma, Washington. His weight had slipped to 132 as the tuberculosis flared up again.

Formerly an Indian school, Cushman had been converted into a U.S. Public Health Service lung hospital. Hammett and the other "lungers" were assigned separate sleeping quarters for a two-week quarantine period.

"It wasn't a bad deal," he later recalled in fiction clearly based on this incident. "We wrangled booze and cigarettes. . . . The booze was bootleg, bad but strong."

Hammett shared a room with "a kid from Snohomish, who liked cards." They would drape the window with a blanket and play poker into the dawn, sipping the bootleg whiskey. This improved their spirits, if not their health. "Overnight passes to Seattle," he said, "were also obtainable from the corruptible head nurse."

Hammett had brought along a Pinkerton blackjack, and this intrigued another patient, Whitey Kaiser, a muscleman from Alaska. "Whitey borrowed the blackjack from me one night and returned it the next morning," Hammett recalled. "That afternoon, in the paper, I read about a guy being slugged and robbed of a hundred and eighty dollars on the Puyallup Road the night before. I showed the clip to Whitey, who said that people who get robbed always exaggerate the amounts."

Boredom set in, and Hammett devised a plan to "liven up the joint." He enlisted the aid of a huge ex-Marine named Bizzarri. They began openly insulting one another, demonstrating more anger with each passing day. Hammett called Bizzarri strong names, and the big man responded with fury. The nurses became alarmed, begging the two men to shake hands and forget their quarrel. No, said Hammett, the only way to end it was "man to man." A slugout.

"We finally went into the yard for our violent showdown, with the entire hospital staff trailing nervously behind us," said Hammett. "After a couple of wild swings we couldn't control ourselves. We both began to laugh—and the gag was shot."

Women were always attracted to Hammett, and he seldom

failed to take advantage of the fact. Now he began flirting with one of the young nurses at the hospital, Josephine Anna Dolan, called Jose.* A pert, dark-haired beauty of twenty-three, she appreciated Hammett's good looks and quick mind. He was soon helping her with ward duties, and she was flattered by his attention.

Decades later, during an interview, Josephine was asked about that early relationship. What had drawn her to Hammett?

"Of all the patients, Samuel seemed to stand out," she replied. "I thought he was very intelligent and striking—and his sleeping area was always very neat. Also, he was gentle."

After Hammett's health improved, they began going out to restaurants in Tacoma and for walks together in the park. "Sometimes we took rides on the ferry boats," Jose remembered. "Mostly we just talked."

She told Hammett of her unhappy childhood, of the desertion by her Irish father when she was still an infant, of her mother's death when she was three. She spent two lonely years in an orphanage, then was raised by an uncle in Anaconda, Montana. In 1912, at fifteen, Jose had entered nurses' training. She enlisted to become an army nurse and, by the time she was assigned to Cushman, she had attained the rank of second lieutenant. ("Samuel used to joke about having to salute me, since I outranked him!")

What had started as a casual flirtation developed into an intense love affair.

During the period of his early writing years in San Francisco, Hammett later fictionalized their relationship in an unpublished character sketch. In this sketch, Jose became "Evelyn" and Hammett called himself "Slim" (his real hospital nickname): "She was a lot of fun," he wrote, ". . . a small-bodied, wiry girl with a freckled, round face that went easily to smiling. We used to leave the hospital around lights-out time, walk a little way . . . to an area where four trees grouped

---

*Pronounced "Josie."

round a level spot. We would stay there until late, looking up through the trees, and loving one another. Our love-making was rough-and-tumble . . . and we cursed one another merrily, ribaldly. She usually stopped her ears in the end because I knew more words. Our love seemed dependent on not being phrased. It seemed as if one of us had said, 'I love you,' the next instant it would have been a lie."

This last line relates directly to a comment by critic Peter Wolfe: "Hammett believed that the key realities of life must be faced indirectly, or with a mask of indifference or reluctance. These realities could be lived, but not discussed." A direct declaration of love might, by its very expression, weaken or destroy the emotional base.

The lovers were soon separated. In late February of 1921 Hammett was sent with Whitey Kaiser and a dozen other disabled veterans to an army hospital at Camp Kearny, near San Diego. Doctors felt that the milder California climate would be beneficial to Hammett's lung condition. Hammett, against orders, was smoking again—and on the train to California, in order to raise cigarette money, he and Kaiser sold a packet of harmless white powder (prescribed to Kaiser for a kidney infection) to a pair of self-declared dopers. ("And they got—or thought they got—a great high out of the stuff all the way to San Diego!")

Discipline at the new hospital was rigidly enforced, and when Whitey drank several bottles of very alcoholic patent medicine and slugged his doctor, he was promptly shipped out.

Whenever he was allowed a pass into San Diego, Hammett would head for a shop selling tonic remedies and purchase several bottles of this same patent medicine. ("In those Prohibition days you drank whatever you could get.") But, unlike Whitey, he never got caught.

Jose had also been reassigned—to the Cheyenne Hospital at Helena, in her home state of Montana. But when she found that she was pregnant with Hammett's child, she left the service and returned to Anaconda. A marriage was arranged by letter, although Hammett was far from certain he could support a wife and baby. He told Jose that he would send for her as soon as his health permitted.

Meanwhile, life at the hospital offered odd pleasantries. Hammett recalled that he staged Gila monster battles in an abandoned boxcar near the hospital grounds, pitting the ugly-tempered lizards against rattlesnakes. ("The lizards always won, but most of the sucker money backed the rattlers.") As his health continued to improve, he was able to take off to Tijuana, Mexico, for an occasional border weekend. One of these weekend "vacations" formed the basis for his autobiographical short story, "Holiday," printed in *The New Pearsons* in 1923.

By the spring of 1921, "with a little fast talking," Hammett was able to obtain his release from the hospital. While his lung problems were far from over, Hammett's file was marked "maximum improvement reached."

"I headed for Seattle," he declared. "Spent a month there. Into the hospital twice. My weight was way down again, and Seattle was a pretty dull town so, by mid-June, I planned to go on home to Baltimore, send for Jose, and get married there. But, first, I had a sudden yen for San Francisco. Figured on a quick stopover."

Dashiell Hammett's "quick stopover" in San Francisco lasted eight and a half years.

2

A PINK IN SAN FRANCISCO

You could feel that Papa was at home in San Francisco. . . . He belonged. Some places, you can live in and never belong. But he belonged in San Francisco.

—MARY JANE HAMMETT

ON JULY 7, 1921, Samuel Dashiell Hammett and Josephine Anna Dolan were married in the rectory of St. Mary's Cathedral in San Francisco. "We went there in a taxi," she recalled. "Samuel gave me flowers." On the marriage affidavit she listed her age as twenty-four, stating that her father had been born in Ireland, her mother in Virginia. Hammett listed his age as twenty-seven, declaring that both of his parents had been born in Maryland.

Hammett had chosen St. Mary's at Jose's urging. Although five months pregnant, as a Catholic she wanted to be married "in a proper church." Adamantly nonreligious, Hammett refused to reveal until after the ceremony that he, too, had been baptized a Catholic. Because of this, they were not allowed to be married before the altar, inside the church itself.

The couple moved into a small apartment at 620 Eddy Street, a four-story structure built shortly after the quake of 1906. Decades later, in reminiscing about this period, Mrs. Hammett vividly remembered the place: "It cost us forty-five dollars a month. There was a bedroom in back, a small living room in front, a folding Murphy bed in the hallway, and a tiny kitchen. Our landlady was a bootlegger, and we'd look out of our window to watch all the policemen coming and going."

Hammett took happy advantage of the fact that their apartment was only a four-block walk from the San Francisco Public Library. "Samuel was always bringing home books," Mrs.
Hammett recalled. "He was really an avid reader. I remember
that he was then very keen on medieval history, classic literature and criminology. I suppose the books on crime helped
him with his work."

Hammett's work, once again, was with Pinkerton. His fifty
percent disability payment each month amounted to just $40,
and with the baby coming he needed to supplement this low
income.

"The Pinks had a branch in the city," said Hammett. "They
hired me right away. Pay was six bucks a day—and when my
lungs acted up I was able to work part time."

Hammett's health failed periodically in those early San
Francisco days. His veteran's record reveals a pattern of physical breakdowns, spaced from two to six months apart, during
which he would require temporary hospitalization. As he re-
built his strength following these breakdowns, he was grateful
for the opportunity to work short hours. He could not have
held a full-time position.

In 1921 the San Francisco branch of Pinkerton's National
Detective Agency was located in Room 314 on the third floor
of the Flood Building, entered through an ornate marble
lobby at 870 Market Street. The agency advertised itself as
being prepared "to undertake all proper detective business
entrusted to it by Railroads, or other Corporations, Banks,
Mercantile Houses, Attorneys, or Private Individuals." The
ads also noted that Pinkerton's "does not operate for [bounty
hunting] rewards nor engage in divorce cases." They listed
branches in thirty-five cities in the United States and Canada,
assuring their prospective clients: "Business transacted in all
parts of the world."

Phil Geauque was chief of the San Francisco office—or resident superintendent. He was a small, canny man who demanded superior job performance from his operatives.

Geauque was partial to veteran detectives, and he was impressed with Hammett's credentials. He assigned him to a wide variety of cases. Hammett tracked down counterfeiters, traced missing daughters, investigated bank holdups. He also got hurt—he fell off a taxi during a chase and, later, got hit in the head with a brick.

Jose Hammett recalled the latter incident: "Samuel was shadowing someone, a man, when a second man got behind him and dropped a brick on him. It left a dent in his skull, but he wouldn't see a doctor." Without complaint, Hammett sat immobile in a chair in the front of their apartment for two full days after the attack. On the third day he stood up, said, "I feel a lot better," and returned to work.

During the afternoon of September 5, 1921, a riotous party took place on the twelfth floor of the St. Francis Hotel in downtown San Francisco. The host of the party was Roscoe "Fatty" Arbuckle, a jolly-faced 320-pound actor who'd gained fame as a member of Mack Sennett's Keystone Kops, and who was then at the height of his career, earning five thousand a week as a top screen personality. San Francisco's gaudy reputation as a wide-open town ("The City That Knows How!") attracted Arbuckle and, with a carload of pals and two cases of bootleg gin, he'd driven up from Hollywood in his custom Rolls.

Among those accompanying the film comedian was Virginia Rappe, an attractive young lady whose party talents far exceeded her doubtful abilities as an actress. She'd left the man to whom she was engaged, a Hollywood producer named Henri Lehrman, to drive up with Arbuckle, hoping to win a role in one of the actor's films.

The hotel festivities were loud and high-spirited, with Arbuckle clowning broadly for the giggling Miss Rappe. Then, from the hall, a maid heard piercing screams—and the manager was summoned. Arbuckle, a pair of silk pajamas draping his huge frame, opened the door. The manager found Virginia Rappe on the bed, semiconscious and moaning in pain.

At left, Hammett in the mid-1920s. Below, 620 Eddy Street, San Francisco, his first home with his new wife, Jose. The Flood Building housed the Pinkerton Agency when Hammett worked for it.

Jose—Josephine Anna Dolan—married Hammett in 1921.

Pieces of her torn clothing were scattered around the room.

Four days later, after admitting she had been intimate with Arbuckle, the young woman died. An inquest was held. The coroner's jury reported: "Virginia Rappe came to her death from peritonitis, due to a rupture of her urinary bladder. This rupture was caused by application of local force which, from evidence, was applied by one Roscoe Arbuckle." Assumption: the film star had raped a helpless girl, rupturing her bladder during the brutal act.

Arbuckle was arrested and questioned by a Captain Matheson of Homicide. The actor denied all charges: Miss Rappe had freely offered her sexual favors, and the bladder trouble was not related to their lovemaking.

But Captain Matheson disagreed, issuing an inflammatory statement to the press which directly accused Arbuckle: "She died as a result of the attack. That makes it first degree murder. . . . Arbuckle can't pull that stuff here in San Francisco and get away with it!"

Reporters in Hollywood rushed to interview the dead woman's husband-to-be. "Roscoe Arbuckle is a beast," Lehrman bitterly declared. "People like Arbuckle don't know how to get a kick out of life, except in a beastly way . . . participating in orgies that surpass those of degenerate Rome." As reporters eagerly recorded his statements, Lehrman continued the tirade: "Arbuckle was a spittoon cleaner when he came to the movies nine years ago. This is what results from making idols and millionaires of people from the gutter!"

Smelling blood, the papers sensationalized the case, printing every anti-Arbuckle rumor they could conjure up. One of the more vicious claimed that a three-quarter-inch tear in Miss Rappe's bladder had been caused by "a soft drink bottle violently inserted into her private parts."

Arbuckle employed the defense services of lawyer Frank Dominguez, who claimed (supported by medical evidence) that Virginia Rappe had died from "a chronic bladder condition, aggravated by bootleg whiskey." (It was later revealed that Miss Rappe had a reputation in Hollywood for "immoral conduct" and that a bungled abortion combined with a venereal disease had caused the bladder trouble.) Dominguez was fighting an uphill battle. He realized that the growing wave of negative public opinion was seriously injuring his client. As he declared: "People want to believe the worst about Arbuckle." Further help was needed—and Pinkerton's was brought into the case.

Hammett was among the operatives assigned to investigate key witnesses. He was working with fellow op Phil Haultain, a young rookie with the agency, teaching him the art of becoming a good shadow man.

Interviewed in 1975, Haultain, who often wore a brown cowboy's Stetson on the job, recalled Hammett during this period, especially one afternoon when they were tailing two witnesses: "We were going down Stockton, past Macy's, shadowing this couple, and Sam was showing me all his tricks. We even circled them, and they still didn't get wise to us. Sam taught me plenty."

How was Hammett rated with the agency in those days?

"High, at the very top," declared Haultain. "Sam was a wonderful investigator. Sharp. Really knew his business. The chief liked him. Hammett was smart and Geauque was smart. They made a good team."

The first Arbuckle trial, which began in late September of 1921, was a misfire. After forty-three hours of heated deliberation, the jury was dismissed because of a 10-to-2 deadlock for acquittal. A second trial was ordered.

The flow of negative publicity continued. Letters were featured from ministers and self-appointed do-gooders across the nation. Typical was a wire sent to the district attorney from the mayor of St. Paul, Minnesota: "In the name of all decent people I thank you for your vigorous action in the Arbuckle case. Do not falter! Fight to the finish! If Arbuckle is not punished, the moving picture business is done for."

Hammett condemned such publicity as "a setup . . . The corrupt newsboys wanted Arbuckle to take the fall. A villainous Arbuckle made good copy."

Shaken by the scandal, Hollywood quickly organized its own film censorship board, headed by Will Hays. The Hays Office was officially launched in January of 1922, the same month Arbuckle was brought to trial for a second time.

The day before this new trial opened, Hammett was in the Plaza Hotel as Roscoe Arbuckle emerged from the elevator, flanked by police.

"He came into the lobby," reported Hammett. "His eyes were the eyes of a man who expected to be regarded as a monster, but was not yet inured to it. He glared at me, which was amusing, in a way, because I was still working for his attorneys, gathering information for his defense."

The second trial proved equally frustrating, and the deadlocked jury (10-to-2 for conviction) was dismissed in favor of a *third* trial—at which Arbuckle was finally acquitted. By mid-April of 1922 he was a free man—yet stood convicted in the public eye. His film career was destroyed, and he died eleven years later, a broken failure at forty-six.

On October 15, 1921, at St. Francis Hospital, Hammett became a father—Jose gave birth to a girl they named Mary Jane. The hospital costs drained them of what little money they'd managed to save, and Hammett took on extra cases to make up the loss. One of his assignments was the holdup of the California Street Cable Company. The criminals responsible were known to be armed and dangerous, and Hammett told his partner, Haultain, to pack an extra gun "just in case we need it."

Haultain recalled that gunwork was a very real part of the profession. "On some cases I carried a weapon," said Haultain, "and so did Sam."

Hammett claimed that he once survived a spectacular gun duel in the streets of San Francisco with "a doped-up kid"— and he had his own strong ideas about gunplay: "Shooting a weapon from another man's hand is often accidental. If you're a fair shot you naturally and automatically shoot pretty close to the spot upon which your eyes are focused. When a man goes for his gun in front of you, you shoot at *him,* not at any particular part of him. Since you are more than likely to be looking at his gun, it isn't altogether surprising if your bullet should hit it."

Hammett recounted an amusing variant to such an incident, involving a deputy sheriff he knew in Montana who tracked a criminal to a remote cabin to find himself confronted by a rifle. As he attempted to shoot over the man's head, to frighten him into dropping the weapon, the deputy's bullet was deflected by a strong gust of wind and ended up knocking the rifle from the criminal's hand. "As time went by," recalled Hammett, "the deputy began to accept his sharpshooter's reputation earned by this incident. He not only let friends enter him in a shooting contest, but he wagered everything he owned on his skill. During the contest, he missed the target completely with all six shots."

Jack Knight, another colleague of Hammett's, was forced to retire after less than four years with Pinkerton's because of job-related gunshot wounds. "I always packed two weapons," Knight stated. "I carried a 9-mm. Luger in a shoulder holster and a .38 Police Positive with a four-inch barrel in a special pocket of my overcoat. When I couldn't reach my shoulder holster all I had to do was slip a hand into my coat pocket, tip up the .38, and the guy was covered."

Knight spoke about Hammett: "The agency had what might be termed 'star performers,' fellows who possessed particular ability. Sam was in that league, known through the agency as a very reliable man. We once worked different ends of the same operation. That was a couple of years before Hammett moved to San Francisco."

He referred to the Kaber murder case, which took place in Cleveland in 1919. Socially prominent Eva Kaber had hired two men, Salvatore Cala and Vitorio Pisselli, to eliminate her husband for the insurance proceeds. The two men entered the couple's home and fatally stabbed Daniel Kaber. To make it look like a robbery, they took the house silverware.

Eva Kaber left Cleveland for Pittsburgh, where she waited

for the insurance money. However, Moses Kaber, the dead man's father, was not satisfied with the police report, and he hired Pinkerton's to probe further. Hammett had investigated the West Coast aspects of the case, tracing the whereabouts of the two killers after they left Cleveland, while Knight went to Pittsburgh, where he impersonated the boyfriend of one of Eva's female friends. He gathered enough hard evidence to convict Eva of her husband's murder.

"When she went to the Ohio State pen for life," said Knight, "she swore up and down she'd get me because I'd done the final rope job on her. But Sam had helped."

The winter of 1921 was particularly chill and foggy in San Francisco, and Hammett's lung trouble began to reassert itself. He developed a deep cough.

"Frisco was a tough beat in the fog," Hammett declared. "The wind off the bay cuts through whatever coat you're wearing, right into you. It was rough on my bum lungs. I wasn't liking it much, working for Pinkerton that winter, but we needed the money."

In order to protect his infant daughter's health, Hammett had been using the hallway's fold-down Murphy bed, while Jose and Mary Jane shared the back bedroom. Sleeping in the drafty hall simply added to his health problems.

In November the local papers were full of headline stories about a massive gold robbery aboard the ocean liner *Sonoma.* The robbery had taken place en route to California from Sydney, Australia. Five boxes of English gold sovereigns, weighing 400 pounds and valued at $125,000, had been taken from the ship's strongroom. When the liner docked in San Francisco, the insurance company hired Pinkerton detectives to find the gold. "I figured it had to be an inside job," said Hammett. "Somebody had keys to that strongroom. Which meant the gold was still on board, or close by, awaiting removal. So we set out to find it."

As senior operative, Hammett led the search, aided by city police. A systematic examination of the liner's fire hoses uncovered a large portion of the gold—and another sizable amount was found in boxes lashed to oil cans floating near the hull of the ship. But a total of $20,000 was still missing.

At this point, time was running out for the Pinkertons. In early December the liner was due to begin its return trip to Sydney. Phil Geauque called Hammett into his office at the Flood Building, telling him that he was convinced the missing gold was still on board the *Sonoma*. "When that steamer leaves next week, I want you on it," he told Hammett. "You'll work undercover. We'll have you signed aboard as a crewman. I *know* that gold's still there somewhere. Whoever has it stashed will likely try to jump ship with it between here and Sydney. When they do, you'll be there to grab 'em."

Hammett was delighted at the chance to escape San Francisco's winter fog via an ocean voyage to Australia, where (the seasons being reversed) it was summer.

"I'll have your seaman's ID papers in a couple of days," said Geauque.

"Oke," nodded Hammett.

The next morning Geauque got a phone call: Hammett on the line. "I *found* the damned gold," he said. "Decided to do a final lookover and located the rest of the stuff. Tucked under the scuppers on the lower boat deck."

"Good work, Sam!"

"Guess I don't get my free trip to Australia?"

"That's right," said Geauque. "I guess you don't."*

The cough got worse as Hammett's lung problems increased; he was rapidly losing weight. He began drinking more to ease the chest congestion and to help ward off the

---

*Previous Hammett biographers, beginning with Lillian Hellman in *The Big Knockover*, have consistently stated that Hammett quit his Pinkerton job in December of 1921, out of disgust at losing a free trip to Australia. In truth, he remained in detective work into mid-February of 1922.

Eleven years later, for the dust jacket of *The Thin Man*, Hammett claimed that he had been "a bit overrated" as a Pinkerton sleuth, "because of the plausibility with which I could explain away my failures, proving them inevitable and no fault of mine."

cold. He was rapidly souring on detective work. "It used to be fun," he told Jose, "but it isn't anymore."

That December, in St. Paul, Minnesota, three men kidnapped the manager of the Shapiro Jewel Company, drove him to the store, and forced him, at gunpoint, to open the main safe. Working with calm precision, they rifled the store of $130,000 in gems and silver, making a clean escape from the city. The Pinkerton Agency became involved in this case, and Phil Geauque received a tip from a local stoolie that the gang was holed up in Vallejo, some thirty miles from San Francisco. Hammett was sent there to ferret them out—in the guise of a wealthy, loose-spending gambler (a natural role for him, since gambling was a lifelong passion). Prowling through Vallejo, he soon marked the three men responsible for the jewel heist. Their leader was a dour-faced veteran criminal known as "Gloomy Gus" Schaefer.

A gang meeting was called one night at a roadhouse, and Hammett determined to hear what was said, since their conversation might reveal the location of the hidden loot. While the gang gathered inside a room on the second floor, Hammett climbed onto an overhead porch in order to eavesdrop; he was making notes on the conversation when the entire roof collapsed. Although bruised and shaken, Hammett managed to limp away into the darkness; when he returned the next day the gang had dispersed.

"I decided to hang around there for a while," he said, "in case any of 'em stayed in town. And I got lucky. Gus showed, and I began shadowing him." Hammett patiently followed the gang leader for weeks. This tail job finally paid off. Schaefer led the detective to his wife in Oakland, a few miles away. Hammett arrested Mrs. Schaefer as she was opening a safe deposit box in a local bank. The box contained Gus Schaefer's portion of the stolen jewels.

"We got 'em all eventually," said Hammett. "But Gus was the only one convicted—and in a few years he was out again on a pardon. So things were right back where they started."

Hammett was clearly fed up with the detective profession

as his health continued to decline. The damp and cold and exhaustion caused shortness of breath; his cough was severe and constant. "I didn't have to quit," he said. "My lungs made the decision. They couldn't take the punishment."

On February 15, 1922, the veteran shadow man handed in his resignation. The Pinkerton years had ended. Sam Hammett's career was over. Dashiell Hammett's career was about to begin.

3

PULPS AND THE PRIVATE EYE

*I have a liking for honest work—and honest work,
as I see it, is work that is done for the worker's
enjoyment as much as for the profit it will bring
him.*

—HAMMETT

HAMMETT HAD A plan in mind when he left the Pinkerton
Agency. He immediately signed up for morning courses in
journalism at Munson's Business College, a vocational school
located on Mission Street in downtown San Francisco. His
original goal was to become a newspaper reporter, but during
the year and three months he attended Munson's he changed
his mind. He would go into free-lance advertising, writing and
designing ad copy for local merchants.

His schooling was paid for by the Veterans Bureau, but
Hammett's shaky financial position forced him into request-
ing a loan from the family. He wrote to his father in Baltimore,
who sent him enough to cover all overdue bills. But in doing
so, Richard Hammett made it clear that he did not approve
of free-lance writing of any kind as a profession and that no
more money would be forthcoming.

Each morning Hammett would get up early, cook breakfast,
then attend class. Each afternoon he'd take his wife and
daughter to the park next to the Civic Center library. Jose and
Mary Jane would sit outside in the sun while Hammett stayed
in the library, prowling the crowded shelves, attacking books
as a hungry man attacks food, devouring one after the other,

subject after subject. He was a fast, retentive reader, and his tastes ranged widely, from classics to modern fiction, from ancient history to abstract mathematics. Those intense afternoons in the library, week after week of them, formed what he later called "my college education."

His illness, however, gradually drained him of energy, and his afternoon trips to the library gave way to long hours in bed, where he would write in longhand with a board across his lap. He began submitting work to commercial magazine markets. Determined to break into print, he found that professional writing was a far more exacting and difficult art than he had imagined.

It was Phil Geauque, the Pinkerton, who had first encouraged Hammett. Admiring the detective's concise, to-the-point case reports, Geauque had told him that he felt Hammett might have a future as a professional writer. Ernest Hemingway had learned to be concise and directly factual in writing stripped-down prose as a journalist; Hammett, too, learned this direct writing technique, in drafting his case reports for Pinkerton. In those early months, Hammett found no real focus for his work. The manuscripts he sent out were brief and formless, little more than clever word sketches. It is not surprising that these esoteric pieces were quickly rejected by magazines seeking more substantial material.

The legendary H. L. Mencken must be credited as the first editor to discover and publish Dashiell Hammett. Mencken was then (in mid-1922) scouting writers for *The Smart Set,* a sophisticated, innovative publication with a reputation for launching new talent. F. Scott Fitzgerald had graduated from college amateur to professional when *Smart Set* printed his early work.

In 1914 the magazine's publisher, Eltinge F. Warner, had offered the job of editor to George Jean Nathan. Nathan insisted on having his friend Mencken hired as co-editor. Warner agreed to this, and the Nathan-Mencken editorial partnership became a functional reality. They had both been writing for the magazine since 1908, under its former editor,

Willard Huntington Wright (who went on to a wide reader-
ship with his series of Philo Vance detective novels under the
pseudonym S. S. Van Dine). Historian Burton Rascoe, in a
piece dealing with the Nathan-Mencken relationship, drew a
sharp portrait of each:

> Nathan, the theatre critic and man-of-the-world with in-
> terests esthetic and hedonistic, not at all concerned with
> sociological or political matters, although quick to see the
> fallacies and weak points in the arguments of demagogues
> and maliciously shrewd in pointing these fallacies out—
> and Mencken, a sturdy bourgeois provincial, with a pas-
> sion for music, an enormous talent for arranging words
> effectively, a great gusto in living, an enthusiasm for liter-
> ature . . . who took hardy delight in the more absurd antics
> of politicians and reformers.

The Smart Set attracted a great many original talents. As
Rascoe pointed out: "It was the one and only place where
writers could sell the stuff they particularly liked and wanted
to write."

One of these original talents was Hammett. He appreciated
Smart Set's boldness and intellectual honesty. There is no
existing record of his earliest submissions to the magazine,
but it is quite possible he wrote and sold a few short "squibs"
(filler items) prior to his first by-lined piece, "The Parthian
Shot," in the October 1922 issue.

Barely over 100 words, this vignette begins: "When the boy
was six months old Paulette Key acknowledged that her hopes
and efforts had been futile, that the baby was indubitably and
irremediably a replica of its father."

Paulette finds that she simply cannot live with another don-
key-stubborn individual. After having the baby christened
"Don Key" (as a Parthian shot at her husband), she sends the
infant home with his nurse. Hammett ends the vignette as she
boards a train for the West, leaving husband and child.

This piece was typical of the material then being printed in *The Smart Set:* intellectually tart, a bit cynical, and daring in its depiction of a mother coldly deserting her infant.

For publication, Sam Hammett decided to drop his first name and use the stronger and more direct by-line of Dashiell Hammett.

Mencken soon bought more from his latest discovery. Hammett's second piece, "The Great Lovers," in the November issue, consisted of an odd assortment of quotes from famous personages, arranged in humorous context. This one-pager is arch and awkward; Hammett was obviously trying too hard, and the strain was evident. He had not found his form or his natural material.

Yet he was much closer to his true direction as a writer than he realized—and it was H. L. Mencken, once again, who was basically responsible for Hammett's next creative step.

Three years earlier, in 1919, Mencken had been nearly broke. He and Nathan had bought into *Smart Set* and were co-owners of the magazine, which was then in shaky financial condition.

Mencken wrote about this situation in a letter to a friend, Ernest Boyd: "I am thinking of venturing into a new cheap magazine scheme. . . . The opportunity is good and I need the money."

Mencken had turned to the pulp market, aware that quick profits in this area were assured. The burgeoning, ragged-edged pulpwood magazines were enjoying wide popularity. In 1915 Street and Smith, the leading pulp chain publisher, had made a strong impact with *Detective Story* magazine; crime star Edgar Wallace wrote for it regularly. Mencken and Nathan had previously involved themselves with a love pulp, *Saucy Stories,* feeding it *Smart Set* rejects; one of Hammett's stories had appeared here. Now they had a new concept in mind, a magazine they would call *The Black Mask.* The publication's trademark was a thin black pirate's mask, with a gun and dirk crossed behind it. (As pulp historian Ron Goulart has pointed out: "Both title and trademark may have come to Mencken while looking at a cover of *The Smart Set,* which each month featured a line drawing of a black-masked Satan in its left-hand corner.")

Mencken appointed Frances M. Osborne, a staff associate with *Smart Set,* as the first editor of *The Black Mask.* In order to project a masculine image, she was listed on the masthead as F. M. Osborne. Unwilling to associate themselves directly with this "lurid thrill book" (launched early in 1920 for a total investment of $500), Mencken and Nathan kept their names out of the magazine. In April, Mencken penned a testy note to Boyd: "Our new louse seems to be a success, but the thing has burdened both Nathan and me with disagreeable work. . . . Reading manuscripts for it is a fearful job." Although crime was offered as the main attraction, the magazine also promised its readers "the best Romances, the best Love stories, and the best stories of the Occult." (Western tales would soon be added.)

Within a year of its debut, a circulation of 250,000 was achieved. By then, Mencken and Nathan had sold out their interest for $12,250 to Eltinge Warner and Eugene Crowe, owner-publishers of *Smart Set.* They had made a fast and solid profit, and wanted no more to do with the magazine.

Mencken had shown an issue of *Black Mask* to Hammett, who'd been shocked by the magazine's crude, unreal melodrama. None of the stories represented the harsh world of crime he himself had experienced. *Black Mask*'s fiction was a continuation of the florid Sherlock Holmes tradition (extending all the way back to Poe's C. Auguste Dupin), a carry-over from the Victorian era of cloaked figures, terrified maidens, and slow deduction. Murder usually took place in musty castles or flowering gardens, in paneled libraries or on fog-shrouded moors. Detectives were tweedy, mustachioed, pompous gentlemen, prone to declarations of Shakespearean intensity. When arresting a villain, they wore the proper frock coat and striped trousers—"detectives of exquisite and impossible gentility," as Raymond Chandler later described them.

An excerpt from a typical early *Black Mask* tale, "The Silvered Sentinel," reflects the ornate, overwritten style: "With a windy shriek De Collyer fell backward upon the bed, the mounting tide of his alcoholic frenzy culminating in an overwhelming wave of insane and blasphemous mouthing, the grim justice of a retributive madness."

In another early melodrama, criminal investigator F. Jackson Melville-Smith smugly summed up his case: "My extensive travels in the Far East, plus a certain deductive faculty, Mr. Pooley, have on occasion resulted profitably for my clients. . . . Now that you have had your valuables returned, I would advise your putting them where they will offer temptation to nobody—especially gentry of this particular persuasion. I believe I can guarantee that you will have no further trouble from Chowdah Singh."

Titles were in keeping with this baroque appraoch: "The Jest Ironic," "The Mysterious Shot," "The Uncanny Voice," and "The Strange Case of Nathaniel Broome."

In disgust, Hammett told Jose that he could do "a hell of a lot better" using his own background with Pinkerton as raw material. She urged him to try.

Hammett wrote a 1,500-word story, "The Road Home," about a gaunt manhunter named Hagedorn who tracks a criminal, Barnes, for two years, from New York to India—finally catching up with him in the wilds of Burma. Captured on a teak boat in the depths of the jungle, Barnes offers the detective a share of "one of the richest gem beds in Asia" if he'll throw in with him. "I'll show you rubies and sapphires . . . that'll knock your eye out!"

Hagedorn won't make any deal. "I'm taking you back to New York," he tells Barnes. The fugitive leaps into the river, reaches shore, and escapes into the jungle, headed for his jewels. The story ends as Hagedorn plunges into the brush after him, thinking about the treasure.

The reader is left with the hint that perhaps the detective

will succumb to greed upon sighting the jewels. Thus, Hammett's career-long theme of man's basic corruptibility is established here, in his *Black Mask* debut. (The story also prefigures Hammett's Continental Op/Sam Spade job-oriented philosophy: "Maybe manhunting isn't the nicest trade in the world," says Hagedorn, "but it's all the trade I've got.")

Printed in the December 1922 issue, under the editorship of George W. Sutton, Jr., and associate Harry North, the story was by-lined "Peter Collinson," since, in this beginning period, Hammett did not want his real name to appear in pulp magazines. (He used Collinson on eight manuscripts during 1922–23: in *Brief Stories, Black Mask,* and *Action Stories.*) Asked how he had come to choose this particular pseudonym, Hammett explained that carnival slang at the turn of the century included the phrase "He's a Peter Collins." Meaning: he's a nobody. Hammett puckishly added "on" to the name, making it, literally, "nobody's son." In *Red Harvest,* written years later, Hammett had a dying hood complain, "I got no more belly left than Peter Collins."

Sleeping only a few hours each night, Hammett wrote—and drank. He held to the theory that whiskey helped arrest his tuberculosis. It also eased the pain and deadened the hacking cough that tore at his chest.

The long hours of work paid off. Fourteen of his stories were printed during 1923, in half a dozen magazines. Seven were in *Black Mask,* where Hammett was drawing more and more heavily on his Pinkerton years.

He was also taking material directly from the city itself. San Francisco, in that era, was rough and wide open. Prohibition had been enacted in 1920—and the town's many smoke-filled speakeasies were jammed with hell-bent citizens out for a maximum of illegal fun. They frequented all-night poker games and swigged vast quantities of rotgut whiskey. There were tong killings in Chinatown, and rumrunners in Sausalito; it was a city of crooked prize fights, fan-tan parlors, white slavery, and opium dens, of rich bootleggers and high-stakes gamblers, where the politicians were on the take and every harness bull had his hand out for a payoff.

Veteran San Francisco columnist Herb Caen vividly described the gritty 1920s atmosphere of this fog-haunted northern California city: "The Hall of Justice was dirty and reeked of evil. The City Hall, the D.A. and the cops ran the town as though they owned it, and they did. Hookers worked upstairs, not on the street; there were hundreds, maybe thousands, most of them named Sally. The two biggest abortion mills—one on Market and the other on Fillmore—were so well-known they might as well have had neon signs. You could play roulette in the Marina, shoot craps on O'Farrell, play poker on Mason, and get rolled at 4 A.M. in a bar on Eddy."

For Hammett, the wicked life of the city provided an ideal background for his fiction. He used what Jose called "a wonderful brain and a wonderful memory" to record what he saw and heard—putting the gaudy town on paper late at night, typing on his used Underwood at the kitchen table while Jose and Mary Jane slept in the back bedroom.

By the end of May 1923, Hammett had completed his schooling at Munson's and was beginning to sell his work on two levels—fiction to the pulps and ads to local stores. He sold his first ad to a shoe store, swapping his fee for a pair of shoes.

Jose recalled that period: "Money was still a big worry, but at least we had Samuel's fifty-dollar monthly disability check to use for the rent. We *were* scraping by, and Samuel was selling most of his stories, and that was the really important thing for all of us."

Although Dashiell Hammett is properly credited as the man who developed and popularized the first-person-narrative hard-boiled detective story, he was not its originator. This distinction belongs to a mild-mannered pulpster named Carroll John Daly, who created, in Three-Gun Terry Mack, the first known example of the tough private eye.

Daly and Hammett were leagues apart as writers, yet one must fully understand Carroll John Daly to appreciate the unique breakthrough Hammett achieved using the same basic "tough guy" materials.

Daly's Terry Mack, who carried twin .45s and a .25 sleeve weapon, made his printed debut in "Three Gun Terry." *Black Mask* featured the story in its issue of May 15, 1923 (four and a half months before the first appearance of Hammett's Continental Op). It is extremely doubtful that Daly's unlettered pseudotough prose had any influence whatever on the Op series. Dashiell Hammett's toughness was genuine, coming from life as he had lived it. Daly was tough only in his mind and on a printed page; his world of pulp violence was purely imaginary. He had no contact whatever with actual crime or criminals. Once he made up his mind to buy a real .45 automatic, curious to know what one was like. Daly purchased the gun—and was promptly arrested for carrying a concealed weapon. As a friend observed: "That was the end of John's criminal research."

Detective Terry Mack, who later functioned as the hero of Daly's third novel, *The Man in the Shadows* (Clode, 1928), was basically lawless, fast-shooting, tough, and illiterate—Daly invariably associated toughness with illiteracy.

Although he was the genre's originator, Carroll John Daly produced what might be termed "instant clichés." His pioneer private eye story, "Three Gun Terry," is remarkable in the sense that almost every cliché destined to plague the genre through the years is evident in this single pulp novelette.*

Mack is tough, but sentimental about innocent girls; he is a knight who rescues the damsel in distress; he is fast with a gun and a wisecrack; he prowls the underworld and avoids the police who wish to "nail" him; he is continually broke and eats from fee to fee, job to job; he stays clear of romantic entanglements; he makes his own laws, although his code is one of crude honesty; he has a cast-iron skull, and never backs down

---

*According to the usage of the pulp magazine business at the time, a novelette was, in length, somewhere between the short story and the novella—from 8,000 to 20,000 words.

in a brawl. The story's opening is a perfect example of Daly's awkward, artificially tough style:

> My life is my own, and the opinions of others don't interest me; so don't form any, or if you do, keep them to yourself. If you want to sneer at my tactics, why go ahead; but do it behind the pages—you'll find that healthier.
>
> So for my line. I have a little office which says "Terry Mack, Private Investigator," on the door; which means whatever you wish to think of it. I ain't a crook, and I ain't a dick; I play the game on the level, in my own way. I'm in the center of a triangle; between the crook and the police and the victim. The police have had an eye on me for some time, but only an eye, never a hand; they don't get my lay at all. The crooks; well, some is on and some ain't; most of them don't know what to think, until I've put the hooks in them. Sometimes they gun for me, but that ain't a one-sided affair.

Daly begins with his detective spoiling for action: "Sometimes things is slow, and I go out looking for business."

On this particular night, prowling the streets of New York, Mack happens upon a kidnap: a lovely young woman is being hustled into a cab. Terry grabs a ride on the tire rack, works his way into the car, and proceeds to get rid of the thugs. After taking the victim home, he is hired by her uncle to recover a secret formula (for a deadly gas) and, as a bodyguard, to protect the young lady. His fee is $50 per day, plus bonus money. (He insists on a $200 boost in his daily fee for every enemy corpse he provides.)

When the young woman disappears, Mack works over a stoolie to obtain information on her whereabouts ("I had seen to it that there wasn't enough left of his map to smile . . .") and invades the house where she's being tortured for her father's secret formula. Mack guns down two hoods and breaks into the torture room, only to get conked on the head. (Instant cliché: "Something like a ton of bricks comes down and . . . after that . . . everything goes black.")

Mack wakes up with a gunman facing him, but uses his .25 sleeve weapon to put the thug out of business with a neat shot between the eyes. The heroine is saved—but Mack must face his old adversary, Detective Sergeant Quinn ("who's been trying to hook something on me since George Washington was a boy.") He uses influence to shake free and nab the villain: the young lady's phony uncle, who's been after the formula from the start. Mack brings in the formula, and the heroine burns it for the good of humanity.

At the windup, Mack gets his fee, plus bonus money for the group of thugs he has dispatched along the way. When the heroine appears to be "going soft" on him, he rejects her. (Instant cliché: "I'm off dames; they don't go well with my business.") And, finally, in the classic tradition of the private eye, Mack goes on to the next case, a free-lance gun for hire.

Terry Mack failed to make an impact on readers. Historians of the period have marked Daly's second detective, Race Williams, as the genre's first "popular" private eye—and it is true that Terry Mack quickly faded from sight once Race came gunning along.

In 1946, writing for Howard Haycraft's *The Art of the Mystery Story*, Erle Stanley Gardner named Daly's 1922 *Black Mask* tale "The False Burton Combs" as the earliest Race Williams story. Gardner was mistaken. Actually, the nameless thirty-year-old narrator of "The False Burton Combs" was not even a detective. He called himself "a gentleman adventurer" and "a soldier of fortune," and claimed to make his living by "working against the law breakers." For a fee, he takes on the job of protecting (and later impersonating) a rich man's son, Burton Combs, who is being pursued by gangsters; he casually proceeds to kill three of them during the assignment. The story ends as he accepts a position with the Combs family, leaving his footloose life behind for a job and a wife.

However, it is easy to see why Erle Stanley Gardner confused this story with one featuring Williams: it is told first-person in the same tough, illiterate style—and the "my ethics are my own" code of the hero is identical to that of Race Williams.

Williams made his first *Black Mask* appearance on June 1, 1923 (just two weeks after "Three Gun Terry"), with a novelette called "Knights of the Open Palm." He introduced himself as "a middleman—just a halfway house between the cops and the crooks. I do a little honest shooting once in a while— just in the way of business [but] I never bumped off a guy what didn't need it."

Race was later described by his creator as age thirty, standing five feet eleven and a half and weighing 183 pounds, with dark brown hair and black eyes. "He admires a clever woman," wrote Daly, "and respects a good one, when he finds her. There is nothing soft-boiled about him." Indeed, there was not. Race was never weaponless, not even when he retired for the night. ("I don't shove a gun under my pillow. I sleep with one in my hand.") He thoroughly enjoyed sending bullets into countless enemies, and he was an incredible marksman. In one story Williams fired both .45s simultaneously— and a *single* hole appeared between the villain's eyes!

During his violent career, Race Williams gunned down several dozen assorted hoods and master criminals ("You can't make hamburger without grinding up a little meat"), operating as a one-man death factory, yet avoiding all legal penalties. Thrill-hungry pulp readers were quick to respond to this trigger-crazed tough guy—and his unlikely exploits filled the pages of *Black Mask* for the next dozen years. Daly had Williams blast his way through eight serials and some two dozen shorter adventures for the magazine.

Carroll John Daly is today unremembered, unread. And the reason is clear: from the outset of his career in 1922, to the end of his pulp productivity in the mid-1950s, he remained an awkward, self-conscious hack, endlessly repetitious, hopelessly false. He had absolutely no ability to characterize, nor did he possess a feel for mood or language. He was cursed with a tin ear, and his dialogue was impossibly stilted, lacking the rhythm and bite of Hammett's street argot.

Thirty-three when he created the prototype private eye, he was a small, mousy-looking man who sported round spectacles and a wispy mustache. He was born in Yonkers, New

York, on September 14, 1889, and claimed to have "attended half the prep schools in the state—with a fling at the American Academy of Dramatic Arts." He studied law ("a short stint") and stenography, but gravitated toward theater work. Fellow pulpster Frank Gruber, who met Daly at a *Black Mask* Christmas party in 1937, later recalled that "John was first an usher, then an assistant manager in a motion picture house. He had tried acting, but didn't like it. He eventually owned and operated the first moving picture theater on the boardwalk in Atlantic City."

A well-to-do uncle helped launch Daly's writing career by financing his early efforts at the typewriter. By 1929, Carroll John Daly was a long-established favorite with *Black Mask* readers, and was challenging Hammett as the magazine's most popular writer. By the close of the 1930s, however, Daly's brand of hokey pulp melodrama faded, and within a decade he could no longer find steady markets.

As Gruber recounted: "John had developed a style of writing he found impossible to change. He could not adapt, and finally left New York for California, where he attempted to break into television without success. Toward the end of his life he was reduced to writing for the low-paying comic book market."

In mid-January of 1958, at the age of sixty-eight, Daly died quietly at his home in California. He ended as he had begun, a man unable to rise above his material—and although his pioneering position in hard-boiled detective fiction cannot be disputed, it remained for Hammett's strong development and superior writing style to revolutionize the genre.

4

ON THE JOB WITH CONTINENTAL

*I see him as a little man going forward day after
day through mud and blood and death and
deceit—as callous and brutal and cynical as
necessary—towards a dim goal, with nothing to
push or pull him [to] it except that he has been
hired to reach it.*

—HAMMETT, on the
Continental Op

THE PUNISHING YEARS as a Pinkerton field operative perma-
nently affected Dashiell Hammett. He had witnessed political
corruption at all levels, had dealt with most forms of crime,
from random street fighting to murder, had been punched,
knifed, clubbed, and shot at; he'd dealt with the rich, the
middle class, and the poverty-ridden, with stool pigeons,
thugs, racketeers, dangerous psychopaths, and elegant blackmailers. He had moved warily through a world of lies, cross-
treacheries, and dark, mindless violence, where his only
stability was the job itself. To survive, he had learned to curb
excessive emotional response, to become hard-shelled and
outwardly impassive, to trust no one, to see the world through
a cynic's eye.

This was the attitude that Hammett brought to crime fiction
in the early 1920s. As novelist Joe Gores has said, "Hammett
was not a writer learning about private detection; he was a
private detective learning about writing."

When he began developing his type of diamond-hard

45

detective tale for *Black Mask,* Hammett was not setting out to
innovate but was simply putting on paper, honestly and directly, the grim world he knew best. Reflectively, he brought
the argot of the streets into print, portraying the people of his
world with total authenticity, allowing them to talk and behave on paper as they had talked and behaved in his Pinkerton
years. The inadvertent result was what Ellery Queen called
"The first 100 percent American . . . truly native detective
story."

Hammett's first major creation was the nameless operative
from the Continental Detective Agency who made his debut
in October 1923, in the story "Arson Plus."

In the year between "The Parthian Shot" in *Smart Set* and
"Arson Plus" in *Black Mask,* Hammett had eight other stories
printed, covering a wide range of style, mood, and subject
matter. But with the Continental Op, Hammett sharpened the
focus of his crime writing and gave it definition—hard-boiled,
realistic. With the Op, the suave, impeccably correct gentleman detective gave way to a dumpy little middle-aged man
who was out to "get a job done." He was no genteel, bloodless sifter of clues: he bled, got bruised, used fist or gun when
he had to, and read *people* more often than clues.

"This business of a detective poring endlessly over clues to
solve a crime is overdone," Hammett declared. "The difference between the knotty problem confronting the detective of
fiction and that facing the real detective is that in the former
there is usually a paucity of clues and in the latter altogether
too many."

The Op, like Hammett, learned that truth must be reached
gradually, by a process of elimination, that it exists behind a
fog of lies and deception. Fearful people seldom speak the
truth; guilty ones, never.

Based on Hammett's Pinkerton mentor in Baltimore,
Jimmy Wright, the Op was tough, shrewd, and tenacious.
Mainly, of course, the Op was Hammett himself, and many of
the Op's cases were thinly fictionalized versions of real cases
Hammett had worked on as a Pinkerton. (One of the Op's

adventures was, in fact, presented in *True Detective Stories* as "by Dashiell Hammett, of the Continental Detective Agency.")

Hammett never gave the Op a name. Early in the series, in a letter to *Black Mask,* he discussed this lack of identity: "I didn't deliberately keep him nameless, but he got through 'Arson Plus' and 'Slippery Fingers' without needing a name, so I suppose I may as well let him run along that way. He's more or less of a type, and I'm not sure that he's entitled to a name. The private detective who's successful is neither the derby-hatted, broad-toed blockhead of one school of fiction, nor the all-knowing, infallible genius of another. I've worked with several of him. . . ."

Hammett kept the Op's biographical and physical details to a minimum in the three dozen stories he wrote about his tough little crook-catcher.* A careful search through the canon reveals that the Op joined the Continental Detective Agency as "a young sprout of twenty"; he left the agency's Boston branch in 1917 to enlist in the American Expeditionary Force; held a captain's commission in wartime military intelligence; lived as a bachelor and was wary of beautiful women; spoke smatterings of French and German; chainsmoked Fatima cigarettes; did no cooking (eating all his meals in restaurants); played poker at posh Sea Cliff; lived in an apartment house classy enough to have a physician as a fellow resident; liked prize fights; had (in the beginning of the series) been with the San Francisco branch of the Continental Detective Agency for some five years, having transferred there from Chicago; was "heavy and thick-waisted" in his mid-thirties when we first meet him, and aged to "around forty" in the eight years Hammett wrote about him; and had a face that was "a truthful witness to a life that hasn't been overwhelmed with refinement and gentility." He was also described as

---

*This total of thirty-six counts the major Op novels, *Red Harvest* and *The Dain Curse,* as eight stories, since each appeared as four novelettes in *Black Mask.* The third Op novel (in order of book publication), *Blood Money,* was originally printed as two linked novellas.

"hard-boiled" and "pig-headed." Although his adventures were narrated in the first person, the Op disliked talking about himself. (Critic Peter Wolfe has noted: "He tells us nothing of his family, education or religious beliefs.") The Op remained, essentially, the faceless observer-participant in the violently unpredictable universe of crime.

And, always, he was a realist. "What's the use of getting poetic about it?" he growled at a client. "If you've got an honest job to be done and want to pay an honest price for it, maybe I'll take it." The Op was quick to fend off emotional females who wanted more from him than his services as a detective. "Well, good God, sister, I'm only a hired man with a hired man's interest in your troubles." (In later years, responding to a sexually aggressive woman, Raymond Chandler's Marlowe would echo these hard words regarding his job. "I work at it, lady, I don't play at it.")

Hammett's first two Continental Op stories in *Black Mask* were by-lined Peter Collinson. "Arson Plus" appeared in the October 1, 1923, issue, with "Slippery Fingers" following it two weeks later. That same October 15 issue of *Black Mask* also contained the third Op tale, "Crooked Souls" (later collected as "The Gatewood Caper"), the by-line of which was Dashiell Hammett. It was the first use of his real name in the magazine. He had grown fond enough of the series to drop his pseudonym, and no further Op stories were printed under Collinson. Writing for the pulps, particularly *Black Mask,* had become "honest work."

In "Slippery Fingers" Hammett wrote about a forger who had coated his fingers with gelatin and pressed them into a copper plate etched with another man's prints in order to mislead the police. When the magazine questioned this method of faking prints, Hammett replied decisively: "The method used in my story was not selected because it is the best, but because it is the simplest with which I am acquainted and the most easily described. Successful experiments were made with it by experts at Leavenworth."

Hammett created several continuing characters for the

series. Dick Foley was the agency's "shadow ace," a character later described as "a swarthy little Canadian who stood nearly five feet in his high-heeled shoes, weighed a hundred pounds minus, talked like a Scotsman's telegram and could have shadowed a drop of salt water from the Golden Gate to Hong Kong without ever losing sight of it." Bob Teal was introduced as "a youngster who will be a world-beater some day." He was short-lived; Hammett disposed of him in a 1924 story, "Who Killed Bob Teal?" Foley, however, figured in a great many of the Op's adventures, as did Detective Sergeant O'Gar, first mentioned in "Crooked Souls." O'Gar, a "squat man of fifty with sharp blue eyes," ran the Homicide Detail and always wore a black, wide-brimmed western hat (inspired, no doubt, by fellow op Haultain's Stetson). Then there was "the Old Man," the white-mustached manager of the San Francisco branch, who gave the Op his orders. He was in his seventies, taciturn, "with no more warmth in him than a hangman's rope." Yet the Op liked him: "We were proud of his cold-bloodedness. We used to boast he could spit icicles in July."

There is little doubt that the author had his ex-boss Phil Geauque firmly in mind when he wrote about the Old Man. They were both prime examples of cold professionalism. Critic William Ruehlmann sees the Old Man as "the mechanically efficient automaton the Op seems bent on becoming. Hammett's stories are the chronicle of that evolution."

The Op stories were populated by real people from Hammett's past. Speaking of his characters, Hammett wrote to editor George Sutton at *Black Mask:* "I doubt that it would be possible to build a character without putting into him something of someone the writer has known." Years later, he flatly stated: "All of my characters are real. They are based directly on people I knew, or came across."

A non-Op story of that period, "The Vicious Circle," dealt with a blackmailer. Again, Hammett declared it to be a composite based on fact. "In the years I tried my hand at 'private detecting' I ran across several cases where the 'friend' called

in to dispose of a blackmailer either went into partnership
with him or took over his business after getting him out of the
way."

By April of 1924, *Black Mask* had a new editor, Phil Cody—
he had been with the magazine from the beginning, as circulation manager—while Harry North stayed on as chief assistant.
Cody and North sensibly concentrated on headlining Dashiell
Hammett, Carroll John Daly, and Erle Stanley Gardner. (The
creator of the famed Perry Mason novels was just beginning
his long career; as "Charles M. Green," Gardner had made
his first *Black Mask* appearance just four months before with
a lurid scare tale, "The Shrieking Skeleton.") "Phil Cody had
a keen appreciation of literature," Gardner later stated.
"With Cody, the action type of detective story took a long
stride forward."

Under Cody's editorship, Hammett published "The House
in Turk Street" and its sequel, "The Girl with the Silver
Eyes." These linked adventures totaled nearly 24,000 words
and brought Hammett much closer to the novel form.

His favorite theme, which these two stories reflected, was
treachery, in which members of a band of crooks would
square off against one another for individual gain. Hammett's
central character in this type of story was usually a woman,
beautiful, soft-eyed, self-seeking, who would not hesitate to
pile one lie upon another in order to persuade and seduce,
who would use her sexuality as a weapon and her charm as a
shield, who was ruthless and totally without scruples. Such a
creature was red-haired Elvira from "The House in Turk
Street"—a direct prototype of Brigid O'Shaughnessy of *The
Maltese Falcon*. The Op described her: "white face between a
bobbed mass of flame-colored hair. Smoke-gray eyes that
were set too far apart for trustworthiness—though not for
beauty. . . . Her red mouth laughed at me, exposing the edges
of little sharp animal teeth."

It is simple to trace the roots of the *Falcon* in these two
related tales. Tai, the fat Chinese gang leader with the oily

tongue, is an early Casper Gutman, and the trigger-happy Hook prefigures gun-toting Wilmer. The Op plays Spade's role in dealing with them, some hidden bonds serving in place of the jeweled Black Bird. The Op had the bonds, but the fat man had *him*—as Gutman had Spade, who had the bird. Hammett was not yet able to develop these characters with the mature brilliance he later evidenced in *Falcon,* but the roots are clearly here. In the sequel story, "The Girl with the Silver Eyes," we have a preview scene of Brigid's attempt to seduce Spade into freeing her—as Elvira, captured by the Op, spins out her lies in hope of release. She loses. The implacable Op turns her in to pay for the lives of the men she destroyed. Truth (and the job) over beauty.

Hammett himself said that "most of the details [of this story] are based on things I've either run into personally or heard second hand from other detectives. Joplin's road-house . . . is exactly as I have set it down. And stoolie Porky Grout's original died of tuberculosis in Butte, Montana, three years ago. . . ." He discussed the role of the criminal informer: "Stool pigeons are almost without exception more cowardly even than the ordinary crook, yet they follow the most dangerous calling in the criminal world. Not only is their world against them, but the detectives who use them seldom hesitate to sacrifice them if anything is gained thereby."

Another Op tale, "Fly Paper," was based on two actual poisoning cases in which Hammett had been involved as a Pinkerton—and featured a tough gangster named Babe McCloor. Hammett revealed his prototype: "The real McCloor was a member of Jimmie the Riveter's mob. They were a nasty bunch of boys we ran down in the winter of 1921. They'd been pulling stickups along the Pacific Coast and knocking over various commercial enterprises—until Jimmie was taken into custody coming out of a post office in Seattle. Just outside, the yegg who was McCloor's original made a dive, handcuffs and all, for a deputy's gun—and shot it out, cowboy-style, right there on the street."

During the course of his career in *Black Mask,* the Op used a gun as often as necessary and, by rough count, killed no less than fifteen men and women, wounding at least another dozen. Hammett did not glorify violence (in the Daly manner), but neither did he *avoid* violence when a story called for it. ("When people shoot at a detective he tends to shoot back.")

In August of 1924 two of Hammett's Op stories were rejected. Cody and North had tightened the editorial reins, and were returning manuscripts which they felt needed additional work. Writing Harry North on the matter, Hammett took full blame: "The trouble is, this sleuth of mine has degenerated into a meal ticket . . . and recently I've fallen into the habit of bringing him out and running him around whenever the landlord, or the butcher, or the grocer shows signs of nervousness. . . . There are men who can write like that, but I am not one of them. If I stick to the stuff I want to write . . . I can make a go of it, but when I try to grind out a yarn just because I think there's a market for it, then I flop. . . . I want to thank you and Mr. Cody for jolting me into wakefulness."

A prime virtue of the Hammett series is that the Op narrates his adventures in the natural language of a hard-working street detective. According to critic Frederick Gardner: "Hammett never merely played lexicographer to the underworld. He selected the witty, colorful elements of the jargon and used them naturally, knowledgeably, without dazzling or digressing for the sake of innovation, but always to advance his story."

We believe what the Op tells us because his behavior and attitudes are inevitable within his environment, and because his methods of crime detection rang true. The Op questioned anyone and everyone connected with the crime at hand, patiently collected bits of verbal and physical evidence (the shape of a man's ear, a woman's tone of voice, the exact layout of several intersecting avenues): he shadowed suspects, examined police lab reports, and requested extra help from his agency whenever he felt the case merited it. He did not panic or bow to pressure or persuasion; he was never in a hurry.

Although the Op used all available outside means to help him run down lawbreakers, Hammett still placed his main emphasis on the man himself. Writing about the devices of scientific detecting, Hammett declared: "Many are excellent when kept to their places, but when pushed forward as infallible methods, they become forms of quackery. The trouble is that criminals are so damned unscientific. The chemist and the photographer make excellent assistants to our old friend, the flat-footed, low-browed gumshoe, but he's the boy who keeps the jails full of crooks in the long run."

Asked, years later, about the job of the writer, Hammett made a statement that applies directly to the Op series: "The contemporary writer's job is to take pieces of life and arrange them on paper. And the more direct their passage from street to paper the more lifelike they should turn out. . . . He needs to make what is set down seem truly contemporary, to give the impression of things happening here and now, to force upon the reader a feeling of immediacy. . . . He must know how things happen—not how they are remembered in later years—and he must write them down that way." Clipped, rapid-fire dialogue and lean, objective description comprised the Hammett style. He was attempting to reproduce the terse speech of men and women who say no more than they have to. Hammett's protagonists, from the Continental Op to Sam Spade, combined the cynic and the idealist. Their carefully preserved toughness formed a barrier against the threatening world. No one could buy them off or bluff them; they were capable of killing, but as the frontier sheriff kills, in the line of duty against a larger evil. Bitterness and cynicism came with the territory. Stripped of sentiment, Hammett's characters moved warily through a fragmented landscape in which sudden death existed as part of the scenery, adjusting their morals to fit the dangers and temptations encountered en route. Taut self-discipline was a tool of survival. Yet, idealistically, they hoped for a better world, worked doggedly toward it. In his stories and novels, Hammett gave such characters organic form; he made them coldly, logically alive to the reader.

Even as Hammett developed the hard-boiled genre, he transcended it. Peter Wolfe has stated: "The vision of depravity Hammett puts forth is too rich . . . to fit under the umbrella term hard-boiled. His lank, spare idiom didn't rule out sophistication, subtlety, or range. Although he developed his fast-moving action without moral commentary, his objective realism cuts deep." And in the words of Ross Macdonald: "As a novelist of realistic intrigue, Hammett was unsurpassed in his own or any time."

Hammett sent the Op on all kinds of cases. The little detective was hired by insurance companies, businessmen, attorneys, and housewives—always working out of the Continental Agency in San Francisco, with the locale usually the city itself or the areas surrounding it.* Mainly, Hammett sent him out to trace killers, investigate robberies, and find missing persons—but the Op also functioned as guard, payoff man, house detective, and town tamer.

Hammett used the San Francisco of the twenties much as Chandler, in his Philip Marlowe novels, used the Los Angeles of the thirties. Chandler allowed Marlowe to describe his locale, to remark at length on its beauty and ugliness, its flowers, trees, architecture. Hammett, however, rarely did more than mention the name of a street or building in order to pinpoint his action. Descriptive passages were terse and compressed. Therefore, Hammett's San Francisco, undescribed, is timeless, while Chandler's old Los Angeles—with its wooden oil derricks along La Brea and its bridle paths dividing Beverly Hills—must now be enjoyed on the level of nostalgia. Hammett's fiction retains amazing freshness and immediacy, even in the 1980s. It has not dated.

William Ruehlmann, in his genre study, *Saint with a Gun*, credits the Op's adventures as "the first [series of] American

---

*Three of Hammett's five novels are set in San Francisco (*Blood Money, The Dain Curse, The Maltese Falcon*), and twenty-eight of his collected short stories and novelettes have a San Francisco locale.

detective stories that might genuinely be called literature." In writing these tales, Hammett had no such grand purpose in mind; he had cigarettes to buy, wine to pay for, rent to meet. Writing kept him alive; it also functioned as catharsis in a period when his despair had become severe. Beset by crippling lung trouble, in and out of VA hospitals, troubled by the civic corruption darkening the city around him, Dashiell Hammett needed to find a sense of mental order to balance the outward disorder of his life. The crime stories he wrote served this end. Through the Op, Hammett was able to create, with the piece-by-piece solving of a crime, a form of completion. His cases were as rigidly disciplined as a chess game, to be played out and won. The Op was Hammett's rational self, surviving within an irrational world of violence and treachery.

As the Op survived, Hammett survived.

5

"ACTION, MORE ACTION!"

*If action, however violent, evolves from character,
there is no higher literary expression—and the
ultimate crystallization of character is likely to be
physical rather than psychological action.*

—ARTHUR S. HOFFMAN,
editor of *Adventure*

LATE IN 1924 Hammett's doctor advised him to separate
from his family. His pulmonary tuberculosis had flared up
again, to a highly contagious stage, and there was a danger
that he would infect his wife and three-year-old daughter.

"We talked things over," Mrs. Hammett stated. "It was
decided that I would take Mary Jane back to Anaconda, Montana, and that we would live there until Samuel was well
enough to have us return to San Francisco. I remember we
stayed in Montana about six months."

Hammett remained in the Eddy Street apartment, spending
up to twenty hours each day in bed, attempting to rebuild his
health. He placed a line of chairs from the bed to the bathroom door to support himself when he arose at night. In the
beginning he ate very little, since his stomach refused to hold
down food, but slowly his appetite returned.

"I did only two things in those months," he later recalled.
"I read and I wrote."

His reading included the magazine *Writer's Digest,* which
helped him keep abreast of current markets. That year the
Digest printed an article by pulp writer H. Bedford-Jones,

warning young writers to stay clear of sexual aspects in their
fiction, asserting that such work would affect both their reputation and their "mental fibre." Hammett was quick to respond. He began by expressing his total disagreement with
Bedford-Jones. "If you have a story that seems worth telling,
and you think you can tell it worthily, then the thing for you
to do is tell it, regardless of whether it has to do with sex,
sailors or mounted policemen. Sex has never made a poor
story good, or a good one poor. . . ."

To back up his argument, he cited works by Anatole France
and Shakespeare. Even in 1924, Hammett was displaying a
wide grasp of classic literature; he was training himself to be
a fine writer in the same thorough manner he had trained
himself to be a fine detective. Hammett was never a man to
do things by half—as he was to prove through the years with
his all-stops-out drinking, womanizing, and gambling.

The writing of fiction, however satisfying, failed to meet his
complete need for intellectual expression. He also placed
verse with *The Lariat,* nonfiction with *The Editor,* and book
reviews with *The Forum.* In the August 1925 issue of *Forum,*
reviewing a book entitled *Everyman's Genius,* Hammett gave
his own definition: "The eternal problem of the creative
worker . . . is to bring his whole mind, his every faculty, to bear
on the task under his hand. To the extent that he succeeds,
granted adequate equipment, he produces what we ordinarily
call a work of genius."

In the late spring of 1925 Hammett's doctor at the Veterans
Bureau advised him that his condition had stabilized; he was
no longer a danger to his family. Hammett's wife and daughter moved back to San Francisco, into a larger apartment that
Hammett had rented in the same building at 620 Eddy. Now
he had enough space to set up his desk in the living room.

During these early professional years, in addition to his
Continental Op stories, Hammett was experimenting with
various themes, ideas, and characters, exploring multiple fa-
cets of the human condition in his fiction. "The Second-Story
Angel" (1923) concerned a sweet-faced young lady crook who

makes fools of several men, including the protagonist, a crime writer. A sharp character study, "The Green Elephant" (1923), featured a small-time crook, Joe Shupe, "an unskilled laborer in the world of crime," who comes into accidental possession of a quarter of a million dollars. Emotionally unable to deal with this kind of "success," Shupe cracks under the burden of such a treasure—and is himself again only after he has been apprehended. In "The Man Who Killed Dan Odams" (1924), Hammett handled the theme of a vengeance murder in stark, memorable fashion.

Also in 1924, *Argosy All-Story* published Hammett's pulp novelette "Nightmare Town." In response to editors' cries of "Action, more action!" Hammett had decided to find out just how much pure action he could crowd into one story; the result was amazing in terms of force and forward movement. A direct forerunner of the "Poisonville" (*Red Harvest*) series, this story treats the same theme: total city corruption. Hammett portrays the town of Izzard, wholly owned by thieves and murderers—a town that hero Steve Threefall enters against his will. In the course of the narrative, Steve links up with heroine Nova Vallance; at the climax, with half the town after them, they head for Izzard's one honest soul, Blind Rymer. That sweet old gentleman hauls out a brace of pistols and reveals himself to be as crooked as all the other townspeople. Armed only with an ebony walking stick, Steve escapes with the girl—but they must fight their way clear.

In that final, wild, tour de force of a climax, Hammett creates total action on the printed page:

> Men filled the doorway. A gun roared and a piece of the ceiling flaked down. Steve . . . charged the door . . . the stick whipped backward and forward. . . . The rhythm of incessant thudding against flesh and clicking on bone became a tune that sang through the grunts of fighting men. . . . [Outside, in the car] Steve was swinging his stick against skin and thigh. . . . The car swerved [against] a building, scraped one side clear of men. . . . Steve fell

into the seat beside the girl. . . . Pistols exploded behind
them . . . a bitter-voiced rifle emptied itself at them . . .
and then the desert—white and smooth as a gigantic hospital bed—was around them.

As the wicked town burns, a biblical Sodom and Gomorrah,
Steve and Nova drive off, with Steve marveling, "What a fight!
What a fight!"

Another strong tale of the period, "Ruffian's Wife" (1925,
published in *Sunset*), marked a departure for Hammett in that
he wrote the story in a subjective third-person style, from the
viewpoint of a woman, the wife of "ruffian" Guy Tharp. The
monumental toughness of Tharp is breeched by a threat from
a perfumed fat man, Leonidas Doucas (another early prototype for Casper Gutman). Doucas is eventually killed by
Tharp, but only with Tharp's wife's help. In saving her brutal
husband, she surrenders the idealistic image she had built;
reality replaces fantasy in her life. This story is extremely well
written, an experiment in style that Hammett brought off
quite successfully.

In 1925 Hammett thought it might be fun to write a "tradi-
tional" western for *Black Mask* featuring the Op. Thus, in
"Corkscrew," Hammett sent his plump little detective out of
San Francisco to the fictional town of Corkscrew, Arizona,
supplied him with cowboy attire, a fast-stepping horse, and a
pair of six-guns, and involved him with rough hombres such
as Gyp Rainey, Milk River, and various Circle H.A.R. ranch
riders. (It must be borne in mind that the Arizona west of
1925, when this story was printed in *Black Mask*, was still
largely rough and untrammeled.) The Op drank at Bordell's
Border Palace, brawled with the town bully, tamed a bucking
bronc, and dry-gulched villains. It was Zane Grey time, and
Hammett thoroughly enjoyed himself.

Westerns were a staple to *Black Mask* readers, and more
often than not the cover featured a western action painting.
Many of the magazine's top talents wrote their share of six-
gun sagas. (Erle Stanley Gardner turned out a lengthy series

of oaters starring gunslinger Black Bart.) Actually, as critics have pointed out, the private detective is a direct carryover from the lone western gunfighter, that mythic folk hero who righted wrongs with a weapon at his hip and who preserved ideals of justice in the face of raw frontier violence. In later years, as *Black Mask* put its full emphasis on big-city crime, the old and new West blended into the figure of the mythic private eye who rode into the sunset at the wheel of a Ford and who packed a .45 in his armpit in place of a Colt at his hip. But, basically, he was the same man.

For the Op, however, the western setting was alien. Almost always, Hammett kept him in San Francisco, using different parts of the city from story to story. One of the most colorful of San Francisco locales was (and still is) its Chinatown district, and Hammett often gambled and drank there, savoring the atmosphere and familiarizing himself with its gaudy sights, sounds, and colors. "In those days," he wrote, "if you ran a joint in Chinatown you had a bodyguard whether you needed one or not, just to rate. There was this roly-poly Chinese muscleboy offered to me by a friend who owned a dive down there, to use if I had anybody I wanted pushed around—a leg broken or something—but I was not to spoil him by giving him money for this service. 'Five or ten bucks is okay for a tip,' I was told, 'but no more.' I didn't take advantage of the offer—but I *did* write the Chinese into a picture much later in Hollywood."

Hammett sent his Continental detective to Chinatown in "Dead Yellow Women" (1925) with spectacular results. In this carefully structured story, Hammett created one of his most memorable characters, the effusive, snake-treacherous Chang Li Ching, who addresses the fat little Op as, variously, the Father of Detectives, the Prince of Thief Catchers, the Emperor of Hawkshaws, the Unveiler of Secrets, the Terror of Evildoers, the Lord of Snares, and the King of Finders-Out. The Op is unruffled; he knows he must never turn his back on Chang. Their cat-and-mouse relationship makes the story a special delight.

Another outstanding Op tale, "The Gutting of Couffignal" (1925), brought Hammett closer to the novel format in terms of plot and characterization. The action takes place on an imaginary island in San Pablo Bay. Like "Corkscrew" and "Dead Yellow Women," it is an extravaganza, a wildly violent example of Hammett at full throttle. The climactic scene, between the Op and tricky Princess Zhukovski, offered Hammett a final rehearsal before he was to pit Spade against Brigid for their memorable *Falcon* showdown.

"I'm a detective because I happen to like the work," says the Op. "And liking work makes you want to do it as well as you can. . . . That's the fix I'm in [and] catching crooks is the only kind of sport I know anything about. . . . You think I'm a man and you're a woman. That's wrong. I'm a hunter and you're something that has been running in front of me. There's nothing human about it."

When she tries to get away, he shoots her in the leg.

Editor Cody had been urging Hammett to attempt a novel, but he did not feel ready for long-form fiction quite yet; he was still learning, still finding his literary footing in new experiments.

In September of 1925 Jose announced her second pregnancy, and by the end of that year Hammett was painfully short of money. No matter how many stories he wrote, he could not earn enough to feed an extra child. He informed Phil Cody, early in 1926, that he could no longer continue to supply fiction to *Black Mask* at his present word rate. Hammett demanded a raise.

Cody replied that, regrettably, a raise was impossible. ("If you got it, then Erle Gardner would have to have more, and if *he* got more we'd have to raise Daly and . . .")

Okay, Hammett told him, he'd just quit the magazine.

In a panic, Cody took the problem to Gardner. *Black Mask,* he said, might very well "go under" without Dash Hammett.

"I found myself in an embarrassing situation," Gardner recalled. "I was practicing law then, and making enough money out of it so I didn't need to depend on writing to get by. But on the other hand, *Black Mask* was my only regular market and if it couldn't stay in business without Hammett I would suffer along with all the other writers."

Gardner made Cody an amazing offer: he would cut a cent a word off his story rate for the magazine, allowing Cody to add it to Hammett's rate. That way, Dash would get his raise and *Black Mask* would not be out of pocket.

Cody agreed, but when he took this offer to Eltinge Warner, the owner of the magazine, he was told that Gardner's idea was "cockeyed." If Hammett wanted to quit, let him.

"He just doesn't realize how much we need those Op stories," Cody complained to Gardner. "What can we do?"

"We can go to San Francisco. I can talk Dash into staying aboard. He'll listen to me."

When they arrived at Hammett's apartment, Jose answered the door. She had never met either of them and was convinced they were bill collectors. "We have business with your husband," they told her.

"He's out of town," she said. "And I have no idea when he'll be back."

They left without seeing him.

Frustrated at his inability to earn a decent living in the pulp market, Hammett decided to go after a full-time job and give up fiction writing. He could not continue to support his family on two thousand a year. In March of 1926 he placed a "position wanted" ad in the San Francisco *Chronicle*, listing his former occupations, from warehouseman to detective, ending with the words "and I can write."

Albert S. Samuels, who had established the oldest jewelry business in the city and was the first local jeweler to use large newspaper ads in place of the usual handbills, needed a writer to turn out his ad copy. Samuels then owned four stores, with the one at 895 Market as his base, the store he called "The House of Lucky Wedding Rings." A friend from the *Chronicle* brought Hammett into the Market Street store and introduced him to Samuels as "your new advertising manager." Impressed with Hammett's wide background, the jeweler hired him immediately, since he fulfilled Samuels' dictum: "Never hire anybody who doesn't know more than you do."

Under the pressures of a full-time job—8 A.M. to 6 P.M. Monday through Saturday—Hammett began drinking heavily again. "He'd write copy for me all day," Samuels remembered. "Then he'd go home to his apartment and drink during most of the night, sobering up enough to report in the next morning. But he always did fine work. I recall particularly his 'romantic' approach, which was ideal for us."

One such Hammett ad depicted two young lovers standing hand in hand atop the globe. The girl is wearing a new diamond ring, and Hammett's tag line read, "A Samuels diamond puts you on top of the world."

With his initial paycheck from Samuels, Hammett rented a second apartment at 408 Turk, at the corner of Larkin. He moved all of his art materials to the Turk address and set up what he called "my studio." At night, as his family slept, he would often work there on ad design and layouts.

In addition to handling the store's regular newspaper advertising, Hammett wrote the weekly "essay ad" in the *Examiner*. At a length of some 300 words, ghosted by Hammett under the Samuels by-line, each ad told a brief story in dramatic form—designed to inspire readers to purchase a Samuels diamond.

Hammett's approach in writing these pieces echoed his objective crime fiction in his use of irony and understatement. In one essay ad, aimed at the parents of graduating students, Hammett pointed out that *no* diamond watch or ring at Samuels would really be a satisfactory reward for all the work of obtaining a college degree. He ended the ad with these soft-sell words: "Is there any gift you can give . . . that will pay [the graduate] in full? Probably not, but you might do what you can."

Samuels gave Hammett an assistant, Peggy O'Toole, to serve as ad artist and secretary. Peggy was young, single, and attractive. A San Francisco girl, she had graduated from Mission High School in 1918.

Hammett liked her, and she was swayed by his cool charm.

The Parthian Shot

By Dashiell Hammett

WHEN the boy was six months old Paulette Key acknowledged that her hopes and efforts had been futile, that the baby was indubitably and irremediably a replica of its father. She could have endured the physical resemblance, but the duplication of Harold Key's stupid obstinacy—unmistakable in the fixity of the child's inarticulate demands for its food, its toys—was too much for Paulette. She knew she could not go on living with *two* such natures! A year and a half of Harold's domination had not subdued her entirely. She took the little boy to church, had him christened Don, sent him home by his nurse, and boarded a train for the West.

Opposite, H. L. Mencken and George Jean Nathan, whose magazines, *The Smart Set* and *Black Mask*, published Hammett's earliest work. Also, two Hammett residences: 20 Monroe Street and 891 Post Street.

Above, the first appearance of the Hammett by-line, in *The Smart Set*, October 1922. Below, the jeweler's for whom he wrote advertising copy.

A relationship quickly developed. They met for after-work drinks—and, on weekends, she would visit Hammett at his studio apartment on Turk.

Hammett's interest in Peggy O'Toole was ill-timed. On May 24, 1926, Jose gave birth to their second daughter, Josephine Rebecca. The Hammett-O'Toole relationship was over.

Hammett was now financially responsible for two children. But the new job was paying him $350 a month, which was a great deal more than he'd been able to earn at his fiction, and Jose was finally able "to keep ahead of the bills."

In late July, less than five months after he had gone to work for Samuels, Hammett suffered a collapse. He fell to the floor of his office, coughing blood, and was taken to the veterans' hospital, hemorrhaging from the lungs.

After eight full weeks away from his job, Hammett reluctantly accepted the fact that he was simply not strong enough to handle the full-time duties of an advertising manager; his weakened health would not permit it.

Al Samuels wrote an official letter to the Veterans Bureau, stating that his employee, Samuel Dashiell Hammett, was unable to continue his duties. The Bureau placed Hammett on a one hundred percent disability pension (amounting to approximately $100 a month). But the Bureau told him that he must live alone, that he might infect his family.

Hammett took a furnished room at 20 Monroe Street and rented an apartment at 1309 Hyde Street for his wife and children. Once they were settled in, he moved to a small, two-room flat at 891 Post, where he again took up the business of free-lance advertising. It was a course Hammett chose deliberately. "Samuel didn't want to go back to writing his stories," Jose recalled. "He thought he could make more as an advertising man."

Hammett's commitment to this trade was reflected in his essay "The Advertisement IS Literature," printed in the October 1926 issue of the monthly journal *Western Advertising*. Sections of this essay are of particular interest, since they convey his views about prose:

Every writer who brings an idea to a blank sheet of paper is faced by the same primary task. He must set his idea on the paper in such form that it will have the effect he desires on those who read it. . . . The selection and arrangement of words is a literary problem, no matter whether the work be a poem, a novel, a love letter or an advertisement. . . . Every man who works with words for effects is a literary worker. . . . Clarity is the first and greatest of literary virtues. . . . Simplicity and clarity . . . are the most elusive and difficult of literary accomplishments. . . . They are the most important qualities in securing the maximum desired effect on the reader.

Hammett goes on to make his point by quoting from a variety of sources, including Joseph Conrad, Anatole France, and Aristotle, again, as he had done earlier in *Writer's Digest,* freely displaying his knowledge of literature.

By that fall, deep into advertising, Hammett considered himself a retired fiction writer. He might never have produced *The Maltese Falcon* or any of his other novels had it not been for a man whose name appeared on the *Black Mask* masthead for the first time in the November 1926 issue. The new editor's name was Joseph Thompson Shaw.

6

LEADING THE *BLACK MASK* BOYS

In only a decade of creative activity Hammett
exerted an influence on the American detective story
greater than that of any author since Poe.

—ANTHONY BOUCHER

"CAP" SHAW WAS fifty-two in the summer of 1926, when he assumed editorship of *The Black Mask* for Pro-Distributors Publishing Company of New York. Shaw knew nothing whatever about pulp magazines, and later swore that until the day he walked into the Forty-fifth Street offices of the publication, he'd never even seen an issue. He had to spend several days reading back numbers of the magazine to familiarize himself with the type of fiction it printed. His first editorial decision was to streamline the title: *The Black Mask* became, simply, *Black Mask.*

Shaw was not at all concerned about his lack of pulp experience, having successfully taken on many challenges in his half-century of life. He was a graduate of Bowdoin College, where he had edited the campus paper and won a national championship in sabers; during the First World War he had served as a captain—earning his nickname, "Cap"—in charge of bayonet instruction; he'd spent five years as chief of a Hoover mission to Czechoslovakia, and he was an accomplished sailor.

Joe Shaw's stated ambition, from the day he took over, was to make *Black Mask* the outstanding publication in its field. (He refused to use the word "pulp," referring to *Black Mask*

66

as a "rough-paper book.") More than any other of the magazine's previous editors, he developed and refined the form of
realistic detective fiction originated by Hammett. Editorially,
Shaw is the man most closely associated with "the *Black Mask*
school" of objective, hard-boiled literature.

At Shaw's arrival, the major names were already established
in *Black Mask:* Hammett, Daly, Gardner, Raoul Whitfield,
Frederick Nebel, Nels Jorgenson, and Tom Curry. (Raymond
Chandler would sell Shaw his first story, "Blackmailers Don't
Shoot," in 1933.) Joe Shaw favored writers who were men of
action—it was said that Shaw himself, as a crack fencer, had
perfected a thrust with the épée against which there was no
known defensive stroke. He boasted of Hammett's Pinkerton
years; Tom Curry was a former police reporter; Whitfield had
been a combat aviator in the First World War; Gardner was
a world traveler, treasure hunter, and sportsman; and Nels
Jorgenson was a New Jersey motorcycle cop.

Shaw recognized Dashiell Hammett's position in the new
genre: "Hammett was the leader in [what] finally brought the
magazine its distinctive form. . . . I wanted to make full use
of his rare ability of observation and his gift to analyze character beneath a surface appearance. . . . Hammett told his stories with a new kind of compulsion and authenticity. And he
was one of the most careful and painstaking workmen I have
ever known."

When Shaw checked the magazine's inventory, he found no
scheduled Hammett stories and was told that the writer was
no longer doing fiction. Hammett had not appeared in *Black
Mask* since "The Creeping Siamese," an Op tale printed in
the March 1926 issue. Shaw was determined to lure Hammett
back to the magazine.

He wrote Hammett a very persuasive letter, telling him that
he wanted fiction of quality in the new *Black Mask.* He would
give Hammett a free hand in creating it and pay him premium
rates for his work (four cents a word, rising to six cents later).
Shaw also urged Hammett to attempt longer, more fully developed stories; he felt that the Op, in novel form, could reach

a large audience of book readers. He suggested extending the Op's fictional range to allow greater depth and character expansion.

Shaw's letter succeeded, and Hammett's reply was enthusiastic: "You've hit on exactly what I've been thinking about. . . . As I see it, the approach I have in mind has never been attempted. The field is unscratched and wide open."

Over the next four years, into late 1930, Joe Shaw became something of a father figure to Hammett. He provided a ready market for Hammett's best fiction, and took immense pride in his star writer's achievements.

In January of 1927 Shaw was trumpeting Hammett's return to the fold in *Black Mask:* "Dashiell Hammett has called back the Continental detective from his long retirement and is setting him to work anew." The Op's retirement had lasted almost a year. In the February issue, the tough-minded crimefighter was indeed back in a long novella, "The Big Knockover," which began with the simultaneous holdup of two large San Francisco banks.

In defending the premise of this spectacular piece of crime fiction, Shaw wrote an editorial blurb to accompany Hammett's story: "Before they actually do it, one is inclined to say it isn't done. But the gang warfare in Illinois, the big mail truck holdup in Jersey, found bandits using airplanes, bombs, and machine guns—and now Mr. Hammett pictures a daring action that is stunning in its scope, yet can anyone be sure it isn't likely to occur?"

The action was indeed stunning: more than 150 gangsters, gathered from around the nation, descend on the Seaman's National Bank and its neighbor, the Golden Gate Trust. In the bloody double robbery, sixteen policemen die along with a dozen spectators. Seven of the bandits are gunned to death while the others speed off. Yet the bloodletting has just begun. As the Op gets into the case, he finds that the gangs are mowing each other down over the stolen loot. He finds fourteen dead crooks on Fillmore, then hits another house to find six more bodies. The roll call on the dead reveals Hammett at his most savagely poetic:

> There was the Dis-and-Dat Kid, who had crashed out of Leavenworth only two months before . . . L. A. Slim, from Denver, sockless as usual, with a thousand-dollar bill sewed in each shoulder of his coat; Spider Girrucci, wearing a steel-mesh vest under his shirt and a scar from crown to chin . . . Bull McGonickle, still pale from fifteen years in Joliet; Toby the Lugs . . . who used to brag about picking President Wilson's pocket in a Washington vaudeville theatre . . . Donkey Marr, last of the bow-legged Marrs, killers all, father and five sons; Toots Salda . . . who had once picked up and run away with two Savannah coppers . . . and Rumdum Smith, who killed Lefty Read in Chi—a rosary wrapped around his left wrist.

In "The Big Knockover," the Op becomes an animalistic man of violence; a fight tones his system, fires his blood: "My blackjack crunched the arm of the man in front . . . I trusted my arms and legs and saved bullets . . . swing right, swing left, kick . . . don't look for targets. God will see to it there's always a mug for your blackjack to sock, a belly for your foot. . . ."

Perhaps Hammett was remembering the all-out brawl with the dynamite gang when he was a Pinkerton; certainly, this sequence has authentic bite.

In a sweep of headlong action, the Op punches and shoots his way through the narrative, wrapping things up by nailing Bluepoint Vance and Big Flora, both in on the double-bank caper. However, he allows the "mastermind" to escape, a string-thin old Greek named Papadopoulos, who takes the woman in the case, Nancy Regan, with him on the runout. The Op vows to get him—which leads into the sequel.

Published in *Black Mask* three months later, "$106,000 Blood Money" (referring to the reward offered) maintained the razzle-dazzle pace of the first story—with the Op surviving an ambush set up by a man he trusted, Jack Counihan, a fellow op out of Continental. At the climax, we learn that Counihan had fallen for Nancy Regan and "gone bad" under her influence. The disgraced young op is shot to death—and Hammett's veteran detective reports it all to the Old Man. Both the Old Man and the Op are relieved that Jack Counihan's death will seem heroic to the press and that the agency will not suffer "a black eye." The Op tells his chief that he needs a couple of weeks off, that he's "tired, washed out." The story ends on this gray note of exhaustion.

There were too many gratuitous killings in this two-parter, too much melodramatic action piled on action, for Hammett to achieve the level of characterization required for a successful novel. (Totaling 38,000 words, it was later brought out in book form as *Blood Money.*) Yet it displays masterful pacing and a tremendous zest for narrative and situation. Philip Durham declared: "If there is such a thing as the poetry of violence, Hammett clearly achieved it in this brief novel . . . with hero, style and setting developed beyond the limits of the short story."

When Willard Huntington Wright left *The Smart Set* to Nathan and H. L. Mencken, he had no intention of becoming a mystery novelist. In fact, he set out to write a series of nonfiction books designed to establish him as an outstanding intellectual. Wright was partially successful in this, but became heavily addicted to opium, and in 1923 his health failed completely. For six months, he was isolated in a Paris clinic, with nothing to read but detective stories. They intrigued him, and after his recovery he decided to create a series of his own: "I've studied the detective novel, and I understand its rules and techniques. I know its needs, and have learned its pitfalls."

He then proceeded to develop plots for a series of novels featuring an eccentric detective he called Philo Vance. Editor Maxwell Perkins of Scribner's accepted the first of these, and Wright's career as a popular crime novelist began in 1926, with the publication of *The Benson Murder Case,* by-lined "S. S.

Van Dine" (a name Wright had chosen for its exotic flavor).

The book was an instant hit with mystery readers, its first edition selling out just a week after publication. The review copy sent to *The Saturday Review of Literature*, however, was treated with open scorn by the magazine's new crime-fiction critic. He attacked Philo Vance as "a bore" whose "conversational manner is that of a high school girl who has been studying the foreign words in the back of the dictionary." The scathing reviewer continued:

> There is a theory that any one who talks enough on any subject must, if only by chance, finally say something not altogether incorrect. Vance disproves this theory; he manages, always and usually ridiculously, to be wrong. . . . The murderer's identity becomes obvious quite early in the story. The authorities . . . would have cleared up the mystery promptly if they had been allowed to follow the most rudimentary police routine. . . . [Van Dine] doesn't let them ask any questions that aren't wholly irrelevant. They can't make inquiries of anyone who might know anything. . . . When information concerning a mysterious box of jewelry accidentally bobs up, everybody resolutely ignores it, since it would have led to a solution before the three hundredth page. Mr. Van Dine doesn't deprive his officials of every liberty, however; he generously lets them compete with Vance . . . in the expression of idiocies.

The caustic critic was Dashiell Hammett, supplementing his income as a fiction writer. He was to review some half-hundred crime titles for *Saturday Review* over the next three years, into late October of 1929. Armed with a hard-won professional knowledge of police procedure, Hammett had no patience with amateurs. He was particularly annoyed by the unrealistic, ornate Vance novels. (Raymond Chandler was later to agree with Hammett, referring to Wright's detective as "probably the most asinine character in American fiction.")

Hammett was confident that his brand of hard-boiled impact fiction would triumph over the outmoded crime writing

of the Van Dine school—but he still had to prove himself to
the reading public as a published novelist.

His initial try at a novel was abortive. He completed only
the first 5,000-word section of "The Secret Emperor," set in
Washington, D.C., and Baltimore. Although unfinished—the
manuscript is now among the Hammett papers at the University
of Texas—the fragment is worth examining for what it
reveals of Hammett's state of mind in the late twenties.

The title comes from character Sheth Gutman's plan to set
up a political power base in Washington and establish himself
as "secret emperor of the United States" by electing his own
man as President (a crooked senator named Jarboe). The
plump, villainous character was yet another prototype for
Casper Gutman—Hammett even appropriated his last name
for *Falcon.* Hammett's protagonist is a tall, "copper-haired"
detective named Elfinstone, whose background includes Secret Service work in Latin America. He is described by Hammett as "a ruthless man, without manners, impatient of the
stupidity of people with whom he comes in contact, with little
love for his fellows."

Elfinstone is hired, in Washington, by General Herbert
Dollard, and assigned to trace a valuable document stolen
from a safe deposit box in Baltimore, Maryland. (The nature
of the document is not revealed.) Elfinstone goes to Baltimore, and seems to be making some headway when he's
called back to Washington by Dollard and abruptly dismissed
from the case. The detective recognizes Dollard's wife, Helene, as an ex-spy he had known in Austria during the war;
she'd been responsible for the death of his partner.

He next meets Sheth Gutman's exotic daughter, Tamar,
and they become involved. Fearing that Elfinstone has found
out "too much" while in Baltimore, Dollard attempts to kill
him. The two men fight, and the general himself dies as a
result. Elfinstone is arrested, charged with manslaughter, and
jailed. Sensing a juicy scandal, the Washington papers accuse
him of having had an affair with the dead man's wife, Helene
Dollard.

On behalf of his daughter, Gutman offers to pay Elfin-stone's bail and spirit him out of the country. Tamar begs him to accept her father's offer, but the moody detective suspects a "frame" and is "angered to the point of insanity." Now everyone seems to be out to destroy him. The manuscript ends at this point, but it is plain that Hammett was attempting to paint a bleak picture of twisted political power in Washington. The twenty-three pages of unfinished manuscript reflect a growing concern with political corruption at high levels, and foreshadow his acidulous treatment of this subject in *The Glass Key.*

Hammett was now established as a writer, but his home life was disintegrating. Between long stints at the typewriter (he worked on one novella for thirty-six straight hours) and his hours of night-prowling in the city (gambling, drinking with other women, attending the Winterland's Friday night fights), Hammett spent less and less time with Jose and the children.

Mary Jane, who was then five, loved her father deeply, but sensed his increasing alienation. Hammett would occasionally try to "make things better" by taking the little girl along with him to the town's speakeasies. She recalled these exotic evenings: "Papa would order sparkling water for me—always insisting that it be served in a champagne glass. He did that to make me feel grown up."

She remembers him as a very strict father, but also very loving. He'd read to her while she sat on his lap. "The Owl and the Pussycat" was one of her favorites. ("He also read to me from *Crime and Punishment,* which I didn't understand.") She also recalled that "Papa's editor, Mr. Shaw, visited us once from New York and brought me a doll."

In the spring of 1927 Jose and the two children moved to San Anselmo, which was north of San Francisco, in order to allow Hammett to "think things out." But they soon returned to the city. At each leavetaking the relationship between Hammett and his wife grew more strained. He was now spending most of his time with an attractive widow and music teacher, Nell Martin. A final break with Jose was inevitable.

Hammett's writing was coming into its full maturity. Encouraged by Joe Shaw and by the response from *Black Mask* readers, Hammett had begun the most ambitious project of his career—his first full-length novel. He was writing *Red Harvest.*

7

OF CORRUPTION AND
COMPASSION

*He speaks in a slow drawl, a glint of amusement
in his eye, yet with a kind of shy, lazy, seriousness. . . .
A tall, thin man with a pale, sensitive face and
quiet voice, he is the last person in the world you
would think of as a former Pinkerton detective.*

—New York *Herald
Tribune,* 1933

OVER THE YEARS between 1917, when he had functioned as
a "politically uninvolved" strikebreaker against the I.W.W. in
Montana, and 1927, when he wrote *Red Harvest,** Dashiell
Hammett had developed a deep political conscience.

As a novelist, he now returned (in his imagination) to the
strife-ridden mining town of Butte, which he nicknamed "Poisonville." In the persona of the Continental Op, he was able
to reverse the position he had taken as a Pinkerton man in
1917; he had the Op make an all-out attack on the anti-union
criminals employed by the mining company. Hammett was
redressing old wrongs.

Although Hammett's own experiences in Butte inspired
Red Harvest, another obvious influence was a book by Allan
Pinkerton, *The Model Town and the Detectives,* dealing with a
situation which took place, according to Pinkerton's account,
in Mariola, near Chicago. Like the Op in Hammett's novel,

---

*Printed in four issues of *Black Mask,* as four novelettes, in November and December 1927 and January and February 1928.

Pinkerton accepted the job of town-tamer, hired to clean out "a gang . . . of desperate criminals existing in and about the city, who were sworn to act in concert and to create a reign of terror." And in the same fashion as the Op, Pinkerton demanded control: "I would undertake to clear the town of its active scoundrels on condition that I be allowed to work in my own way without interference by anyone, and that my instructions be obeyed implicitly." Pinkerton got the job done, aided by other operatives. He claimed that criminals, as a group, lacked organization and were therefore "basically unable to maintain a position of lasting power in the community."

Hammett's bleak portrait of Poisonville opposes this view. He makes the point that crime is deeply entrenched in our society. He describes the power of old Elihu Willsson (Sheth Gutman revived!) as president of the main bank in town, majority stockholder in the Mining Corporation, and owner of the city's two newspapers. "Along with these," Hammett added, "he owned a United States senator, a couple of representatives, the governor, the mayor, and most of the state legislature."

The Op arrives in Poisonville on a call from Elihu's son, who is the publisher of the local paper. A civic reformer, the son is shot to death that same night. The Op then goes to old Elihu, who has been working with ganglords Pete the Finn, Lew Yard, Max "Whisper" Thayler, and Noonan, the corrupt chief of police. Having seen his son gunned down and fearful for his own life, the old man hires the Op to "clean up Poisonville." The Op accepts the job, shrewdly deciding to play one gangster off against another. He is with Chief Noonan on a raid against Thayler's place, but ducks inside to warn him that Noonan is closing in, thus setting off a chain of killings, dynamitings, and shootouts.

From chapter to chapter, the Op uses his veteran's knowledge of human weakness to drain the poison from Poisonville. Although he drinks with the town's brassy playgirl, Dinah Brand, he does not make love to her; such entanglements leave a detective open to attack, and the Op wants no flaws in his armor. Yet even the implacable manhunter himself almost cracks in the course of the bloody events. The Op says: "I've got hard skin over what's left of my soul, and after twenty years of messing around with crime I can look at any sort of murder without seeing anything in it but my bread and butter . . . but this getting a rear out of planning deaths is not natural to me. It's what this place has done to me."

He becomes uncertain in his role as mass executioner. Early in the action he declares: "Poisonville is ripe for the harvest. It's a job I like, and I'm going to do it." But the job turns sour and ugly; the callous detective sees too much death. "This burg's getting me," he says. "If I don't get away soon I'll be going blood-simple like the natives." He finishes—and gets out.

With a Hammett detective, it was always the job that mattered, the job assigned, the job that had to be done against lawbreakers—the small, near-futile, but necessary acts that shored up the crumbling banks of society against the tides of corruption. Hammett and his Op were fatalistic—they felt that things wouldn't really change (". . . you'll have your city back, all nice and clean and ready to go to the dogs again")—but someone had to do something, and that was the Op's job.

In each Hammett episode the red harvest mounts; at the climax more than two dozen people are dead, including twelve of the nineteen main characters. Thayler is gone; so is Dinah Brand and Noonan and Yard and Pete the Finn. As Dante used his native Florence as a model for hell, as Dickens depicted the horrors of London with its poverty and crime, as Melville projected his Gothic vision of New York as "an inferno into which the hero falls"—so Hammett used Poisonville. André Gide called *Red Harvest* "the last word in atrocity, cynicism, and horror."

Some critics have described the novel as a Marxist assault on capitalism, and certainly Hammett forcefully dramatized the evils of a system driven by greed. His message, however, was not overt. Hammett mixed his politics with his fiction, and he often dealt with the theme of political corruption, but his primary purpose was to tell a story, not to convert his readers. He was several years away from active political commitment—and by the time he entered the political arena he was no longer writing crime fiction.

Yet his anger against injustice was genuine. His portrait of Poisonville, like that in *Blood Money,* is bitter and unrelenting. Along with many similarly frustrated writers of his generation (Steinbeck, Farrell, Dos Passos, et al.), Hammett was projecting a strong, personalized viewpoint into a fictional framework. Clearly, *Red Harvest* offers far more than entertainment; it is an expression of moral outrage, exposing (as one critic phrased it) "the cancer of crime." The darkly pessimistic *Blood Money* was simply a rehearsal for *Red Harvest.*

"The enemy that Hammett found beneath the decadent facade of twentieth-century capitalist society," wrote pop culture critic John Cawelti, "was the universe itself. More than [that of] any other hard-boiled writer, [his] work reflects the vision of a godless naturalistic cosmos—ruled by chance, violence, and death—that dominates such major writers as Conrad, Crane and Hemingway . . . man alone in a meaningless universe."

Cap Shaw was delighted with the reader response to Hammett's violent saga. "We are hearing about this series from all over the country," he wrote in the magazine after the first segment, titled "The Cleansing of Poisonville," had appeared. The subsequent three segments were printed as "Crime Wanted—Male or Female," "Dynamite," and "The 19th Murder."

Hammett was now eager to break into the book field. In February of 1928 he sent *Red Harvest* (then called *Poisonville*) to the editorial department of Alfred A. Knopf. The submission was unagented, and the odds against its being accepted were astronomical. Very few manuscripts move from the "slush pile" to publication. But all manuscripts are sampled, if not read, and the good ones stand out against the general run of dross. Hammett's manuscript was called to the attention of Knopf's wife, a brilliant woman with a keen appreciation of good writing. Blanche Knopf was a major asset to her husband's publishing house—she had signed up André Gide as a Knopf author during her first tour of Europe. Subsequently, she helped secure several other international talents—but she also maintained a lively interest in the modern American scene. Hammett's manuscript impressed her, and she wrote to him, suggesting revisions. For one thing, the story was much too violent. Would Hammett be willing to revise his material a bit?

He replied that he'd be happy to cooperate. After an agreement had been drawn up, he began working with house editor Harry Block on the changes desired by Knopf. This reworking process involved the entire manuscript; Hammett went over it word for word. Thus, the sentence "You're mistaken, my dear" became simply: "Wrong." The magazine version's "and ran out to follow my advice" was changed to the more direct "and went away." In another dialogue change, "Who for?" took the place of a stilted "For whom?"

Like F. Scott Fitzgerald, Hammett would sometimes cannibalize sections of his early magazine stories for his books. He lifted a full description of the agency's Old Man directly out of "The Big Knockover" and inserted it into the book version of *Red Harvest.*

In a March 20 letter to Blanche Knopf, Hammett declared that he was quite serious about the potential of the detective story, and predicted that "someday somebody's going to make 'literature' of it." Actually, Hammett was only three months away from beginning his masterwork, *The Maltese Falcon,* the book that *would* achieve the stature of literature. He was on the verge of a breakthrough in the genre.

Alfred A. Knopf published *Red Harvest,* which Hammett had dedicated to Joseph Thompson Shaw, in February of 1929.

The Bookman, in March, found the novel's crime elements impressively modern: "It reads like the latest news from

Chicago. . . . It is doubtful if even Ernest Hemingway has ever written more effective dialogue than may be found within the pages of this extraordinary tale. . . . Hammett's characters speak the crisp, hard-boiled language of the underworld." In *The Outlook,* W. R. Brooks also praised the novel's authenticity: "It is written by a man who plainly knows his underworld and can make it come alive for his readers. The action is exciting and the conversation racy and amusing."

In 1941 the poet Robert Graves called *Red Harvest* "a literary landmark." Writing for *Saturday Review* in 1952, Ben Ray Redman observed: "With *Red Harvest,* the hard-boiled school of detective fiction, bound in hard covers, moved out from the back room of the pulps into the bright lights of the bookstores." In 1962 critic Martin Maloney wrote that with *Red Harvest* the Conan Doyle image was completely shattered: "It is a long step from Holmes pondering the significance of a flake of cigar ash . . . to Hammett's Op, who, on one occasion, stuffs a length of copper wire into his pocket because it's just the right length to go around somebody's neck. The verb 'to pursue' now becomes 'to destroy' . . . and the black-and-white universe of Holmes vanishes. . . . The burden of guilt for crime tends to spread, so that no one is free of it."

Hammett's second full-length novel, *The Dain Curse,* quickly followed *Red Harvest* into the pages of *Black Mask.* The Continental Op was again the protagonist narrator in what was, in many ways, the most romantic of Hammett's Op stories, involving symbolism, allegory, and mysticism.

This four-part history of the "Black Dains" (written as separate novelettes to please Shaw, who disliked serials) is notable for its dazzling invention, intricate cross-plotting, and multiple dramatic climaxes. On a surface level, however, the story lends itself to parody—and crime specialist John Bartlow Martin found the plot elements wildly overdone: "In this single Hammett novel the detective shot and stabbed one man to death, helped shoot another dead, was himself attacked with dagger, gun, chloroform, and bomb, fought off a ghostly manifestation barehanded, wrestled with five women, cured the heroine of narcotic addiction—and was obliged to deal with one seduction, eight murders, a jewel burglary, and a family curse."

Hammett was attempting to use the basic crime-puzzle framework of the formal mystery and overlay it with his own brand of objective realism, but this ambitious plan was only partially realized. He was not satisfied with the final result, and later dismissed the novel as "a silly story . . . all style."

His charge is too harsh; the unique Hammett style is certainly in evidence, but this novel displayed a sensitivity, an aura of compassion and hope, that far surpassed the dour *Red Harvest* in depth of feeling. While *Curse* fails structurally, it succeeds philosophically. Also, on a sheer entertainment level, it is a rattling good action yarn, with its bizarre Gothic melodrama, surprise murders, and richly atmospheric scenes. The segment titles convey the special flavor of the story: "Black Lives," "The Hollow Temple," "Black Honeymoon," and "Black Riddle."

In execution, *The Dain Curse* is confusing and fragmented, and the four segments (even after Hammett revised them for Knopf) never wholly meshed. Lacking the cohesion of a single locale, the story jumps from seacoast to city to country. The reader is forced to cope with over thirty characters (including Eric Collinson; Hammett was paying tongue-in-cheek tribute to his old pen name). That he could bring the story off at all is to his credit—and there are few writers who could have unified the narrative's disparate parts as well as he—yet, to some extent, *The Dain Curse* marked a plateau, not an upward step, in Hammett's career.

Threading her way through this complex saga was a young woman Hammett called Gabrielle Dain Leggett, who bore "the terrible curse of the Dain family." In contrast to the female villains Hammett was fond of portraying, Gabrielle was victim rather than aggressor. Pursued by many men who were destroyed in seeking her love, she turns to morphine in an effort to escape a dark reality.

The Op undertakes her cure, and Hammett came closer to outright tenderness in this relationship than in any previous Op story. "Let yourself go," the detective says, soothing her in the midst of the harrowing therapy. "I'll take care of you."

She later asks the Op how he could have put up with her. Why did he do it? "I'm damned if I'll make a chump of myself by telling you why I did it, why it was neither revolting or disgusting, why I'd do it again and be glad of the chance." She takes this as a declaration of his love, but he quickly covers: "I don't mean anything that I'll admit."

Philip Durham wrote that with this novel the Op had grown "old and soft." Durham charged that Hammett had "traded a hard-boiled hero for a part-time sentimentalist." He was wrong. Hammett actually added emotional qualities to the Op's character, allowing him to become more humanly sensitive. He was *never* sentimental, remaining clear-headed and practical, moving warily within a world of masks and contradictions. He only pretended to be in love with Gabrielle in order to provide her with a vitally needed stability during the agony of her cure. Yet he *did* feel tenderness and emotion.

The Op was capable of heroic actions, but his attitude remained that of the cool observer. Unlike Chandler's Marlowe, the little detective never saw himself in a heroic role. Yet, in *The Dain Curse,* Hammett gave him a knightly task.

Gabrielle's mother, father, husband, stepmother, doctor, and "religious counselor" all die during the story, but the Op breaks the "black curse," and Gabrielle is allowed to live, to find a final happiness; the knight has dissolved the magic spell and set the maiden free. His escape has been a narrow one, and he learns that it is easier to turn an evil woman over to the law than to walk away from a good one.

A dark, Gothic atmosphere permeates *The Dain Curse,* and there is a splendidly chilling scene staged in San Francisco's Temple of the Holy Grail, home of a fake religious cult. Drugged with chloroform, the Op must battle what seems to be a ghost, yet a ghost that bleeds as he lashed at it: ". . . the thing squirmed and writhed, shuddered and shivered, swirling wildly now, breaking apart, reuniting madly in the black air. . . ." The blood is his own, the Op discovers, as he staggers into unpolluted air, regaining his senses. Yet no sooner is he clear of this "ghost" than he is forced to use his gun against a knife-wielding fanatic, the Temple's Joseph Haldorn, who considers himself God. The Op is shaken by Haldorn's seemingly supernatural defense against bullets: "I fired. The bullet hit his cheek. I saw the hole it made. No muscle twitched . . . not even his eyes blinked. He walked deliberately, not hurrying, towards me. I worked the automatic's trigger, pumping six more bullets into his face and body. I saw them go in. And he came on steadily, showing in no way that he was conscious of them. . . . The knife in his hand went up high above his head . . . he was bringing retribution to me." The Op, too, has a knife—a dagger—and now he uses it. "I drove the blade into his throat, in till the hilt's cross stopped it. Then I was through." The cross—the dagger—has killed the demon; the knight has triumphed over evil.

In reworking *Red Harvest* from magazine to published book, under Harry Block's supervision, Hammett made changes, deletions, and additions. Aware that the story's excessive violence worked against it, he toned down the shootings, removing a scene in which the Op uses his pistol to kill a certain Mrs. Fink, and he also eliminated two dynamitings.

A lengthy sequence in the *Black Mask* version involved a seedy dwelling, the Primrose Hotel, run by a former tent showman, Felix Weber, who had once drunkenly fired a .45 slug at the Op. This entire sequence was dropped and Hammett turned the Primrose into the Temple of the Holy Grail, with Joseph Haldorn taking Weber's place as a character. (The Temple did appear in the original *Black Mask* version, but not until much later.) Hammett also extensively reworked the story's ending for Knopf.

The opening section of *Dain Curse* demonstrated a specialized knowledge of diamonds, and Hammett credited the source by dedicating the book to his ex-employer Albert S.

Samuels. Also, several of the characters in *Dain Curse* were named after store employees. "Leggett was our switchboard operator," Samuels later recalled. "A doctor in the novel was named after David Riese, who worked for us—and another book character was named after our Mrs. Priestly, who was in silverware."

Hammett's fictional killer in the novel turns out to be a longtime friend of the Op, novelist Owen Fitzstephan, who reveals himself as a Dain: "My mother and Gabrielle's maternal grandfather were brother and sister." He tells the Op that he will plead insanity, that "the cursed Dain blood" is in him, then adds: "But it's no fun if I'm really cracked." Ironically, he is judged insane and put away.

This is Hammett having his joke: the novelist naming a novelist as mad villain. His portrait of Fitzstephan was obvious self-description: "a long, lean, sorrel-haired man of thirty-two with sleepy gray eyes, a wide, humorous mouth, and carelessly worn clothes; a man who pretended to be lazier than he was, who would rather talk than do anything else, and had a lot of what seemed to be accurate information and original ideas on any subject that happened to come up, as long as it was a little out of the ordinary."

Hammett reflected a split personality; he was half the pragmatic, tough-minded ex–Pinkerton detective and half the imaginative novelist conjuring up Gothic curses and doomed heroines. In the Dain book, he simply put these two opposite halves of himself on paper, playing them against each other as hero and villain. The detective is the final winner; the dreamer is defeated by the realist. Hammett respected a working detective more than he respected a working novelist.

The Dain Curse remains the least appreciated of Hammett's books. Its obvious structural flaws and overt melodrama have often been cited by its detractors. Yet the overall attempt was a bold one, and though performance fell short of aspiration, the novel clearly possesses many virtues.

In this, his last full-length case, the Op from Continental was fully humanized, allowed to demonstrate compassion and sensitivity. His creator had taken the fat little detective as far as possible along the road to fictional maturity. It was time for Hammett to move on, to create an even more engaging and emotionally complex code hero.

It was time for Sam Spade.

8

THE STUFF THAT DREAMS ARE MADE OF

Hammett shows that truth to one's profession, truth to the way things are, and self-truth all become one. Hammett's moral vision can be understood only in these terms.

—GEORGE J. THOMPSON

TODAY, IN A San Francisco alley on Burritt Street, set into a building at the corner of Burritt and Bush, is a bronze plaque. Its words are simple and direct:

> ON APPROXIMATELY THIS SPOT
> MILES ARCHER,
> PARTNER OF SAM SPADE,
> WAS DONE IN BY
> BRIGID O'SHAUGHNESSY

No reference is made to the fact that the murder was fictional or that Archer, Spade, and O'Shaughnessy were not real people. In truth, after more than half a century, they are as real as the man who created them; they have taken on a classic life of their own, owing to the power of Dashiell Hammett's imagination.

The overt corruption of San Francisco had added color to Hammett's Continental Op fiction, but it also sickened him. At thirty-four, Hammett had experienced too much of life's uncertainty. Nothing was stable; no person could be relied upon entirely. Ill health had brought him close to death, and detective work had revealed its dark face to him many times. Cynicism had been replaced by bitterness; troubling visions of a meaningless universe possessed him—and his method of dealing with such visions was to write about them. Balanced against this bleakness of spirit was the soul of a poet, a romantic.

In *The Maltese Falcon,* he mixed hope and disillusionment to create his masterpiece. Like a series of upward steps, all of his previous fictions led to this perfectly balanced expression of romantic imagination and doom-haunted philosophy. He had never written anything as fine—and he would never write anything finer. Here the disparate parts of Hammett's nature achieved perfect fusion.

"When a man's partner is killed he's supposed to do something about it," detective Sam Spade says, after his agency co-partner, Miles Archer, is gunned down in the fog.* What Spade does about it, and to whom, fuels the plot of Hammett's most famous novel, the prototype of a thousand others, the book which in the very act of remaking its field transcends it.

San Francisco, in 1929, was a made-to-order backdrop for the brutally staged melodrama of the lethal falcon. The mayor, that year, was James "Sunny Jim" Rolph, a jolly, flamboyant little man in cutaway and cowboy boots whose corrupt city rule ("You make a buck, I make a buck") embraced every form of vice and political graft. An example was the McDonough brothers, Pete and Tom, who listed their business as bail bonding. In his autobiography, *A Life*

---

*An earlier Hammett story, "Who Killed Bob Teal?" (1924), prefigures the Archer gundown. Writing in *The Armchair Detective,* Christopher Bentley cites the parallels: "In both the short story and the novel the murderer stands in the same relationship to the victim, and the murder is committed for identical reasons. Both detectives are killed premeditatedly by their clients who intend that a criminal associate (who has become a nuisance to them) will be blamed for the murder. In both cases the murder weapon had been previously obtained from the associate, and the victims are both killed at night and in similar locations."

in My Hands, attorney J. W. Ehrlich describes these two enterprising gentlemen:

> From their scrubby little office on Kearny, close to the Hall of Justice, these squid-handed brothers supervised the many-splendered nightlife in San Francisco. They kept an eye on the take of every hustling girl on Eddy Street, knew to the dollar how much Russian Mike or Bones Remmer or Eddie Sahati folded into their pockets after a night's play, and had the drawings of any burglary, con-game, or safeblowing that happened, *before* it happened—or it *didn't* happen. . . . They had their own lawyers. They created judges and uncreated them. They got city and county ordinances passed, defeated, amended, and shelved. . . . They "laundered" soiled money, cooled overnight beefs . . . and, oh yes, they wrote bail bonds.

Although the McDonough brothers do not appear anywhere in the pages of *The Maltese Falcon,* their spirit permeates it; they are there, invisibly, along with Sunny Jim and his crooked politicos.

The history of the falcon, as given to Spade by Casper Gutman in the novel, was partially based on fact. Hammett later recalled: "Somewhere I had read of the peculiar rental arrangement between Charles V and the Order of the Hospital of St. John of Jerusalem." He was referring to the agreement of 1530, between the order and Emperor Charles V, under which, as "rent" for the island of Malta (then under Spanish rule), the order would pay Charles an annual tribute of a single falcon. One of these birds, according to Hammett's fictional account, was "a glorious golden falcon encrusted from head to foot with the finest jewels in their coffers." Down through the years it moves from country to country, leaving a trail of theft and deceit and death. Some seventeen years before the story opens, Casper Gutman goes after it. That the bird is a worthless fake when Gutman finally obtains it is no real surprise to Spade. He never believed in it anyhow; men who live in seedy apartments and work out of seedy office buildings may dream of fabled riches, but they know such riches, for them, are illusion.

Hammett reworked fact to suit his dramatic purposes. There was no jeweled bird. According to Diane Moore, assistant curator of the order, the presentation each year of a Maltese bird of prey was indeed "one of the conditions attached to the grant of Malta and Tripoli made to the Order by Charles V in 1530." But the actual birds were living ones; the jeweled falcon, with its complex blood history, is entirely Hammett's invention.

Was there a real-life model for this treasure object? Hammett's ex-partner, retired detective Phil Haultain, believes that he can pinpoint Hammett's inspiration for the falcon. "I had this jeweled skull when I knew Sam," Haultain stated. "Had it in my apartment. An uncle of mine, who lived in Calcutta, India, sent it to me. Had a gory history . . . it was taken as loot by a member of the British Expedition to Lhasa, Tibet—the jeweled skull of a holy man. I've still got the thing. When *The Maltese Falcon* came out, the book rang a lot of bells."

The characters in Hammett's novel remain firmly in the reader's memory: Casper Gutman, the florid fat man seeking the elusive statuette, who speaks effusively in a "throaty purr" and whose eyes are "dark gleams in ambush behind pink puffs of flesh," who finds the always resourceful Spade a more-than-worthy opponent; red-haired, blue-eyed Brigid O'Shaughnessy, the culmination of Hammett's good-evil women, the lying temptress who changes identity as often as she changes her old lies for new ones; Joel Cairo, the soft-voiced, perfumed homosexual; Wilmer Cook, the sadistic, baby-faced killer—and Sam Spade himself, with his V-shaped face and sharp predator's teeth ("He looked . . . like a blond satan").

Effective, too, are Lieutenant Dundy and Detective Polhaus of Homicide, who dog Spade closely throughout the narrative. ("I've warned you your foot was going to slip one of these days," Dundy tells him. Spade remains unruffled. "It's a long while since I burst out crying because policemen didn't like me.")

Hammett never told his former secretary Peggy O'Toole that she was his primary model for Brigid. ("O'Shaughnessy had two originals . . . the other was a woman who came to Pinkerton's to hire [me] to discharge her housekeeper.") Gutman—Hammett's second direct try at the same-named villain (after Sheth Gutman in "The Secret Emperor")—was based on the fat man he'd shadowed in Washington, D.C., who was suspected of being a German secret agent. Effie Perine, Spade's good-hearted secretary, was based on a cousin of his named Effie.

"The Cairo character I picked up on a forgery charge in 1920," Hammett revealed. "Wilmer, the boy gunman, was picked up in Stockton, California . . . a neat small smooth-faced quiet boy of perhaps twenty-one. . . . He was serenely proud of the name the local papers gave him—'The Midget Bandit.' He had robbed a Stockton filling station the previous week . . . and had been annoyed by the description the station proprietor had given of him and by the proprietor's statement of what he would do to that 'little runt' if he ever laid eyes on him again. So . . . he'd stolen an automobile and returned to . . . stick the guy up again and see what he wanted to do about it."

Hammett also revealed real-life origins for other *Falcon* characters: "Polhaus was a former captain of detectives; I used to buy books from Iva [Archer's wife] in Spokane. I worked with Dundy's prototype in a North Carolina railroad yard."

Although he gave Spade his own first name of Samuel (the last name is said to have originated with a boxer of the period, John Spade), Hammett always insisted that "Sam had no original. . . . He's a dream man in the sense that he is what most of the detectives I worked with would like to have been and what quite a few of them, in their cockier moments, thought they approached . . . a hard and shifty fellow, able to take care of himself in any situation, able to get the best of anybody he comes in contact with, whether criminal, innocent bystander or client."

Samuel Spade is, of course, like the Op, a direct extension of the author, a man caught up in an unstable universe of random violence, who survives by following a rigid self-imposed code of honor, who seeks to sift truth from lies, who trusts no one but himself.

W. Somerset Maugham, who admired Hammett's work, found Spade to be "a nasty bit of goods . . . an unscrupulous rogue and a heartless crook. . . . There is little to choose between him and the criminals he is dealing with." Yet this is precisely the character Spade wants to project to Gutman; it is imperative that the fat man think him capable of anything; he must play villain to defeat a villain. Later he says to Brigid, "Don't be too sure I'm as crooked as I'm supposed to be. That kind of reputation makes it easier to deal with the enemy."

Spade wears a variety of masks throughout the book. He pretends to go along with Brigid although he knows she killed Archer, stringing the police, working himself into a false rage for Gutman's benefit. As each mask is removed a new one appears; total honesty is a luxury Sam cannot afford. "Everybody has something to conceal," he says.

It is a mistake to see Spade as "unscrupulous" and "heartless." In the climactic scene, in which he finally turns Brigid over to the police, we realize that his heart is with the woman, but his code forbids his yielding to her. Spade would be finished if he betrayed his principles and went off with Brigid; she killed his partner, and it doesn't matter that Spade felt that Miles Archer was "a louse" and that the agency is better off without him. Sam can sleep with Iva, the dead man's widow; he can bed down his secretary (". . . his hand on her hip. . . . 'Don't touch me now—not now' "), and he can spend the night with Brigid, but he must never make a permanent alliance with any of them. He must remain, like the Op, a free man for hire. He may love Brigid ("I think I do") but cannot trust love any more than he can trust the woman herself ("I

am a liar," she tells him, "I have always been a liar"). Spade
refuses to "play the sap"; but admits that after she's jailed "I'll
have some rotten nights." Finally, emotionally, he tells her he
won't let her go free "because all of me wants to—wants to
say to hell with the consequences and do it—and because—
God damn you—you've counted on that with me the same as
you counted on that with the others."

Spade is far from Maugham's heartless crook as he ultimately rejects Brigid with the line: "You're an angel . . . and
if they hang you I'll always remember you." He means it
literally.

In the midst of the case Spade tells Brigid a long, seemingly
irrelevant story she does not understand, about a man named
Flitcraft who left his wife and family suddenly one day to start
a whole new life—all because, while walking along the street,
he had narrowly missed being killed by a falling beam, and
"he felt like somebody had taken the lid off life and let him
look at the works." Spade is telling Brigid, in parable, that life
is a series of falling beams and that some of us find out about
them and some of us don't. He is telling her, in effect, not to
be surprised when one hits her—as it finally does. Spade lives
longer because he knows the beams are falling, and is watching for them.

The Maltese Falcon, when closely studied, is basically a series
of brilliant dialogues, set in motion by offstage events. In this
respect, it is totally unlike Hammett's first two books, in which
violence was a major ingredient of the plots. It is as if Hammett had set himself the challenge of creating a violent novel
without the *use* of violence. Aside from a bit of scuffling and
a punch or two, all of the physical action takes place beyond
the reader's vision; the four killings are done offstage. We are
shown the *effects* of murder rather than its execution, what its
factual existence does to the men and women who share in it.
Hammett gives us implied violence: guns are drawn and flour-
ished, never fired; threats are made, tempers flare, accusa-
tions and cross-accusations abound—but Hammett keeps the
tension taut as a stretched wire without ever resorting to overt

violence. There is the constant, immediate feeling that, at any given moment, the scene will explode into bullets and blood, but Hammett resists the temptation, and suspense is therefore greatly intensified.* Even at the climax, when one expects a shootout, we are given only conversation—crackling, menace-laden conversation, laced with double and triple meaning—designed to do the job we have come to expect from overt violence. When Gutman is finally killed by one of his own gang, we learn this as it is reported to Spade—just as we learned of the deaths of Archer and Thursby. (Jacobi, the doomed ship's captain, staggers into Sam's office and dies there, but he has been shot elsewhere.)

Spade, a man of potential violence, uses only his personality, his shrewdness, to hold the game in check. True, in the course of the novel, he disarms two of Gutman's hoods, but casually and with no fuss. Unlike the Op, he does not carry or use a gun.

The Maltese Falcon ran as a 65,000-word, five-part serial in *Black Mask* (from September 1929 into January 1930). Joe Shaw was stunned by it. "I have never encountered a story as intense, as gripping or as powerful as this one," he told the readers. "It is a magnificent piece of writing. With all the earnestness of which I am capable, I tell you not to miss it."

Strong editorial censorship existed in the popular magazines during this period. When Hammett's manuscript arrived, Shaw checked it carefully. Sex was a problem. Brigid's line "I'm not ashamed to be naked before you" was dropped, as was a line from Cairo directed to her regarding a boy she had failed to seduce ("The one you couldn't make"). A *damn* or a *hell* was permitted, but outright swearing was not. (Hammett got around this neatly, losing none of the intended impact: "The boy spoke two words, the first a short guttural verb, the second 'you.' ") Hammett's line from Spade "How

---

*During a lecture on "tempo in the novel," Hammett declared: "The essence of suspense is that while it lasts nothing happens."

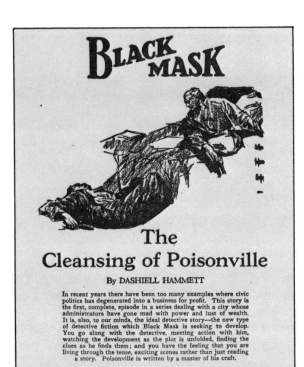

BLACK MASK

The Cleansing of Poisonville

By DASHIELL HAMMETT

In recent years there have been too many examples where civic politics has degenerated into a business for profit. This story is the first, complete, episode in a series dealing with a city whose administrators have gone mad with power and lust of wealth. It is, also, to our minds, the ideal detective story—the new type of detective fiction which Black Mask is seeking to develop. You go along with the detective, meeting action with him, watching the development as the plot is unfolded, finding the clues as he finds them; and you have the feeling that you are living through the tense, exciting scenes rather than just reading a story. Poisonville is written by a master of his craft.

I FIRST heard Personville called Poisonville in 1920, in the Big Ship in Butte, by a red-haired mucker named Hickey Dewey. But he also called his shirt a shoit, so I didn't think anything of what he had done to the city's name. Later, when I heard men who could manage their r's give it the same twist, I still didn't see anything in it but the meaningless sort of humor that used to make richardsnary the thieves' word for dictionary. In 1927 I

9

The first part of *Red Harvest* as it appeared in *Black Mask*; editor Joseph Shaw wrote the boldface blurb. Hammett used John's Grill as a hangout for his fictional detective Sam Spade.

At right, the world's first glimpse of Hammett's masterwork. Below, a way station on the tour of San Francisco's Hammett sites.

long have you been off the gooseberry lay, son?" was changed
to "How long have you been off the lay?" since Shaw was
certain Hammett had something gamy in mind. He was mistaken. A "gooseberry lay" was crook slang for stealing wash
from a clothesline.

However, Shaw did not touch the line "Keep that gunsel
away from me . . ." He assumed the word "gunsel" meant
gunman. Actually, it was a homosexual term meaning a "kept
boy." Homosexuality, in fact, was not censored nearly as
much as heterosexuality during those early pulp days. In the
published book version, when Spade questions a house detective about Joel Cairo, the man answers with a leer, "Oh, that
one." The original magazine version was bolder: "Oh, her!"

Another interesting Hammett magazine-to-book change,
having to do not with censorship but with clarity, consisted of
his switching "You'll want to sleep if you've been in the grease
all night" to "You'll want to sleep if you've been standing up
under a police storm all night." He made innumerable minor
alterations in the book version to improve narrative flow, to
sharpen dialogue, and to clarify.

Hammett took equal care in his treatment of the novel's San
Francisco locale, but it is difficult to verify certain locations,
since Hammett deliberately obscured them; he'd often use a
real hotel, for example, but under a fictional name. In the
novel, Gutman has rooms at the Alexandria (the Sir Francis
Drake), Joel Cairo lives at the Belvedere (the Bellevue), and
Brigid is shadowed from the St. Mark (the St. Francis).

Spade's address is never revealed, but Joe Gores (who patiently tracked down many of the book's locales) showed
Spade's apartment to be one of Hammett's own, the one at
891 Post Street. Working from internal evidence in the novel,
he located Spade's office at 111 Sutter (now the Hunter-Dulin
Building), and pinpointed Brigid's fictional Coronet Apartments as the Cathedral Apartments, at 1201 California Street.

"The most famous location in Spade's San Francisco,"
wrote Gores, "is the dead-end alley where Miles Archer was
shot. It is on Burritt, at Bush, atop the Stockton tunnel. Just

across Bush is 20 Monroe, a white-brick apartment house where Hammett lived briefly in 1926. Two buildings have been added to the east side of Burritt since then, and would today prevent Archer's body from rolling down the dirt slope toward Stockton Street below. Of course, that dirt slope is long gone—but it *was* there in Hammett's day."

Hammett named several real cafés and restaurants in his novel, including John's Grill, at 63 Ellis. Spade ate chops with tomatoes at John's, which still operates at the same address and is now official headquarters for the Dashiell Hammett Society of San Francisco.

Hammett presented Samuel Spade's dark world in terms of lies and treachery. As a working detective, Spade moved warily, each day, through this minefield of psychological and physical dangers, knowing that his next step, if miscalculated, could destroy him. John Cawelti speaks of Hammett's "vision of an irrational cosmos, in which all the rules, all the seeming solidity of matter, routine, and custom can be overturned in a moment."

To maintain a hold on reality and sanity, Spade employs ceremony in his daily habits. There is a stylized pattern in the rolling of a cigarette or the opening of an apartment door. Mysticism mixed with hard practicality. Yet no more mystical than Hemingway's war veteran (and Spade is a veteran of many wars) ceremoniously fishing the Big Two-Hearted River to keep his mind off the horrors of his past. It is pertinent to note that in his magazine-to-book revision, Hammett substituted "They shook hands ceremoniously" for "They shook hands with marked formality." This same resort to calming ritual is present in the way Spade dresses, ransacks an apartment, disarms a gunman. A cigarette is real, a room key is real, a gun is real. His love for Brigid is *not* real, and cannot be relied upon; she's the wrong woman to love, for all the wrong reasons. Had he succumbed to her, allowed her to escape the police, chaos would have been unloosed. The mine would have exploded under him.

The falcon is a symbol for the falseness and illusion of life itself; we seek jewels and find only lead. In the definitive John Huston film version of Hammett's novel, when Spade is asked about the falcon, he says that it is "the stuff that dreams are made of."

Spade is the messenger who delivers Hammett's disturbing vision to us. At the story's end he is left alone. He knows that in allowing himself to love Brigid he courted self-destruction. He "sends her over" and survives, but the cost is high. As always, he has only himself and the ceremonial realities of his daily existence; he has sent away the one woman he allowed himself to love.

At the completion of *The Maltese Falcon,* in the spring of 1929, Hammett also ended a relationship. His marriage to Jose was over; he was in love with Nell Martin.

For Hammett, the early dream of a stable family life had proved as unreal as the mythical falcon itself. Jose was no longer with him when *The Maltese Falcon* was published, but he was grateful for the good years they'd had together—and that gratitude was reflected in the book's dedication: "To Jose."

9

THE WINNER TAKES NOTHING

*No matter how . . . a man alone ain't got no
bloody . . . chance.*

—HEMINGWAY'S HARRY
MORGAN

IN THE FALL of 1929, Hammett moved up in the world; he
was now living on Nob Hill, at 1155 Leavenworth, in an attractive, gable-windowed apartment house a few blocks west
of the Mark Hopkins with an impressive view of downtown
San Francisco. He was working here on the manuscript of a
new *Black Mask* novel, *The Glass Key*.

Proudly, Joe Shaw placed an ad in *Liberty*. Above a smiling
photo of Hammett was the boldly printed question: DO YOU
KNOW THIS MAN? And, under the photo, Shaw's hyperbolic
pitch:

> He is the greatest living writer of detective stories. His
> books . . . have been lavishly praised by the most compe-
> tent critics. He is a true genius! . . . His name is Dashiell
> Hammett, and his latest story is called THE GLASS
> KEY. . . . It will hold you gripped fast, tense with excite-
> ment and completely oblivious to your surroundings,
> from beginning to end. You will find it in the new issue
> of BLACK MASK!

Although he was now the most popular of the *Black Mask*
authors, Hammett declined to repeat himself. He felt that he
had no more to say about the Op, or Sam Spade, and he did

97

not wish to continue their adventures. He no longer believed that the private detective made a realistic protagonist. As his view of the world continued to darken, Hammett became convinced that the problems of society could not be dealt with one-to-one. The tide of universal corruption was running too strong for a lone detective to combat it successfully.

He had replaced the knightlike Op of *The Dain Curse* with antihero Sam Spade, who knew how to deal with crooks by playing their game, by assuming a criminal role, if necessary. Now, with Ned Beaumont of *The Glass Key*, * Hammett moved a step beyond; Beaumont does not fight against the ills of society. On the contrary, he has long since been corrupted. He works for political boss Paul Madvig, who is battling rival racketeer Shad O'Rory for ultimate city control. (The city Hammett had in mind, but did not name, is Baltimore.)

The Op and Sam Spade were outsiders, men of intense personal honor, code-directed, who did their jobs and maintained their integrity. Ned Beaumont is an insider, on the wrong side of the law, in the service of a man the Op would have happily put behind bars. As Peter Wolfe writes: "Beaumont has sold out to the machine. A believer in the spoils system, he hands out bribes, sinecures, and patronage jobs in return for political favors. His ability to handle people [including the police] makes him valuable to Madvig. Beaumont's neglect of the poor, the sick, the jobless makes him . . . an unlikely Depression hero."

Of course, Ned Beaumont is not a hero, he's an outright crook, gripped by a single, consuming fear: he hates to lose. As a gambler, he has lost often, and is bitter about it. When a bookie, Despain, runs out on a gambling debt he owes Beaumont, Ned becomes enraged: "I've got to get this guy. . . . The money . . . is not the real thing. It's what losing and losing and losing does to me."

---

*Printed in four issues of *Black Mask* as four novelettes, in March, April, May, and June of 1930.

This obsessive fear of loss is at the heart of the novel. When Paul Madvig is accused of murdering Taylor Henry, the son of a senator he's backing in an election, Beaumont is *compelled* to solve the crime in order to prove Madvig's innocence. Paul Madvig is more than a boss to him; he is Ned's only close friend, and a father figure. If this boss-friend-parent is actually a murderer, then Beaumont loses again, on the deepest personal level. Thus, his efforts to find the real killer are not based on any type of hero's code, or job-oriented quest for justice; Beaumont must find the killer for his own psychic survival. His amoral quest separates him starkly from Hammett's previous protagonists.

Beaumont fakes an argument with Madvig, in order to gain Shad O'Rory's confidence; he miscalculates and suffers a terrible beating. Many critics have been confused by this brutal sequence: why does Beaumont so docilely allow it to happen? He seems, in one sense, to invite the punishment. "I can stand anything I've got to stand," he says. Hammett clearly gives the beating a touch of sadomasochism. He is telling us that Ned Beaumont is a willing victim of his own self-loathing and that Ned believes, on a subconscious level, that he *deserves* such treatment as punishment for being a continual loser. This self-loathing is revealed when Janet Henry, the senator's daughter, calls him a "gentleman." Ned acidly corrects her: "You're wrong. I'm a gambler and a politician's hanger-on."

Even more than novelist Fitzstephan in *The Dain Curse,* Beaumont is a virtual carbon copy of Hammett in habits and physical appearance: he wears a mustache and dresses neatly (as Hammett always did); he is tall and lean, with the flat chest of a consumptive (like Hammett, he has suffered from tuberculosis). He drinks, enjoys good cigars, and knows how to lay on the charm when the occasion demands. His passion for gambling (horses, dice, cards) is, of course, Hammett's own. ("If you have fooled around with crap games as much as I have," Hammett once wrote to *Black Mask,* "you know what chance can do to the laws of probabilities.")

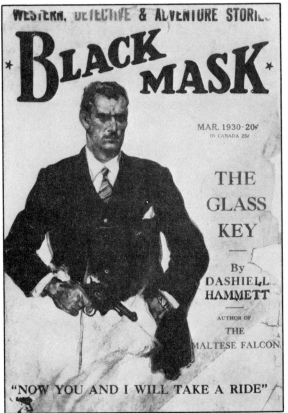

The Glass Key was Hammett's own favorite. Below left, 1155 Leavenworth Street, where he lived after leaving Jose and where he wrote *The Glass Key*. At right, Hammett during this period.

Dashiell Hammett
133 East 38th Street
New York City

THE THIN MAN

Dashiell Hammett [signature]

By Dashiell ~~Hammett~~

THE train went north among the mountains. The dark man crossed the tracks to the ticket-window and said: "Can you tell me how to get to Mr. Wynant's place? Mr. Walter Irving Wynant's."

The man within stopped writing on a printed form. His eyes became brightly inquisitive behind tight rimless spectacles. His voice was eager. "Are you a newspaper reporter?"

"Why?" The dark man's eyes were very blue. They looked idly at the other. "Does it make any difference?"

"Then you ain't," the ticket-agent said. He was disappointed. He looked at a clock on a wall. "Hell, I ought to've known that. You wouldn't've had time to get here." He picked up the pencil he had put down.

"Know where his place is?"

"Sure. Up there on the hill." The ticket-agent waved his pencil vaguely westward. "All the taxi-drivers know it, but if it's Wynant you want to see you're out of luck."

"Why?"

The ticket-agent's mien brightened. He put his forearms on the counter, hunching his shoulders, and said: "Because the fact is he went and murdered everybody on the place and jumped in the river not more than an hour ago."

The dark man exclaimed, "No!" softly.

The opening of the first version of *The Thin Man*, written in 1930, signed by the author.

The attraction between Ned Beaumont and Janet Henry is subtly developed; Hammett employs extreme understatement, never allowing either of them to express tenderness or love. No outward sign of affection is permitted, yet the attraction is there. At the novel's end, as Beaumont is about to leave for New York, she says, "Take me with you."

Off-handedly, as if he doesn't really care one way or the other, he agrees: "I'll take you if you want to go."

The coolness of the novel's style keeps the reader at a distance—and Hammett has been criticized for it. We are never allowed inside any of the characters; we are forced to judge them strictly on what they say and do, which presents a perplexing challenge—since they often say one thing and do another. Hammett was well aware of this paradox in life itself, once revealing that one of the reasons he drank was that "I was confused by the fact that people's feelings and talk and actions didn't have much to do with one another." Because of this stringent, unwavering objectivity, *The Glass Key* is Hammett's most difficult book. Motivation is never stated, only implied. Beaumont's emotional mask is kept firmly in place throughout, and it is easy to misinterpret his actions. The reader must follow the subtle clues of character that Hammett provides as carefully as Beaumont follows the clues of murder to solve his case. An interviewer once asked Hammett which of his books he favored, and he named *The Glass Key*, "because the clues were nicely placed, although nobody seemed to see them."

The novel's title seems overtly symbolic. Most critics have assumed that it refers to a dream of Janet Henry's. In the dream, as she relates it, Janet and Ned are together, and very hungry. They reach a house with food inside, but the door is locked. They have a glass key to open the door with, but if they use it they will release the snakes writhing on the floor. In her first recounting of the dream, Janet lies to Beaumont, telling him that they were able to eat the food and escape the snakes. He does not believe this. When they are about to go away together at the end, Janet admits the truth: that the glass key shattered, and "we couldn't lock the snakes in . . . they came out all over us."

Hammett is telling us that the lovers are due for a bad time, that they should not feed their hunger for one another, because the snakes will, in turn, devour them. (If Spade had fed his hunger for Brigid, the snakes would surely have had him.)

Ned's luck has again gone bad. ("What good am I if my luck's gone?") Although he solved the case and proved Madvig innocent, their father-son relationship has been ruined—Madvig wanted Janet, but she chose Beaumont. In winning, by unmasking the true killer, Ned has actually lost again, matching the constant pattern of his life. Hammett obviously means to tell us that he will lose again in New York with Janet.

Ned Beaumont himself is the key of glass, fragile in character and, at the end, broken.

The Glass Key represents an updating of *Red Harvest*. In *Harvest,* the gangsters are crude in the Old West manner, using bombs and machine guns to control Poisonville. In *Key,* the racketeers are glossy and refined, their methods much more sophisticated. In place of guns, they use political persuasion and blackmail. They represent the pernicious advance of twentieth-century crime, which was replacing the open street violence of the Capone era.

Since it featured a racketeer protagonist, Hammett's novel shocked many *Black Mask* readers; they could not identify with Ned Beaumont as they had identified with the Op and Sam Spade, and they felt that Hammett had "glorified crime and criminals." Editor Shaw rushed to defend his star writer with a strong letter printed in *Writer's Digest:*

> *Black Mask* never has and never will make money by appealing to the appetite for stories which present crime in an alluring light. *The Glass Key,* a story of modern gangsters, is a seriously written and highly dramatic presentation of the present day alliance between corrupt politicians, public officials, and organized crime. In this

story, virtue comes out on top. The crook who has ruled
a city is destroyed, his gang is broken up, and the politicians who made his career possible are swept out of office
by the voters. Publication of it, and of all stories like it, is
a public service. Not until our citizens realize that modern
crime cannot exist without the collusion of corrupt police
and public officials, will it be possible to cure what is
undoubtedly one of the most serious illnesses that our
body politic has ever suffered.

The Glass Key was Hammett's most ambitious attempt to
write what he termed "a serious novel, which happened to be
about crime." Through the decades since its publication, it
has been hailed as his "masterwork" or dismissed as his
"worst novel." Both Maugham and Raymond Chandler
greatly admired it, the latter praising its "gradual elucidation
of character." Novelist James M. Cain has often been accused
of imitating Hammett. (His *The Postman Always Rings Twice* was
published by Knopf in 1934.) Cain used *The Glass Key* to back
up his denial of the charge: "In 1931 I worked for *The New
Yorker* . . . and had to go out to Greenwich, Connecticut, every
Sunday to the printer and put the magazine to bed. Lying
around there was this book, *The Glass Key.* I would pick the
thing up and try to read it and, at the end of four or five
Sundays, when I'd read only about twenty pages, I said forget
this goddamn book. And that's my total knowledge of Hammett."

One can sympathize with Cain. *The Glass Key* is surely not
meant for browsing, and it is easier to admire than to enjoy.
Lacking the vigorous action of *Red Harvest* and *The Dain Curse,*
as well as the romantic flamboyance of *The Maltese Falcon,* and
centered upon an unsavory protagonist, the novel has far less
surface attraction. But it is an important step in the development of Hammett, the writer and the man.

By that fall of 1929, according to Hammett's doctors, his
tuberculosis was in total remission. He felt strong again—and

restless. After eight years, having solidly established himself in American crime fiction, Hammett was ready to leave San Francisco. The town had served him while he was a developing novelist, but now he felt the need to move on to the beckoning excitement of the East.

Nell Martin agreed to go with him, and in October they boarded a train for New York.

10

AN UNFINISHED DETECTIVE IN NEW YORK

New York after the Crash . . . with its nervy,
slanderous parties, sporadically violent speakeasies,
disintegrating boozing, and permanent hangovers.

—A. ALVAREZ

HAMMETT'S CROSS-COUNTRY trip to New York was financed in part by a $500 loan from Al Samuels, the jeweler. Hammett had continued to write ads for Samuels as a free lance after leaving his full-time employment, and the two had become good friends.

With Nell Martin, Hammett took an apartment at 155 East Thirtieth Street and settled down to the job of revising *The Glass Key* for Knopf. Although he dedicated the book to Nell, their love affair was soon over; she moved out of the apartment early in 1930.

The nation was reeling from the collapse of the stock market. The bleak Depression years were beginning. For Hammett, hard times would be a boon. People needed to forget their troubles, to lose themselves in novels and films. As an established storyteller, Hammett was insulated from the poverty surrounding him; he earned solid money for his fiction. Hammett also agreed to review mysteries for the New York *Evening Post.* * He would provide a biweekly column, "Crime Wave," in which he would assess up to a dozen new books.

---

*Hammett reviewed mysteries for the *Post* from April 5 through October 11, 1930.

104

Typically, his reviews were caustic and negative; Hammett had no patience with sloppy crime research or with unbelievable plotting. He felt the mystery genre was poorly served by most of its writers.

One of the few books he praised that season was *Green Ice* by fellow *Black Mask* author Raoul Whitfield. While he had some reservations about the story, he liked the style: "The plot does not matter. . . . What matters is that here are 280 pages of naked action pounded into tough compactness by staccato, hammerlike writing."

Not all reviewers were as kind to Whitfield. In *Judge,* a critic attacked him as a shameless Hammett imitator: "Mr. Whitfield has evidently dosed himself thoroughly in the best detective writer of the times . . . and has helped himself to the master's style, tricks, and ideas—right down to the commas. Furthermore, he has gotten Knopf to publish *Green Ice* and they even used Hammett's type on the thing."

However, Will Cuppy, in the *Herald Tribune,* declared that the book was superior to Hammett, rating *Green Ice* "by several miles the slickest detective job of the season."

Hammett and Whitfield were friends. They had met—when Hammett was living in San Francisco—after years of correspondence. Whitfield had badgered *Black Mask* editors in the early twenties to "give us more Hammett," and had modeled his own writing style on that of the ex–Pinkerton detective. In appearance, Whitfield was (in period slang) "a dapper Dan." Photos show him with cane, elegant leather gloves, and a silk scarf at his neck, looking aloof and imperious. His mustache is carefully trimmed, his dark hair slicked back and parted in the middle. Every inch the gentleman.

Like Hammett, he was a chain smoker and a hard drinker; Whitfield had been a steel mill laborer and a Pittsburgh newspaper reporter, and had "bummed around China for a while after the war." In 1926, at the age of twenty-nine, he had chosen a career in writing.

He first appeared in *Black Mask* with a series of aviation thrillers; he had been a fighter pilot in France during the First

World War, and this background lent color and authenticity to his early stories. Whitfield quickly developed into one of the magazine's top five writers. Much of his work was extremely terse and ultra tough. While he lacked Hammett's subtlety and range, his work found favor with pulp readers. Through the mid-1930s, Whitfield published some ninety pieces of fiction in *Black Mask*. Only Erle Stanley Gardner exceeded this total.

Green Ice was his first novel, printed as a *Black Mask* serial in 1926. Hammett had suggested that it be sent to Knopf, and Whitfield was deeply appreciative. Knopf became Whitfield's main publisher and eventually issued seven of his books. When he moved to New York in 1930, he contacted Hammett and they became drinking companions. They would sit for hours at a booth in a New York bar, discussing the craft of fiction. According to a mutual friend, "Whit and Dash talked shop endlessly. Whit maintained, given characters and a general plot, that it was a cinch to write a detective story. When in a spot, all one need do is use well-known props. Hammett argued that this was cheating; a good writer should produce novels without any of these appurtenances to achieve effect." Hammett would assert that the structure of a crime story limited possibilities for character development. They would then argue over how many murders a novel could sustain, "debating whether a story should have seven murders or twenty-seven for maximum effect. As they got drunker, the numbers increased!"

Another *Black Mask* writer, Frederick Nebel, also drank with Hammett in the bars of New York. "We did a lot of clowning around," Nebel remembered. "Hammett and I got stoned one night and decided to pull off a gag. We wanted to see how New Yorkers would react to a couple of guys huddled under an umbrella on a perfectly clear, cloudless night. So we walked up Lexington from 37th Street to the Grand Central Terminal under this open umbrella. At the station's Oyster Bar we checked the umbrella, but insisted it remain open, to 'dry out.' The bet was that no one would pay any attention to us. And no one did. I still have a copy of *The Maltese Falcon* with Hammett's inscription: 'To Fred Nebel, in memory of the night when we were companions under the umbrella.' "

Knopf published the book version of *The Maltese Falcon* in February 1930. That same month, in a letter to critic Herbert Asbury, Hammett said, "It's the first thing I've done that was, regardless of what faults it had, the best work I was capable of at the time." The book received enthusiastic attention in the press, and gave Hammett a national reputation. William Curtis, in *Town & Country,* claimed that "until Mr. Hammett appeared, no American writer had taken the detective novel seriously enough to do more than ape the outstanding characteristics of the British school." When it was published in England, the *Times Literary Supplement* said: "This is not only probably the best detective story we have ever read, it is an exceedingly well written novel." *Judge* stated: "He writes with a lead pipe [and] stands alone as ace shocker. . . . The writing is better than Hemingway, since it conceals not softness, but hardness." Knopf responded with ads headed: "BETTER THAN HEMINGWAY!" and quoted the respected critic Carl Van Vechten: "Hammett is raising the detective story to that plane to which Alexandre Dumas raised the historical novel."

The strongly favorable reception for *The Maltese Falcon* changed things for Hammett. He put aside the rough-draft crime novella he was working on, "The Darkened Face"—he had written nine pages—to finish one last Continental Op story for Joe Shaw, "Death and Company" (printed in the November 1930 issue of *Black Mask*). That was it; Hammett was through with pulp-writing. Although Shaw wrote many letters urging him to revive the Op, and once enclosed a $500 check to jog his imagination, Hammett's work for *Black Mask* was over. That farewell November issue appeared almost eight years to the month after Hammett's first story, "The Road Home." In all, during these eight years, his work had been included in fifty-two issues of *Black Mask*. No other writer had made such a total impact on the magazine. At his departure, Hammett was still the readers' favorite.

Joe Shaw bragged to the end: "We knew he was great . . . but it took the *Black Mask* stories published in book form to wake up the country as to how great he really is."

During 1930 Hammett did a considerable amount of work on a new novel, the original version of what he later revised into *The Thin Man.*

It is impossible to determine just how successful this incomplete novel would have been. It bears very little resemblance in plot or style to the book eventually published under the same title. The bantering humor, the zany husband-wife relationship of Nick and Nora Charles, the bright social chatter, the weird characters, and the sexual by-play all came later. This original version is stark and humorless; one can hardly imagine Asta barking her way into its dark pages.

In the original, Hammett returned once again to the detective-as-protagonist pitted against the forces of murder and deceit. Hammett's op, John Guild, worked for Associated Detective Bureaus, Inc., in San Francisco's Frost Building (an obvious twin to Pinkerton's, in the Flood Building). Guild drinks beer, carries a gun, is a chain smoker, and has blue eyes and a sun-darkened complexion. (Hammett continually refers to him in this third-person narrative as "the dark man.") He is a veteran sleuth, wary, remote, and implacably committed to his job. When a woman in the story attempts to seduce him and Guild does not respond to her advances, she calls him "bloodless," a "ghost" of a man; he is "unreal, untouchable," she says. ". . . trying to really come in contact with you is like trying to hold a handful of smoke." The detective is amused. "It's an advantage when I'm working," he replies.

Hammett's objective style is as tightly controlled as it was in *The Glass Key;* the reader is removed from the characters' thoughts. Guild trusts no one, believes nothing until it becomes proven fact. Hammett stripped him of all emotion; he is machinelike, coldly efficient, more robot than man. Perhaps, at this stage of his life, Hammett believed that only an emotionless automaton could survive in a crime-universe of murder and sudden treachery. Even Sam Spade seems warm and outgoing in comparison. Guild would never allow himself to love Brigid; he would "send her over" without a qualm. There would be no "sleepless nights" for John Guild.

The plot involves a missing scientist-philosopher, Walter Irving Wynant, who has "apparently" shot his secretary dead and vanished. This murder has taken place in Hell Bend, a small community beyond San Francisco. (As a nod to his *Black Mask* buddy, Hammett placed the town in Whitfield County.) The victim is young, attractive Columbia Forrest, who was on the verge of leaving Wynant to marry a San Francisco man, Charles Fremont, involved in the rackets.

Guild is sent to Hell Bend by the Seaman's National Bank of San Francisco in an attempt to clear up the mystery of a Wynant check that had been altered from $1,000 to $10,000. Wynant had been writing out a number of checks to one Laura Porter. The name proves false; Porter was actually Columbia Forrest—and all evidence points to Wynant as the killer. He is described as tall, thin, and whiskered, and is reported to be "on the goofy side . . . likely his mind has cracked." Guild believes he is innocent and sets out to prove it.

The detective talks to Charles Fremont, who is tied in with mobster Frank Kearny, owner of the Manchu, a club in Chinatown. (The nightclub sequence at the Manchu did appear, in revised form, in *The Thin Man.*) Guild is introduced to Deep Kee, the brother of a tong killer he had sent to prison—and he also meets Fremont's sister, Elsa, who sings at the club (and who later attempts to seduce the "bloodless" detective).

Shortly thereafter, Charles Fremont becomes the second victim; he's found dead in the basement of his home. The murder is rigged to look like suicide, but Guild isn't fooled.

The murderer is not revealed in this unfinished manuscript, but in addition to racketeer Kearny, Guild also suspects Deputy Sheriff Ray Callaghan (once involved with Miss Forrest) and Elsa Fremont, who had shown no real shock at the death of her brother. Certainly, Wynant himself was not guilty and (as in *The Thin Man*) would likely have been found dead during the course of the narrative, another victim of the mystery killer.

Why did Hammett stop writing the novel at 18,000 words? Discussing this manuscript in a letter, he explained that since Knopf had moved up publication of *The Glass Key* (from the fall of 1930 into 1931), he felt he had "plenty of time" to finish the new novel, and had decided to put the draft aside.

Hammett's major reason was financial. In late June of 1930 Warner Brothers had paid Knopf $8,500 for the film rights to *The Maltese Falcon*, alerting Hollywood to Hammett's potential. Producer David O. Selznick, who was then working for Paramount, heard about the Warner deal and decided that Hammett was worth going after. In mid-July he dictated a memo to his Paramount boss, B. P. Schulberg:

> We have an opportunity to secure Dashiell Hammett. . . . I believe that he . . . might very well prove to be the creator of something new and startlingly original for us. . . .
>
> Hammett is unspoiled as to money, but on the other hand anxious not to tie himself up with a long-term contract. . . . So far, I have tentatively discussed the following:
>
> Four weeks at $300 weekly. An option for eight weeks at the same salary—and a bonus of $5,000 for an original. . . .

Responding to this memo, Schulberg authorized Paramount to offer Hammett a contract under Selznick's suggested terms. In addition, the same studio purchased film rights to *Red Harvest* and put writer Ben Hecht to work on adapting it for the screen.

Hammett accepted the bid from Paramount. This was not his first try at Hollywood; in April of 1928 he had been called to town by the William Fox Studios, which planned to purchase several of his stories for filming. At the time Hammett had also plotted an original screenplay, but the deal collapsed and he had returned to San Francisco.

This time, two years later, he was certain that he could succeed. On the way to California, he stopped off in Baltimore to visit his sister. Reba was very proud of her famous brother and welcomed him warmly; as always, Hammett felt close to her, but found it very difficult to relate to the others in his family. He was happy to put the city behind him and head west.

David Selznick was correct in stating that Hammett wished to avoid a long-term tie-up with Hollywood; he had promised himself that he would soon begin what he termed "more serious work." He wanted to write plays in Europe and create "mainstream" novels. He was thirty-six and confident of his ability to move beyond the crime-fiction field. For Dashiell Hammett, Hollywood was to be "a stopping-off place" in a writing career he felt was just beginning.

In California, however, he would meet a woman who would alter the pattern of his life and reshape his future. Her name was Lillian Hellman.

11

HOLLYWOOD AND HELLMAN

The town was loud with wild hearts and the
poetry of success.

—BEN HECHT

WHEN DASHIELL HAMMETT arrived in Hollywood, during
the late summer of 1930, the motion picture industry was just
emerging from the Silent Era of Chaplin, Fairbanks, and the
Keystone Kops into its Golden Age of Sound ("Jolson sings!
Garbo speaks!"). The "talkies" were launching stars at an
astonishing rate, and it was common practice for the studios
to assign a writer to develop "originals" for a particular box-
office attraction. At Paramount, young Gary Cooper was in
demand. A star at twenty-five in his first feature role, *The
Winning of Barbara Worth* (1926), Cooper had scored heavily
in *The Virginian* and *Wings*. The studio was eager to advance
his career. When Hammett reported to the lot, he was told:
"We want a gangster film for Coop. Something with class.
Something different."

As open criminal warfare broke out across the country, the
gangster film was rapidly becoming hot in Hollywood. Vapid
musical numbers and sentimental romantic dialogue were
giving way to the roar of a low-slung black sedan and the rattle
of gunfire. Each day the nation's headlines provided a new
kind of excitement, which soon was reflected in films such as
Edward G. Robinson's *Little Caesar* and James Cagney's *Public
Enemy*. Crime gave films a new vigor, a sense of immediacy
and raw reality. As one of the most popular crime writers in

America, Dashiell Hammett was riding the crest of this wave.

Knowing he could earn a bonus of $5,000 if he came up with the right idea, Hammett tackled his Cooper assignment with determination, working in his room at the Hollywood Knickerbocker, cigarette in mouth, a bottle of Scotch on the table beside him.

He wrote six short screen outlines with Cooper in mind, and two of these, "Dynamite Carson," and "The Devil's Playground," were given serious studio consideration—but ultimately rejected. Then Hammett came up with a story mixing gangsterism with carnival life, dealing with a young sharpshooter, "the Kid," who falls in love with a tainted heroine whose stepfather is "in the rackets." She tries to persuade him to quit his job with the carnival and work outside the law "for some big money." He refuses, but when she's sent to prison he joins the gangster world to obtain evidence for her release. Out of jail, she rejects her past and attempts to go straight. Complications arise, and the Kid must save her at the film's climax, when she's framed for murder.

Paramount assigned Oliver Garrett and Max Marcin to develop Hammett's story into a shooting script for a film to be titled *City Streets*. Rouben Mamoulian would direct. Hollywood's celebrated "It" girl, Clara Bow, was set to star but had a nervous breakdown. She was replaced by a new talent, Sylvia Sidney. (Later, when Hammett saw the film, the only thing he really liked was Sidney's performance.)

Hammett met Cooper on the set, and the lanky star told him he'd read *The Glass Key* and wanted to play the part of Ned Beaumont. "Don't tell me, tell Paramount," said Hammett. "I'm just a hired hand around this joint—same as you."

Having earned his first $5,000 bonus, Hammett promptly gambled it away at the Clover Club. Like his character, Ned Beaumont, Hammett lost far more often than he won, but these losses failed to dim his abiding passion for cards, horses, and crap games.

Now living in rented quarters at 1551½ North Bronson Avenue, Hammett became friendly with fellow writer Ben

Hecht, who in 1927 had scripted the first popular gangster film, *Underworld,* and who was then working on *Red Harvest* for Paramount—it had been given a new film title, *Roadhouse Nights.* Hammett's novel was radically altered for the screen. Afraid of the book's violence and political implications, Paramount insisted on a neatly laundered "action-comedy." Garrett Fort was credited with the final screenplay, from Hecht's treatment, and nothing of Hammett's novel remained. This film marked the debut of a new comic, Jimmy Durante, and was reviewed as "a nifty talker, with laughs and thrills."

Hecht had been a Chicago news reporter, and had experienced the Capone era firsthand; Hammett was intrigued by his lurid stories of guns and gangsters. Similarly, Hecht relished the Pinkerton anecdotes recounted by Hammett.

"Of the thousand writers huffing and puffing through movieland," Hecht later wrote, "there were scarcely fifty men and women of wit or talent." Obviously, he considered Hammett to be one of them. Hecht recalled the era vividly: "Most of the important people got drunk after one o'clock, sobered up around three-thirty and got drunk again at nine. Fist fights began around eleven. Seduction had no stated hours, and the skimpy offices shook with passion [as] the mingled sounds of plotting and sexual moans came through the transoms."

Of the town itself, he wrote: "I remember fine homes with handsome butlers . . . vivid people, long and noisy luncheons, nights of gaiety and gambling, hotel suites and tented palaces overrun with friends, partners, secretaries. I remember yelling matches in the lairs of the caliphs, swimming parties, all-night card games—and a picnic of money-making."

Hammett quickly grew restless under the restrictions of his Paramount contract. He entered marathon poker games, amused himself with starlets, cheered favorite boxers at the local fights. And he drank. Sometimes for days. With Hecht, or others. At parties or alone. It was the drinking that counted, not the who or where of it.

The night he met Lillian Hellman, at a Hollywood restaurant in the fall of 1930, Hammett was emerging from a five-day drinking binge, feeling lonely and disoriented, needing to talk to someone. The bright, intense young woman in her mid-twenties met this need—they talked all night. Hellman recalled that one of the subjects they discussed was the work of T. S. Eliot; she also remembered how "tired and rumpled" Hammett looked. Still, she thought he had a "wonderful face."

Hellman was then married to Arthur Kober, a former theatrical press agent who was writing for the studios. He had aided her in obtaining a position at MGM as a scenario reader, but she was not happy with this job, or with her marriage. She shared Hammett's affinity for alcohol; drinking helped her forget the ridiculous stories she was paid to read. Drinking also helped her deal with her prime frustration: she wanted to write.

Born on June 20, 1905, in New Orleans, Lillian Florence Hellman was the only child of German-Jewish parents, Max Hellman and Julia Newhouse. She spent her childhood alternating between family groups in New York and New Orleans. In 1922, at New York University, she was introduced to the works of Kant, Marx, and Engels—and a lifetime of radicalism. In the summer of 1924, at nineteen, she left college to write ad copy for the Liveright publishing house. (Hemingway's first U.S. book was issued from Liveright in 1925.) She began an affair with Arthur Kober, and they were married the following year. Kober took her to France, and he printed her first short stories in a magazine he edited, *The Paris Comet.* By 1926 she was reviewing for the *Herald Tribune* in New York. During a trip to Germany in 1929, Hellman considered entering the university at Bonn, but changed her mind when she encountered anti-Semitism there.

After their return from Europe, the Kobers moved to Hollywood, where Arthur went to work as a Paramount writer. Hellman had become a play reader during her New York years, and this background sufficed as a critical credential with MGM. But the job of scenario reader bored and annoyed her.

A few weeks after their long night of talk, Hammett and

Hellman met again, and each was attracted to the other. Hammett was very much in charge of the relationship at this point, and biographer Richard Moody, in writing of Hellman, described the power Hammett exerted over the young woman: "His charm was irresistible. . . . She was awed by his adventurous former life as a Pinkerton private eye, by his best-seller success as a detective-story writer, and by his top rank in motion pictures."

Hellman told him she wanted to become a professional writer, but was totally discouraged by her attempts thus far. Hammett agreed to help her "when and if" she ever became "really serious about it."

"That may be sooner than you think," she told him.

Hammett could now afford a manservant, and hired one named Jones. He also rented a chauffeured limousine to take him to and from the studios. Hearing that his old friend Al Samuels was ill in San Francisco, Hammett set out to visit him, motoring up from Hollywood in the hired limo.

"I owe you this and I figured it might come in handy right now," he told Samuels, handing the sick man a $500 check.

With tears misting his eyes, Al gratefully accepted the money, but was startled to see Hammett again just a week later. ("He told me he'd spent all of his 'loose cash' in San Francisco and was unable to pay his sizable hotel bill. Could I be a good fellow and let him borrow back the $500 *plus* an extra $300 to cover his expenses back to Hollywood?")

Upon his return, Hammett worked on the script of *Ladies Man* for actor William Powell, who had gained a wide following for his portrayals of Philo Vance. Privately, Powell shared Hammett's distaste for Vance and wanted to escape the role.

Ladies Man was Hammett's last job for Paramount (following some "polishing" on *Blonde Venus,* for Marlene Dietrich). Early in 1931, on behalf of Warner Brothers, Darryl Zanuck offered Hammett $15,000 to create an original crime film for Powell. Warners had three other writers working on his *Maltese Falcon,* and what Zanuck wanted from Hammett was a story about a *crooked* Sam Spade.

Hammett developed a screen story for Zanuck called "The Private Detective," based on a seedy operative Hammett had known when he worked for Pinkerton. Columnist Louella Parsons, writing for the Hearst newspaper chain, ran a feature item on the project, describing it as "an exposé of the unscrupulous methods employed by private detective agencies."

A trade-paper item, in early March, announced the completion of *The Maltese Falcon*, with the title changed to *Woman of the World*. By its release that summer, the title had been changed again, to *Dangerous Female*, but soon thereafter the studio was marketing the picture under Hammett's original title. Fashioned by a trio of writers (Maude Fulton, Lucien Hubbard, and Brown Holmes), the screenplay followed Hammett's novel in most of the basic details, but added a ludicrous finale: after Spade has turned Brigid over to the police for his partner's murder, he is offered a job on the D.A.'s staff as a reward for his fine work on the case. And there is the strong suggestion that Brigid will soon be out of prison and back in Sam's arms. (Hammett's comments on the new ending remain unrecorded, but he could not have been pleased.)

The direction, by Roy Del Ruth, was clumsy and heavy-handed, and the story was played as semicomedy (probably because Bebe Daniels, starring as Brigid, was an established screen comedienne. Her performance was flat and unconvincing). Dudley Digges achieved solid believability as Gutman, but his contribution could not offset the severe damage inflicted on Hammett's concept by Ricardo Cortez's portrayal of Spade.

Says historian Ron Goulart: "Cortez, real name Jacob Kranz, was a sleepy-eyed lover with Valentino hair and Ramon Novarro postures. His Sam Spade was a strange hybrid, half-tough, half-sultry. In some scenes he is terse and cynical. In others he looks as if he's about to carry the heroine off into the desert. When Spade talks to Brigid in his apartment he wears a silk lounging robe and sits before a giant fireplace—hardly typical of Hammett's austere detective."

To protect his writing interests on both coasts, Hammett employed two agents: Dan Leonardson in Hollywood, for film work, and Ben Wasson in New York, for magazine and book sales. It was Wasson who resurrected Hammett's unfinished 18,000-word "Thin Man" manuscript, which the author had abandoned in 1930. On the phone from New York, Wasson told him he felt certain he could sell the story for "top dollar." The question was, would Hammett be willing to complete it?

"Not now," Hammett told him. "Send out what you've got and try for a deal. If the money's right I'll finish the damn thing."

Wasson reached an agreement with *Cosmopolitan*. The magazine would pay Hammett a total of $26,000 for the completed manuscript, which, in 1931, was indeed "top dollar." But the deal had to be called off when Knopf claimed first publication rights.

However, Wasson *did* make two other deals for his client that season. He sold film rights to RKO on Hammett's *Liberty* serial, "Woman in the Dark" (actually a novelette), and he sold stage rights for *The Maltese Falcon* to Benjamin Glazer.

Another Wasson project involved an anthology edited for the John Day Company that year, *Creeps by Night*. For this 1931 book, Hammett selected twenty tales of terror—by William Faulkner, John Collier, Irvin S. Cobb, Conrad Aiken, Stephen Vincent Benét, André Maurois, Philip MacDonald, and others. Hammett's introductory remarks dealt with the reader's ability to believe in the supernatural, and he summed up his position by stating: "If you believe in werewolves, then it can make little difference to you, except perhaps academically, whether your heroine is eaten by one of them or shot down by a Cicero muscleman." Again, it was the sardonic Hammett speaking.

He also responded sardonically to a *New Yorker* "bit" that season. The magazine had reprinted a reader's complaint from the Baltimore *Observer* regarding *The Maltese Falcon:* "This fellow Hammett is the same fellow that wrote *The Dain Curse* and there is something creeping up my back to tell me that it was punk, too, but I don't know what it is. Just something."

Hammett supplied *The New Yorker* with the two-word editorial riposte: "Your undershirt?"

Lillian Hellman and Hammett had been spending so much time together at the Brown Derby that they became a gossip item, which amused them. She recalled an incident at the Derby revealing Hammett's casual attitude toward money. A tall, dark-skinned man in full Indian regalia (who sold tourist postcards) had come over to their table to confront Hammett. He accused him of having arrested an Indian for murder during the Pinkerton days.

"That's right," said Hammett.

The dark man then claimed that his grandfather was a Sioux chief who felt that the white man had exploited his tribe.

Hammett grunted, took out his wallet, tossed it on the table. The dark-skinned man counted out a hundred dollars, telling Hammett that it was "only a loan." Then the man bowed, kissed Lillian Hellman's hand, and quickly exited the restaurant with Hammett's money. Hellman was moved, impressed with the proud dignity of the Indian. But Hammett told her that he was no Indian, that he was a black man pretending to be an Indian. Actually, he was "a no-good stinker." Then why, she wanted to know, had he given him the money?

Hammett grinned. "Because no-good stinkers get hungry too."

In early March of 1931 Hellman visited some friends in New York. Hammett's film work kept him in Hollywood, but he wrote to say how much he missed her: "The emptiness I thought was hunger for chow mein turned out to be for you."

Ironically, Hammett and Arthur Kober had become good friends, regularly attending "the fights" together on Friday nights. Kober knew his marriage to Hellman was over, accepted the fact, and had no qualms whatever about her

intense relationship with the personable ex-detective. Two
more of Hellman's close friends took a liking to Hammett—
humorist S. J. Perelman and his wife Laura. Writing to Hellman about seeing them at the Derby, Hammett added: "I
tried to pump Laura about your conduct in New York. . . .
Suspected you of the loosest sort of conduct. Just a she-
Hammett." In the same letter he told her that he had been on
the wagon for seven days. His head was clear, and he was
eager to get back to real creative prose. He told her that his
ambition was to earn enough money from film work to let him
spend two full months completing his unfinished John Guild
mystery—"which, God willing, will be my last detective
novel."

Hammett was determined to break free of the crime genre
and do "something entirely new"—but he had become one of
the hottest talents in Hollywood and was in constant demand
as a "story man." The new prose would have to wait. Dusting
off one of the early Paramount outlines ("Dynamite Carson,"
his story of a hobo), Hammett talked with MGM's Irving Thal-
berg about developing it as a vehicle for Wallace Beery. RKO
was "seriously considering" purchasing *The Dain Curse* for the
screen, while Paramount had already purchased rights to *The
Glass Key.*

At publication of *The Glass Key,* in April of 1931, novelist-
critic Dorothy Parker raved over Hammett in a breathless *New
Yorker* piece, calling him "as American as a sawed-off shotgun . . . a good, hell-bent, cold-hearted writer, with a clear eye
for the ways of hard women and a fine ear for the words of
hard men. . . . Anybody who doesn't read him misses much
of modern America."

Parker then sent a letter to Hammett in which she admitted
"I have never written to an author before [but] I think you are
great."

Such extravagant praise disturbed Hammett. He wanted his
novels to be popular, but he disliked being fawned over in the
manner of a "literary pet."

In the fall, when he was able to join Hellman in New York, they were invited to a cocktail party given by William Rose Benét. Hammett was sober, and therefore uncomfortable; his tolerance for literary cocktail parties increased in direct proportion to his alcoholic intake. He had just accepted his first drink of the evening when a small woman with bright, birdlike eyes dropped to her knees in front of him and enthusiastically kissed his hand. The woman was Dorothy Parker, and Hammett stared down at her in stunned shock.

Lillian Hellman and Dorothy Parker were to become close lifelong friends, but Hammett (though he saw much of her through the years) never liked Parker from this moment forward. In later decades, he would vanish for days when she visited at Hellman's farm. He appreciated coolness and control in people, and was put off by Parker's affectations and hypocrisy; her eccentric behavior and sharply barbed remarks failed to amuse him.

Hammett did become quite friendly with another writer he met in New York, fellow southerner William Faulkner. Their rapport was immediate, and their respect for one another's talent was genuine. They disagreed on many levels— political (Faulkner was extremely conservative) and intellectual (when, for example, Hammett disputed the worth of a Faulkner favorite, Thomas Mann's *Magic Mountain*)—but spent long evenings in Hammett's hotel room swapping stories about the South and putting away vast quantities of Scotch. Hellman tried to keep pace with them, but would finally fall asleep in a chair as they continued to talk and argue into the dawn.

Editor Bennett Cerf recalled the time he met Faulkner and Hammett for lunch at a bar-restaurant. During the meal, Cerf mentioned that he had been invited to dinner that evening by Alfred and Blanche Knopf.

"Bill's never been introduced to Blanche," said Hammett, a hand on Faulkner's shoulder. "So we'll go along—and *I'll* introduce him."

Cerf pointed out that the dinner was several hours away and

Members, with Hammett, of the New York literary set of the 1930s: James Thurber, Dorothy Parker, William Faulkner.

Hammett, 1933.

Hammett's publishers, Alfred and Blanche Knopf, and their son, Pat. At right, Hollywood cronies Ben Hecht and Charles MacArthur.

Lillian Hellman, 1935.

that he had to return to work, then go home and dress for the evening.

"You do all that," nodded Faulkner. "We'll just wait for you here."

"Yeah," agreed Hammett. "In the bar. Pick us up around seven."

Cerf protested that the dinner was black tie and that they were in tweeds!

"Nobody will notice," said Faulkner.

Cerf had no choice; they wouldn't allow him to leave until he'd agreed to the plan.

By the time he arrived back that evening to pick them up, both writers were flushed and staggering under the effects of their day-long drinking.

The dinner party was elegant. Novelist Willa Cather was there, as well as Hammett's first editor, H. L. Mencken. Hammett introduced Faulkner to Blanche Knopf, then sat down on the couch, a fresh drink in his hand. His eyes glazed, and he slowly toppled forward, sprawling onto Knopf's thick carpet. Faulkner wheeled, weaving drunkenly toward his friend, intending to aid him. Instead, with a sigh, he collapsed next to him.

Faulkner always enjoyed his evenings with Hammett; he admired the ex-detective's hard-headed honesty. One of Faulkner's complaints about himself was that he had written the novel *Sanctuary* simply to make money, without regard to creative pride. Hammett claimed that Faulkner was deluding himself, that no honest writer could ever turn out a "deliberate potboiler." Only hacks could do that; a good writer always wrote his books as well as possible, or not at all. There were other ways to make money from writing, and he knew about them, but hacking out novels was not one of them.

Hammett's vehemence on this subject stemmed from his respect for novelistic fiction as a vehicle for artistic expression and his growing fear that his Hollywood screen work was replacing his efforts at creative prose.

The question that continually troubled Hammett was: could he do *both*? Could he go on earning money in films, yet turn out the novels he desperately wanted to write?

At this point in his life, he was determined to try.

12

THIN MAN IN A BLIND CORNER

I see life as ferocious and sinister.

—HENRY JAMES

AFTER A FULL year's absence from the magazines, Hammett was finally persuaded by Ben Wasson to turn out some new fiction for the high-paying "slicks." He had been urging Hammett to try a serial for *Cosmopolitan*—and told him that several editors had expressed strong interest in new Sam Spade material.

Hammett wrote three new short stories about Spade, two for *American Magazine,* and one for *Collier's.* They were well crafted but lacked the intensity and wry passion of his work for *Black Mask.* Here, Hammett's detective was far inferior to the complex, richly textured Spade that Hammett had created in *The Maltese Falcon.* The "new" Spade could have been named Smith or Jones; his character was bland, all but invisible. As one critic rightly observed, "These stories were written against the grain of Hammett's creativity."

Joe Shaw knew that he had lost his star writer to the slick markets, that there was no way for him to compete with their higher word rates. In frustration, Shaw ran an editorial in *Black Mask,* responding to numerous reader requests for more of their favorite author:

> Dashiell Hammett's *Maltese Falcon* has been screened . . .
> his *Glass Key* will also appear and be heard in movie-talkie
> theaters . . . we have many letters asking when he'll have

124

another story for us . . . but when a fellow is pulling $100,000 a year out of Hollywood we just don't have the heart—or is it nerve?—to suggest that he knock off and turn out one of those great old Continental Op stories. Anyway, we keep hoping.

Shaw's hopes were futile. In truth, money had nothing to do with Hammett's failure to write more Op fiction. He had developed a pessimism that prevented him from returning to the Op; by 1931 Hammett had long since moved beyond the emotional environment of the series.

Hammett did write one excellent piece of fiction that year, for *Harper's Bazaar,* a brief, bitter vignette which was strangely self-prophetic. "On the Way" (which was printed in the March 1932 issue) is set in Hollywood and deals with a man on the way down and a woman on the way up. As the story begins, Gladys, a starlet, has just landed a film contract, while Kipper, her partygoing lover, is out of work and almost out of money. Their dialogue gives an eerie preview of the developing Hellman-Hammett relationship: "Up the ladder for you now, hey?" he asks, and she replies, "For both of us. You're as much a part of it as I am. You gave me something . . ."

He cuts her off with "You always had things—just a little trouble knowing what to do with them."

Hellman, indeed, always had things—dedication, intelligence, writing talent—but, at the time she met Hammett, had trouble knowing what to do with them. Her successful career as a playwright was to be launched and nurtured by Hammett ("You're as much a part of it as I am"). Within two years, thanks to Hammett's help, Lillian Hellman would be "on the way."

Late in 1931, Hammett submitted to his first extensive interview, printed in *The Bookman* early the following year. He evidently charmed his interviewer, Elizabeth Sanderson, who described him in his thirty-seventh year as "tall, slim, and sophisticated, with prematurely white hair above a young face." He named Hemingway, Faulkner, and Hecht as three writers he admired, and told her that he didn't want to continue with detective fiction. He did not like *The Dain Curse* and considered *The Maltese Falcon* "too manufactured."

"Mr. Hammett wants to write a play," Sanderson reported. "He wants to go abroad [and] stay in Europe for a year or two while he finishes his play and tries his hand at a straight novel."

By the summer of 1932, as the nation entered the depths of the Depression, with fifteen million people unemployed, Hammett was prospering in Hollywood. He never got to Europe, nor did he work on his play. What he did do was attend parties, parties, parties. Ben Hecht, who hosted some of the wildest and gaudiest, reminisced:

> At that time . . . Leland Hayward, Charles MacArthur and I were living in a rented wooden castle on a Hollywood hill. There were two hundred and fifty turkeys on the grounds. There was a big mosaic fountain on the front terrace. The drawing room was large enough for a baseball diamond. We never counted the bedrooms. Two chefs in ballooning white hats cooked for us, and there was a printing press in the cellar on which we printed our dinner menus. We called the joint Turkey Hill . . . and we worked, drank, swore, and sinned there.

It was to Turkey Hill that Hammett came one evening that summer, mounting the grade with his long-legged stride— grinning happily at Ben and Charlie as they promptly led him to the bar. The Hollywood Greats had gathered: Jean Harlow, all sex and blazing blond hair, holding the hand of her fiancé, Paul Bern (who would die a suicide); John Gilbert, idol of the silents, with three giggling prostitutes he'd hired for the evening; Harpo Marx and Ernst Lubitsch playing craps; director Howard Hawks, listening with sad eyes as George Antheil stroked the piano. Bootleg booze and industry small talk flowed in equal measure.

"The two drinkers out front were MacArthur and Hammett," Hecht recalled. "They took the lead early in the evening and were holding on to it without sign of strain. . . . Dash remembered a gun duel in San Francisco [as] the party climbed a high perch."

When Hellman wasn't in town, Hammett usually brought home another woman to share his bed. Once, she claimed, she arrived unexpectedly and found *two* women there, with a startled Hammett in the middle. Even when a woman had not intended spending the night, Hammett's charm usually prevailed. But there were exceptions. Actress Elise De Vianne sued Hammett for $35,000, claiming that he "forced his sexual attentions" upon her. A Los Angeles judge awarded Miss De Vianne $2,500 in damages.

This was not the only court action against Hammett. He used hired limousines daily and would often ignore the monthly limousine bills, and so he was regularly sued in small-claims court for nonpayment.

Although, as Joe Shaw had written, Hammett was now earning more than $100,000 a year from the studios, he was usually broke. He spent the money as fast as he got it—on himself and on anyone else who happened to be in his vicinity. To capture the attention of one young woman, Hammett had a taxicab full of fresh red roses delivered to her apartment each morning. After a week of this, buried in flowers, she agreed to go out with him. He would buy lavish gifts on impulse for his friends and lend money to anyone who seemed to need it, for any purpose, without asking for or expecting repayment. One Hollywood friend said of him: "Dash was the only guy I ever met who really didn't care about hanging on to money. He sure loved to make it and have it, but he didn't give a damn about *keeping* it!"

Hammett and Hellman were back in New York for the summer of 1932, and these summer months blended into a dizzy round of Manhattan parties. Bright talk. Bright faces. Weekend celebrations. Smoke-filled hangouts in Greenwich

Village. A drunken blur of nights and days. One of their New York watering holes was Tony's, a speakeasy, and Hellman recalled a night there with humorist James Thurber, who called himself "a wild-eyed son of a bitch" and who could be anything but humorous when he was drinking heavily.

They were talking politics, and Hellman said something with which Thurber disagreed. Abruptly, he pitched a glass of whiskey at her. Hammett stepped between them, pinning Thurber to the wall. "That'll be enough," he told the red-faced humorist.

Satisfied that Thurber had calmed down, Hammett turned away, only to have Thurber snatch up another glass and throw it at his head. Hammett ducked, and the glass struck a waiter—who just happened to be Tony's cousin. Suddenly, the argument turned into a general melee, which continued until the police arrived. They were all hustled down to the local stationhouse. Hammett was amused at the prospect of being arrested, which annoyed Hellman, who saw nothing attractive about being thrown into a jail cell. But the matter was settled with Thurber's apology, and all charges were dropped.

By summer's end, Hammett's publisher was pressing for his new novel. Blanche Knopf wrote to his agent, asking when they could expect to receive *The Thin Man*. Hammett's other novels were still selling briskly, and Knopf wanted to take full advantage of his current popularity.

Hammett settled into Manhattan's elegant Hotel Pierre in September of 1932 with the firm intention of finishing *The Thin Man*. But when he reread his original 18,000-word, two-year-old manuscript, he realized he could not complete it. Life had changed radically for him since 1930, and the terse, humorless *Black Mask* style was no longer appropriate. Hammett's present life prompted a shift in background: he would draw upon his relationship with Hellman and his exposure to the New York social world. Now involved in this hedonistic microcosm, Hammett lost interest in the hard-boiled working detective and recast his protagonist. Nick Charles (Greek name Charalambides) is an ex-operative of the Trans-American Detective Agency of San Francisco, married to Nora, a lumber heiress. Nick was tough in his heyday, but now the toughness has been replaced by cockiness; he refuses to take anything seriously unless backed to the wall.

John Guild, Hammett's morose, job-holding detective of the unfinished first version of *The Thin Man,* would have quickly rejected the spoiled heiress and her millions (Nick has quit the detective business to manage Nora's properties), and he would certainly have never had a drink before breakfast. The job-holder was replaced by the partygoer; the new Hammett protagonist was a self-indulgent fellow who just wanted to be left alone with Nora and her dollars, and who came out of retirement to solve the case of the missing thin man only because his wife nagged him into it. What on the surface is amusing and fresh in this published version simply reflects Hammett's own cynicism. He could no longer believe in, or write about, detectives who resisted life's pleasures to get a case solved. Nick Charles is, in many ways, an unattractive, self-centered character—made attractive on the printed page only by Hammett's wit and clever style.

Nora is delighted with the caper. ("I love you, Nicky, because you smell nice and know such fascinating people.") But when Nick gets serious he admits that he's worried by "riddles and lies—and I'm too old and too tired for them to be any fun." At first he wants to get back to San Francisco, but by the novel's end he's changed his mind; the old habits have returned. "Let's stick around awhile," he says to Nora. "This excitement has put us behind in our drinking."

Nora Charles was modeled directly on Lillian Hellman, whose intense curiosity about Hammett's Pinkerton days prompted her to urge him back into detective work so that she could follow him around and discover how a sleuth really behaves.

Hellman's fascination with detectives can be traced back to her childhood in New York. When she was twelve, Lillian and a friend started their own counterespionage service. As biographer Richard Moody tells it: "They were seeking to break up a German spy ring they imagined operated along this section of Riverside Drive. They would pursue anyone carrying a briefcase or a violin case." One afternoon they tailed a pair of suspicious-looking types for ten blocks. When Hellman was sure that she had unearthed a pair of German spies, she asked a policeman to arrest them. Says Moody: "One spy turned out to be a professor of Greek, the other a concert violinist."

According to Hellman, Hammett would become "very angry" each time she suggested he return to detective work—until he suddenly realized that the situation was tailor-made for a mystery story. In the novel, Nora manages to nag her husband back into the detective game (a success Hellman never actually achieved with Hammett). In *The Thin Man* Hammett also used much of the bright, wise-cracking Hammett-Hellman repartee for Nick and Nora. Hellman claimed that she recognized their word-for-word dialogue in several of the novel's sequences.

With the new *Thin Man* barely under way, the Knopf advance ran out. Unable to pay their hotel bill at the Pierre, they contacted a friend, Laura Perelman, whose brother, Nathanael "Pep" West, was then night manager at the Sutton Club Hotel at 330 East Fifty-sixth Street. West agreed to provide lodging for Hammett until he could finish his novel.

West, a writer, had already published his first novel, *The Dream Life of Balso Snell,* and the next year would publish his second, *Miss Lonelyhearts.* Fellow writers were always welcome at the Sutton, and some of literature's brightest stars had accepted free lodging there during periods of financial stress. The roster included S. J. Perelman (West's brother-in-law), Erskine Caldwell, James T. Farrell, critic Edmund Wilson, and journalist Quentin Reynolds.

The Sutton had been built as a women's club but opened as a hotel. Owing to its small lobby and odd room arrangements, it was never successful. West always had rooms available for his "writer guests." He told Hammett and Hellman that they could occupy what he jokingly called the "Royal Suite"—three cramped upper rooms.

"What about meals?" Hammett wanted to know.

"You can charge 'em," West said.

They arrived without bags, having skipped on their bill at the Pierre. For the first time in his adult life, Hammett actually looked overweight; he was wearing all of his clothes, in layers, shirts over shirts, coats over coats, pants over pants. They had carried nothing from the Pierre except his manuscript. Even Hammett's typewriter remained behind.

Now, as Hellman reported, the parties and the drinking stopped. Hammett refused to leave the hotel, even for a walk, fearing that "something creative might be lost." The novel occupied his total attention, his discipline extending to the manuscript page itself; each sheet was neat, clean of errors, precisely typed. A normal night's sleep became an intrusion. As he had done so often back in the San Francisco days, Hammett worked steadily for thirty-hour stretches, chain-smoking, pacing the small rooms, typing, correcting, rewriting.

Hellman felt unwanted; she spent several hours each day at the Sutton's indoor swimming pool or at Child's Restaurant near the hotel, nibbling at the "awful food" and drinking endless cups of coffee with West and the Perelmans.

West was using many of the guests at his hotel as characters in his darkly pessimistic books. Like Hammett, West's perception of a godless killer-universe formed the core of his fiction.

West was repelled and fascinated by the half-dozen suicides he had witnessed at the Sutton. (One jumper crashed through the glass ceiling of the hotel dining room just as the guests were sitting down for their evening meal.) He wanted to know more about the "inner lives" of his tenants, and enlisted Hellman's aid in steaming open letters addressed to various Sutton residents. For West, it was an act of "creative necessity."

Weeks passed. When Hammett had half a first draft, he

allowed Hellman to read it. That's when he told her, "You're Nora."

Hellman said that she was pleased and flattered.

"Don't be," Hammett muttered. "You're also the villainess."

He was referring to Mimi Jorgensen, a woman definitely not to be trusted. "When you catch her in a lie, she admits it and gives you another lie to take its place and, when you catch her in that one, admits it and gives you still another." This description, from the novel, could apply equally well to Brigid in *Falcon;* both women were skilled at playing the game of falsehood.

Asked, years later, if the portrait of Nora was accurate, Hellman said: "I don't really see myself. Nora is Hammett's picture of me." But she admired the relationship between Nick and Nora, calling it "one of the few marriages in modern literature where the man and woman really like each other and have a fine time together."

Hammett's other characters in the novel were a bizarre lot. Clyde Miller Wynant, the missing inventor, is described by Nick as "one of the thinnest men I've ever seen." He is suspected of murdering his secretary, Julia Wolf. (Hammett retained this basic plot bit from his original 1930 version.) Dorothy Wynant ("cute, but cuckoo") carries a rusted pistol in her purse. Gilbert, Mimi's neurotic, crime-obsessed son, is fascinated by cannibalism. Herbert Macauley is the crooked lawyer who has done away with the missing thin man. Shep Morelli is a nervous gangster who almost kills Nick. And tough Studsy Burke runs the Pigiron Club. ("Studsy leaned over . . . and smashed a big fist into the fat man's face. . . . 'I ain't running a dive, but I ain't trying to run a young ladies' seminary neither!' ")

Hammett gave the name of his 1930 detective, John Guild, to a police lieutenant involved in the case—but this Guild bears no relationship to "the dark man" from Hammett's unfinished first-draft manuscript.

On the surface, Hammett's novel is merry and clever. The

dialogue snaps and crackles. The setting of New York at Christmas adds a festive atmosphere. Nick and Nora even have a dog, Asta, named after Laura Perelman's pet. And, as critic Hugh Eames observed: "Charles is the first Hammett character to have an agreeable relationship with a woman."

But this glossy surface, like Melville's sea, covers a depth. Philosophically, *The Thin Man* is the bleakest of Hammett's novels. George Thompson states: "The moral vision of *The Thin Man* is dark indeed. The plot does more than unmask a villain; it shows that the villain survives only because of the corresponding greed and savagery in those around him. . . . cannibals like Macauley the killer can feast off others because the world is so devoid of values that he can appear as a natural part of the landscape."

In spirit, despite his charm, Nick Charles stands shoulder to shoulder with *The Glass Key*'s Ned Beaumont in Hammett's canon of antiheroes. Both are hollow men, empty of moral commitment. They are passive; they do not act, they react. A direct line can be traced from the reluctantly heroic Continental Op, through the more cynical Sam Spade, to the final emptiness of Beaumont and Nick Charles.

This line of degeneration reveals why Hammett abandoned the crime novel. There was nowhere for him to go beyond *The Thin Man*. He had written himself into a blind corner.

Ironically, Hammett's saga of Nick and Nora Charles touched off a wave of crime comedies—in films, radio, and television—and many regard *The Thin Man* itself as a comic novel. Howard Haycraft, writing in *Murder for Pleasure,* saw the book as "one of the first works to bring humor, of a distinctly native brand, to the detective story in this country."

But the laughter is empty—the sound of a creator wise-cracking against the encroaching night. In his final genre novel, Samuel Dashiell Hammett was having the last laugh. On himself.

13

FROM SEX TO SECRET AGENTS

He is an indefatigable and charming host, a
connoisseur of fine liquors, and an expert
ping-pong player. He likes dogs and loves music.
Hammett reads . . . everything but detective
stories. His favorite book is Spengler's Decline of
the West. *. . . He likes tweeds . . . smokes*
enormously [and] when in New York he may be
found several nights a week at Tony's.

—ALFRED A. KNOPF,
promotion folder for
The Thin Man, 1934

WHEN *The Thin Man* was completed in May of 1933, Hammett's agent had difficulty placing the serial rights with a
major magazine. The novel's sexual aura, with its hints of
perversion and incest, was considered too strong for the mass
market. Finally, however, *Redbook*'s Edwin Balmer bought it
for $5,000. He did insist on the right to edit the manuscript
"for public consumption." Hammett needed *Redbook*'s money
and agreed to cuts.

When the check arrived, Hellman and Hammett left New
York. They spent the summer of 1933 at a remote area in the
Florida Keys, "fishing every day, reading every night." Hellman had by then obtained a divorce from Arthur Kober, who
remained a close friend to both Hellman and Hammett.

More Hammett fiction, written earlier, appeared in the slick
magazines that year. A new men's magazine, *Esquire,* obtained
work from both Ernest Hemingway and Hammett for its first

134

(August) issue. Hammett's contribution was a clever crime short, "Albert Pastor at Home."

By the fall, Hellman and Hammett were back in New York, drinking with William Faulkner. They spent many weekends at S. J. Perelman's newly purchased hunting lodge in Bucks County, Pennsylvania. Hammett, like Faulkner, loved the woods, and they hunted there together, sharing these outings with Robert Coates and Pep West. Hellman would often join them in the woods, and she noted that Hammett and Faulkner were both excellent shots.

During the previous year, Raoul Whitfield had received an offer from Hollywood on his novel *Death in a Bowl* and had gone to work for Warner Brothers. He earned a screen credit in 1933 for *Private Detective 62*, the William Powell crime drama that Hammett had created in 1931. Although Whitfield reworked the plot and added new material from a *Black Mask* story of his own, he retained Hammett's premise—the corruption of a private detective. The fact that Whitfield received the story credit on this film did not disturb Hammett; he had often worked on screen projects without recognition, and would again. It was the money the job brought him that counted, not the final credit. With books, he felt, it was different. They were important; films were not.

At the end of 1933 Whitfield was stricken with tuberculosis. Unlike Hammett, he was unable to overcome this disease and was forced to end his writing career. He had a final story printed in 1937, and died eight years later at the age of forty-eight.

Hammett's final writing project for 1933, undertaken in the closing months of the year, presented a fresh challenge. He was about to enter a new arena: newspaper comics.

On October 4, 1931, a revolutionary adventure strip had made its debut for the Tribune-News Syndicate in Chicago. The artist was young Chester Gould, and the strip was called *Dick Tracy*. The first hard-boiled police drama to appear in newspaper syndication, it featured a detective who was not afraid to "shoot it out, gun to gun, with the rats of society." Gould declared: "We had a crime situation during Prohibition that was beyond coping with legally. . . . So I brought along this guy Tracy . . . who could dish it out to the underworld, who could toss the hot iron right back at them along with a smack on the jaw thrown in for good measure."

Dick Tracy caught on with readers. Other syndicates became aware of potential profits in this area. By 1933, Publishers Syndicate was featuring *Dan Dunn, Secret Operative 48* as a competitor to Tracy. The success of these two newspaper strips proved that an active market existed. William Randolph Hearst, who controlled the powerful King Features Syndicate, phoned his president, J. V. "Joe" Connolly, in New York and told him he wanted to launch a crime strip immediately— "and I want Dash Hammett to write it."

Connolly contacted Hammett, who agreed to create the strip for "top money, and a totally free hand in the concept." That fall Hammett began work on *Secret Agent X-9* under a $500-a-week contract calling for him to deliver dialogue and continuity on four stories over the following year.

It was not uncommon for a writer of Hammett's stature to associate himself with a newspaper comic page. Authors Ring Lardner, Anita Loos, and Gene Fowler had all signed to write original strips. The money was good, and the artist did most of the work. It was not difficult for Hammett to come up with a character and concept; he simply borrowed heavily from his own novels, even from the Hammett-Whitfield film, *Private Detective 62*, in which William Powell is first a government agent, then a private eye.

Ron Goulart, an authority on the comics, finds in *Secret Agent X-9* "characterizations which are part *Falcon*, part *Dain Curse*, and part *Thin Man* . . . with a good innocent blonde in trouble, a doublecrossing older woman who continually lies, a wacky professor who keeps disappearing, and a fat con man named Sidney George Harper Carp who talks like Casper Gutman."

Hammett combined the Continental Op and Sam Spade in the character of X-9: he is cool, efficient, quick with a gun or a wisecrack, and, like the Op, a man without a name. As French critic Maurice Horn pointed out: "In his struggle against crime, X-9 is not satisfied merely to fight criminals; he mingles with them, borrows their habits, jargon, even their methods. . . . The fact that he possesses no known name, only an FBI number, and that he always works alone, further heightens his mystery."

In the pulp tradition of action, Hammett kept things moving. The opening adventure—"The Top," which ran daily for eight months beginning in January of 1934—was full of gunfights, car crashes, gold shipments, piracy, explosions at sea, mysterious code messages, and multiple murders.

The artist for *Secret Agent X-9* was twenty-four-year-old Alexander G. Raymond, an ex–stock market employee who had been earning $20 a month ghosting *Blondie.* At the time he was hired for *X-9,* he had just sold two creations of his own to King Features, *Flash Gordon* and *Jungle Jim.* He would handle these as Sunday features, while drawing *Secret Agent X-9* as a daily strip. Raymond's characters wore clothing of the period. The natty X-9 was outfitted in trench coat and snapbrim. He also wore silk smoking jackets and neat double-breasted suits. Raymond's hoods sported derbies and spats, striped shirts and straw boaters, while his gang molls flounced about in gaudy flapper attire.

The hoods are Hammett-tough ("You're liable to get slapped around whether you behave yourself or not!"), and the gun molls are equally potent. One of them visits a society woman and clips her smartly on the jaw, knocking her to the floor. "You'll pay for this!" says the victim. "OK, Baby, and you can put this on my bill, too!" replies the snarling young woman, kicking her in the stomach.

X-9 is a hard character. He *uses* the gun he carries, once killing four men in four panels. And not only can he "dish out" punishment, but he can also take it. In his second adventure ("The Mystery of the Silent Guns"), he is hit over the head, is placed inside a tunnel of burning oil, survives an auto crash, is blackjacked—and has his parachute fired upon as he leaps from a plane after the villain. In "The Martyn Case" (which ran into March of 1935), he is thrown from a cliff and almost drowned, and spends the greater part of his adventure with one arm in a sling.

In the first *X-9* story an attractive, Brigid-like character, Grace Powers, attempts to charm the tough agent in a typical Hammett exchange:

> GRACE: I like you. I really do.
> X-9:   I don't like you. I really don't.
> GRACE: Why must we be enemies?
> X-9:   One reason might be that the last time I saw you you tried to hire a guy to kill me.

She offers to help him find the criminal he's after (known as "The Top"), but he accuses her of lying and says he can't trust her. Obviously, like Spade, he is fascinated by her, attracted to her, but knows he must not let down his guard. Hammett had written such scenes many times before.

King Features launched the new strip with much fanfare, announcing in papers across the nation that "there has never been a sleuth like X-9. He matches racketeers' cunning with his finely trained wits . . . fights gun-fire with gun-fire." They blurbed Hammett as "the greatest detective story writer of the 20th century, today's most popular, fastest-selling author."

A photo of Hammett accompanied an "exclusive interview," showing him at his desk, cigarette in mouth, hair tousled, pounding out *X-9* copy on his typewriter. Columnist Joseph Harrington asked him where he got his characters. "From life," he replied. Hammett bragged about being lazy. "I'm a two-fisted loafer," he told Harrington. "I can loaf longer and better than anyone I know." Did he have a hobby? "Sure. I drink a lot."

Simultaneously, Knopf was conducting its own newspaper and magazine ad campaign for Hammett's new book, *The Thin Man*—which became an overnight best seller upon publication in January 1934. Knopf chose to tease the public with a reference to a bold question in the novel, asked of Nick by Nora. She wants to know if he got sexually aroused during the time he was tussling with Mimi: "Didn't you have an erection?" The *New York Times* carried a Knopf ad in which the publisher protested: "We don't believe the question on page 192 of Dashiell Hammett's *The Thin Man* has had the slightest influence upon the sale of the book. It takes more than that to make a best seller these days. Twenty thousand people don't buy a book within three weeks to read a five-word question."

Redbook editor Edwin Balmer was upset by this ad—and wrote a piece for *Esquire* in which he spoke of the shocking "new candor" of modern publishers. He was proud of the fact that he had eliminated the sexual question when he'd edited Hammett's book for slick-paper publication. "My own magazine cannot be accused of being crinoline minded," he wrote, "but we seem to be welcoming a common condition of literary nudism."

At the book's publication, several novelists and critics expressed their admiration. Sinclair Lewis stated that "Dashiell Hammett is undoubtedly the best of American detective story writers, and *The Thin Man* is certainly the most breathless of his stories." Alexander Woolcott called it "the best detective story yet written in America." Herschel Brickell praised "the punch of Mr. Hammett's streamlined dialogue." In England, Peter Quennell of *New Statesman and Nation* wrote: "Dashiell Hammett is almost alone in being praised by writers as a serious writer and by good novelists as a master of their business. Hemingway continues to admire him." Quennell went on to call the novel "absorbing and extremely ingenious [with] lurid glimpses of New York drinking society, but . . . what will the British public say of a detective—now happily married—who has once had 'immoral relations' with the woman he suspects of having murdered her divorced husband's mistress?—whose first thought, when he wakes up in the middle of the night, is to ask his wife to pour him a whiskey and soda?"

The notorious five-word question was excised from the

British edition since, as critic Julian Symons said solemnly, "Erections did not, at that time, exist in the English novel."

Naturally, all of this *Thin Man* publicity helped *Secret Agent X-9* to flourish.

Will Gould, creator of the *Red Barry* comic strip, was obliged by King Features to call on Hammett regularly to have Hammett inspect the *Red Barry* continuity. He would show up at Hammett's hotel each week as instructed, but the atmosphere was anything but businesslike. "I kept mixing Bacardi and ginger ales for his friends," Gould recalled, "who were constantly dropping in on him—producers, song writers, artists. . . ." Gould described Hammett as "the original thin man. He was above six feet, weighed maybe one-forty-five with rocks in his pockets. Had a crewcut. Wore tweeds. He handed me an autographed copy of *The Thin Man*, which had his photo on the front. He said the book had been banned in Boston." Finally, when all the guests had departed, Gould and Hammett would sit down to discuss the week's work on *Red Barry*. He described one of these sessions: "It lasted far into the night—and we talked about everything *but* comic strips. Talked a lot about fighters—and also about his days as a Pinkerton cop. Hammett would keep pouring drinks—and, past midnight, I noticed a slight, telltale flush on his cheekbones. He was beginning to slur his words and his speech wandered. I helped put him to bed.

"Hammett told me I ought to get out to California and grab some of that Hollywood dough," said Gould. "He'd say to me, 'You can come up with more stuff [good ideas] in a half hour than you'll hear in a month of story conferences out there.'"

When Joe Connolly grew concerned about a certain *Red Barry* sequence, he sent Gould over to Hammett's hotel to check it out. Hammett phoned the editor: "For Christ's sake, Joe, why don't you leave the kid alone? He knows what he's doing with *Barry*. And he sure as hell doesn't need *me* for a wet nurse!"

The editor finally agreed to let Gould handle *Red Barry* on his own. The strip became a hit and was described years later by mystery critic Anthony Boucher as being "vigorously in the Hammett tradition."

In time *Secret Agent X-9* began having problems. "King Features didn't seem to appreciate the subtlety and realism of Hammett's work," wrote comic strip historian Bill Blackbeard, "and [they] began to tamper with his material. As a result, the strip deteriorated markedly as it was diluted and rewritten by other hands. The end result was totally unlike Hammett's orderly, coolly reasoned detective fiction."

Hammett lost his enthusiasm and grew lax about deadlines. The strip was finally turned over to Alex Raymond. Hammett was relieved to end his King Features assignment. MGM had bought screen rights to *The Thin Man* for $21,000, and they wanted to discuss the film version with him.

Producer Hunt Stromberg had been responsible for the studio's purchase. He brought Hammett's book to director W. S. Van Dyke who was immediately excited about it. They both agreed that the only actor who could play Nick Charles with total conviction was William Powell. And for Nora? Another mutual choice: Myrna Loy.

MGM's Louis B. Mayer told Van Dyke he was "nuts" to suggest Powell and Loy for a lighthearted comedy-mystery. To begin with, Myrna Loy could never play comedy. ("For heaven's sake, she's Fu Manchu's daughter! *That's* the role people remember her for!") And Powell was due to begin a new Philo Vance film in less than a month.

"Get me Powell and Loy and I'll wrap up this one in twelve days," Van Dyke promised.

Van Dyke's reputation as one of the speediest directors in the industry tipped the scales in his favor, and Mayer gave him a grudging go-ahead, expecting *The Thin Man* would amount to no more than another cheaply made "mystery programmer."

The writing team of Albert Hackett and Frances Goodrich completed a screenplay based on Hammett's novel in just two weeks—and Van Dyke cranked the picture out in another eighteen days, bringing in the project for just $231,000. Cinema historian Jon Tuska revealed Van Dyke's time-saving methods: "He would have one setup behind the camera and one in front of it. As soon as he finished shooting the scene in front of the camera he would have the crew turn around, the cast change positions, and shoot until that scene was finished while the other stage was being readied for yet the next scene."

Although Nick and Nora were husband and wife, the Hays office censors insisted on separate beds for them in the film, and the novel's sexual atmosphere was considerably muted. Despite this, the Powell-Loy team projected a sense of zany erotic camaraderie which gave the film life and sparkle. The hard-drinking party sequences were directed with an easy, graceful style that added sophistication; in these, Van Dyke demonstrated his command of camera and situation.

William Powell thoroughly enjoyed himself as Nick Charles. "Powell really loved the role," Tuska declared. "Being a steady drinker (at his home in Palm Springs he was never without a glass in his hand), he could be entirely natural."

Mayer liked the final film—and by the time Hammett rejoined Hellman in a rented summer house on Long Island, he was already planning a return to MGM. His agent had arranged for a payment of $20,000 for an original screen sequel to *The Thin Man*.

By the summer of 1934 Hammett's career as a creative prose writer was over. His last three short stories were printed in *Collier's* that year: a boxing story, "His Brother's Keeper"; a crime tale, "Two Sharp Knives"; and a film story, "This Little Pig," featuring a hack writer, Chauncey "Bugs" Parish, who interrupts a play he's doing to heed a producer's frantic request to "go sex up my Western." Working on location, Parish finds intense jealousy among the actresses, centered around a young starlet, Kitty Doran, who yearns for a larger part in the film. Parish writes her into the picture to teach her a lesson, knowing that the leading lady will make certain Kitty's scenes end up on the cutting-room floor. When this happens, Kitty apparently attempts suicide—and Parish rushes to her, stricken with conscience over the "game" he played. Another actress, who knows Kitty, exposes her suicide attempt as a fake. Parish, his cynicism restored, goes off with this actress, leaving a furious Kitty to work her wiles elsewhere. The "little pig" of the title has been too greedy. The climax of Hammett's story finds Parish still hacking at the end, as he accepts another quickie film job. ("Max Rhinewien had bought a Hungarian comedy which he said needed more epigrams, and talked me into doing the adaptation.")

In flavor, mood, and general structure, this story is much like F. Scott Fitzgerald's Pat Hobby tales, which appeared several years later in *Esquire.* Since Fitzgerald knew and read Hammett, it is possible that his hack screenwriter, Pat Hobby, might have been inspired by Bugs Parish.

As a prose writer, in just twelve years Hammett had completed over ninety pieces of fiction. (This total includes two stories printed after his death and some thirteen unprinted stories found among his papers.) He had also written a dozen nonfiction pieces and well over a hundred book reviews.

Hammett had no intention of ending his career as a novelist at this point in his life. When he spoke of *The Thin Man* as "the last of the damned things," he referred only to mystery novels. He intended doing "straight stuff" and continued to think of himself as a working writer. But in truth, at the age of forty, his fiction-writing career had ended.

Lillian Hellman's career was just beginning. With Hammett's help, she was on the verge of becoming one of America's major playwrights.

14

LIFE IN THE DREAM FACTORY

A kind of purgatory, a place where it was
necessary to come from time to time to do penance.

—WILLIAM FAULKNER on
Hollywood

IN A 1942 introduction to four of her collected plays, Lillian
Hellman stated that by 1930 she had unhappily abandoned
creative writing. She had been striving all of her adult life to
become a writer, and had decided that she could not successfully reach this goal. "That I tried again is entirely due to
Dashiell Hammett," she declared.

In her introduction, she described Hammett's method. He
would begin by "attacking" most of what she had written,
showing her what was weak and wrong and false in it. He
would speak of a writer's integrity, would say that it was better
never to write at all if what was written failed to be really good.
She must learn, he would tell her, to *think* like a writer; she
must study the craft as a doctor studies medicine. Read, study,
and practice, practice, practice. If she turned out to be a bad
writer, *then* she could quit. The world would not miss her.

Listening to this "tough logic," Hellman started working
again, and wrote her first play in 1932 as a collaboration with
Louis Kronenberger. A comedy called *The Dear Queen*, it was
"about a royal family who wanted to be bourgeois." Hammett
did not like the play. He told her he knew it was no good
because Kronenberger laughed only at his lines and she
laughed only at hers. It was never produced.

144

Hammett urged Hellman to try a novel, but she was terrified of the form; she felt far more comfortable with plays. She had turned out a few short stories, but novels seemed beyond her grasp.

"Okay," said Hammett, "but if you're going to do another play, then start with something solid."

He gave her a book by William Roughead, *Bad Companions,* and suggested she base her play on a chapter entitled "Closed Doors; or The Great Drumsheugh Case," the true narrative of an episode in 1810 wherein a pathologically disturbed girl attending a Scottish boarding school accused two teachers of a lesbian relationship. Her accusation caused the school to be closed. The teachers sought a court trial in order to prove that the girl was lying, and the House of Lords eventually exonerated them, but the adverse publicity had done its work, and they were destroyed by the scandal.

Hellman liked Hammett's idea of transforming this case into a play. She decided to call it *The Children's Hour.*

Beginning in 1933, she worked on various drafts for a year and a half, redoing scenes as many as twenty times. Hammett criticized each page, each act, each bit of dialogue. Draft after draft he would tell her, "It's getting better, Lily. But you're not there yet."

By May of 1934 Hellman felt confident enough to show the playscript to theatrical producer Herman Shumlin (who had successfully produced *The Last Mile,* with Spencer Tracy, and *Grand Hotel*). She waited nervously in his office as he read the script.

Shumlin put down the last page, looking at her intently.

"Well . . . what do you think?" Hellman asked.

"I like it. I'll produce it."

Hellman was stunned. The most she had hoped for was a bit of encouragement, perhaps some suggestions for improvement. Instead, in one dazzling moment, she had become a professional playwright!

Shumlin, who was destined to produce many of Hellman's plays, began production plans immediately. With polish work still to be done on the manuscript, Hellman remained in New York that fall. Hammett took a train west, to fulfill his contract for the new Nick-and-Nora adventure.

The Thin Man was a box-office hit, and the studio was eager for Hammett to deliver the outline for a sequel. Powell and Loy had agreed to return in their original roles. Again, Hunt Stromberg would produce and Van Dyke would direct.*

From his suite at the Beverly Wilshire Hotel, Hammett wrote Lillian Hellman in October of 1934 to inform her that the new film would be called *After the Thin Man* and would relate directly to the first novel and film, involving many of the same characters. He had no detailed plot worked out yet but knew he wanted to "devise a murder that grows with some logic out of the setup we left everybody in at the end of *The Thin Man.*"

Hammett's return to Hollywood was news, and a local paper asked him to write about the new film.

He obliged with a tongue-in-cheek account of his plot problems: "In this sequel somebody must be killed—but I am at loggerheads to determine which character shall die. It would not be a mystery if somebody does not pay the supreme sacrifice. I'm sure I will spare William Powell and Myrna Loy. None but Frankenstein could eliminate either of these fine people. Yet the dilemma haunts me. Who shall die? Shall it be poor little Asta, the wire-haired fox terrier? God forbid! It shall not be Asta!"

In his first eight-page plot outline, Hammett attempted to carry through his plan to revive several characters from the novel. He had the original killer, Macauley, escape from New York (disguised as a woman) and follow Nick to San Francisco. The lying Mimi Jorgensen was also featured, as was her son Gilbert.

---

*At this point, Powell (as Nick Charles) had become "the thin man" to the screen-going public, although in Hammett's novel the actual thin man was the missing eccentric, Clyde Wynant.

Stromberg didn't like this idea of a carryover—and by Hammett's second thirty-four-page outline Macauley, Mimi, and Gilbert had all been discarded. A whole new storyline was substituted, involving a murder within Nora's family. Hammett set much of the action in Chinatown, using some scenes and plot bits from his original 1930 John Guild version. Nora insists on "playing detective" and gets herself kidnapped, slugged with a blackjack, and drugged. When she's safely back in their apartment, Nick lectures her about amateur sleuthing: "There's more to being a detective than just blundering into jams that people have to pull you out of."

Stromberg liked this second outline much better, but told Hammett that it needed "a lot more work."

In another letter to Hellman that season, Hammett mentioned attending parties and "town-roaming" until 5 A.M., bragging that he was up by 10 A.M. and back to work at MGM on his film story. But in a follow-up letter, written five days later, he said that he was "back on the booze pretty heavily" and that he had been neglecting his studio work and was suffering from massive hangovers. He expressed surprise at the impact that MGM's *Thin Man* was having on the town. "People bring the Joan Crawfords and the Gables over to meet me instead of vice versa! Hot-cha!" He said he had visited Edward G. Robinson, "who's going to play Spade in Warner's new version of *Falcon.*" (Actually, Robinson never played Spade in films, but he *did* take over the role in a 1943 adaptation of Hammett's novel for a broadcast on the *Lux Radio Theater.*) He also told Hellman that he was "house hunting."

On MGM's money, supplemented by income from Knopf (who had sold *Thin Man* syndication rights to King Features), Hammett resumed his rich style of living. The house he finally rented was the two-million-dollar Harold Lloyd mansion in Pacific Palisades, with forty-four rooms, vast gardens, a pool, and tennis courts—and an ice-cream parlor in the basement. Hammett considered it "a great joint for parties" and was soon entertaining a string of women there. They usually remained as overnight guests.

On November 20, 1934, *The Children's Hour* made its debut on Broadway and was an opening-night success. Even George Jean Nathan, a difficult critic, applauded it. At the postperformance party, Hellman was acclaimed as "the new Chekhov" and as "the American Strindberg." It was heady praise indeed for a starting playwright, and Hellman was in a daze of happiness when she phoned Hammett later that night from her hotel. She was startled when a woman answered.

"Who are you?" Hellman demanded.

"I'm Mr. Hammett's secretary. He's sleeping now and cannot be disturbed."

Hellman slammed down the phone. She knew that Hammett *had* no secretary. Her anger mounted into rage, and she booked a flight to Los Angeles.

By the time she arrived at Hammett's house in Pacific Palisades, she'd been drinking steadily, and was in no mood for talk. Hellman entered the house, proceeded directly to the basement, walked into the ice-cream parlor, and "smashed it to pieces."

Then, calmly, her anger appeased, she took the next flight back to New York.

The Children's Hour swept Lillian Hellman into the front rank of American playwrights. One hundred and forty-five plays were produced in New York during the 1934–35 season, including works by Eugene O'Neill, Sean O'Casey, Marc Connelly, Maxwell Anderson, and Archibald MacLeish. Yet Hellman's play ranked with the season's best, *Vanity Fair* calling it "one of the most literate, sensitive, and humane dramas in the contemporary theater."

She was suddenly newsworthy. One reporter described her as "five feet three inches tall, slim, with reddish hair, a fine aquiline nose and a level, humorous mouth." Her status as an unknown amateur was over. Lillian Hellman was now a celebrity.

In Hollywood, Hammett alternated his daylight hours between MGM and Musso & Frank's restaurant in Hollywood, where he maintained a special "drinking booth" in one corner. He would sit there for hours each afternoon, "soaking in the booze" and talking happily to "whoever happened to sit down." Alcohol loosened Hammett's tongue, allowing him to bypass his reserved, introverted nature and indulge in marathon conversations with a variety of drinking companions. Once he'd sobered up, he would reject such people, withdrawing abruptly.

Film director Howard Benedict knew him well in those Hollywood years. "Dash was wonderful with sick people," recalled Benedict. "Maybe it was because he'd been so sick himself, in so many hospitals. We had a mutual friend, a woman, who was quite ill. She wasn't responding to postoperative therapy. Deeply depressed. Wouldn't talk to anybody. Dash decided to make it his business to cheer her up. He'd visit her every day with flowers. Brought along gag gifts. Wrote wacky little poems for her—until she began smiling, talking again. In a week Dash had her back to normal.

"Dash had a way with kids, too," Benedict said. "Children of his friends. He'd remember their birthdays, send 'em presents through the mail. He was really a very sweet, gentle man. A real charmer when he put his mind to it."

In 1934 Universal purchased a ninety-page Hammett film treatment he called "On the Make." It represented another attempt (following *Private Detective 62*) to tell the story of a corrupt private investigator. The protagonist was Gene Raymond, an unsavory character in the tradition of Ned Beaumont; again, the word "hero" does not apply. When we encounter Raymond in the opening scene, he is being "escorted" out of town by two police detectives. They warn him not to come back. Cool and unaffected, Raymond sets up his private detective business in another city (unnamed by Hammett, but obviously Los Angeles). He becomes embroiled in a case of murder and blackmail centering on a wealthy

stockbroker, Herbert Pomeroy. Raymond meets Ann, Pomeroy's twenty-one-year-old daughter, who thinks he is a legiti-
mate, honest detective. Actually, Raymond is working "both
ends of the street." At the climax of the story he loses Ann
because of his attempted double-dealing. Joe King, a narcotics officer, accuses Raymond of being "always on the make."
Gene does not deny it; he's proud of it.

"Maybe you boys like working for your lousy little salaries,"
he tells King, "but I'm in the game for money."

"Lousy little salaries is what we get," King agrees. "But we
can sleep at night."

Hammett plays the final scene in the detective's office, as
Raymond accepts the fact that he's lost the only woman he's
ever cared for and there's nothing he can do about it.

Universal found this story far too downbeat, and assigned
Doris Malloy and Harry Clork to write a new version. When
the film was released, as *Mr. Dynamite*, almost nothing remained of Hammett's treatment. Edmund Lowe, as a detective named Dynamite, is dapper and charming in the Nick
Charles mold. The picture was reviewed as "a comedy, with
homicidal interruptions." Hammett's hard-bitten antihero
had been totally erased.

Early in 1935 Lillian Hellman joined Hammett at the house
in Pacific Palisades. She had returned to California on her
own terms, as a $2,500-a-week scriptwriter for Samuel Gold-
wyn, to work on *Dark Angel*.

In Hollywood, she renewed her friendship with Dorothy
Parker, who (according to Hellman biographer Richard
Moody) "introduced her to political activism when they campaigned together for the passage of the Wagner Act (estab-
lishing a National Labor Relations Board) and for the revival
of the Screen Writers Guild."

Hellman recalls indulging herself with ice-cream sodas at
the now-repaired basement soda fountain—but she also
drank much more potent concoctions at the endless round of
parties she and Hammett attended. He would often pass out

during these affairs, remaining unconscious for twelve-hour periods; Hellman grew accustomed to overnight stays "while Dash slept off his drunk."

They engaged in many heated arguments over his sexual escapades. She was aware that he did not form any emotional ties with his "casual women," that they were only temporary diversions, but she resented having to put up with them.

After one such argument, she decided to fly to New Orleans for a family visit. (She had spent much of her childhood there, with her two aunts, Jenny and Hannah.) She phoned Hammett at her arrival, telling him she was not coming back to Hollywood "for quite a while."

When she mentioned she was seeing her uncle Willy and might go with him on a trip, Hammett grew angry and accused her of wanting to sleep with a murderer. (Willy's firm had been involved in worker slayings.)

Shaken by his reaction, she abandoned plans for her trip and flew back to Los Angeles that same night. ("And I never saw Willy again.")

Paramount produced *The Glass Key* in 1935, starring George Raft (as Beaumont) and Edward Arnold (as Madvig). Raft met Hammett during the shooting and later confessed to feeling uneasy around the tall writer. "He was really a very distinguished man," Raft said. "He'd read all these different books. Me, I was never much for reading—and I didn't have a lot to say to him."

Adapted by Kathryn Scola, Kubec Glasmon, and Harry Ruskin—a typical example of Paramount's "mass production" approach to screenplays—the script took a considerable amount of Hammett's dialogue directly from the novel, particularly in the scenes with the apelike Jeff Gardner, chillingly played by Guinn "Big Boy" Williams. But the man-woman climax was dropped, and Raft's role was made much more heroic. It is generally agreed among film critics that he gave the best performance of his career as Ned Beaumont.

Paramount hyped the film as "the swellest yarn Dashiell

Hammett ever spilled!" and billed Raft as "the Thin Man's hard-boiled brother. . . . He carries love in his iron fists!"

In the spring of 1935 literary lioness Gertrude Stein, early mentor to Hemingway and Joyce, traveled from Paris to California, announcing that the two men she most wanted to meet in America were Charles Chaplin and Dashiell Hammett. A dinner party was set for early April at the home of socialite Lillian May Ehrman in Beverly Hills. Chaplin came with Paulette Goddard, and Hammett with Lillian Hellman. Alice B. Toklas, Stein's constant companion, sat next to Hellman, while Miss Stein devoted her full attention to Chaplin and Hammett.

She told Hammett that she very much admired his detective novels and that he wrote about women better than any other American male. Why was it, she wanted to know, that American men seemed to write "only about themselves"?

"Maybe it's due to a loss of masculine confidence," Hammett replied.

Indeed, she agreed, this might very well be the answer. In Hammett, she saw what she termed "the perfect fusion" of writer and writing; he seemed to "exist as one with his creations." Later, in statements, articles, and public lectures, she spoke glowingly of Hammett, ranking him alongside Sherwood Anderson and Thornton Wilder as "one of the best contemporary American writers."

In June of 1935 Hammett's Hollywood agent arranged a lavish three-year contract with MGM. Hammett would be paid $1,000 a week to function as an executive assistant to Hunt Stromberg and would receive an additional $750 a week if any writing was required on the job. One of Hammett's drinking pals, a fellow writer at MGM, recalls his shock at hearing about the deal: "We all knew that Dash would make a terrible film executive. We figured he'd get drunk, ignore studio meetings, never attend story sessions, and refuse to meet with other writers on Stromberg projects . . . all of which he did!

But somehow, he stayed on the payroll. Don't ask me how. It was a real tightrope act."

Hammett persuaded MGM to purchase film rights to Albert Halper's *The Foundry* as a future Stromberg production. He was in the process of adapting this novel to the screen when Nathanael West, just in from New York, contacted him regarding screen work. He was looking for an assignment. Hammett invited West to "a party I'm throwing tonight," telling him, "We'll talk there."

According to West, things went very sour that evening. No one remembers what triggered the outburst, but, drunk and aggressive, Hammett ridiculed West for not having "a pot to piss in." West stormed away from the party, hurt and angry.

Such behavior reflected Hammett's growing unhappiness. He and Stromberg were having serious arguments over *The Foundry*. At the same time they were also in sharp disagreement over the final outline Hammett was writing for *After the Thin Man*. With each Stromberg plot change, Hammett's concept was diluted. Despite Hammett's objections, Stromberg insisted that Nora announce her pregnancy by Nick at the end of the film (setting things up for a "son of the Thin Man"), and he also insisted on softening the role of the killer to fit the stammering, shy-schoolboy style of James Stewart (who was then a young contract player being groomed for stardom at MGM).

Hammett turned in his final 115-page outline that September, and *After the Thin Man* was released in 1936 with Stromberg's changes incorporated into the Hackett-Goodrich script. The contrived plot emerged on the screen as a confused cross-mixture of disappearing husbands, a strangling, a dead janitor, and blackmail. The final revelation of Stewart-as-killer was unconvincing and hokey, with one critic complaining about the actor's having "turned into a raging, snarling maniac at the moment of his denunciation by Nick Charles—after almost two hours of stumbling speech, wistful eyes, and humble, self-effacing mien."

Yet the charm and attraction of the Powell-Loy team carried the film to box-office success, and MGM began planning more screen adventures for Nick and Nora. In creating the couple as co-detectives, Hammett had established a genre—the man-woman, sophisticated comedy-thriller. Over the next decade, rival studios would produce a host of imitative films in *The Thin Man* formula. Nick and Nora Charles, like Sam Spade, had entered American folklore.

15

OF POLITICS AND POTBOILING

*You can get plenty bored cooped up in a 3-room
New York apartment, making the same rounds
every night—the Stork Club, 21, Dempsey's . . .
seeing the same old faces and hearing the same
damned chatter and lies.*

—HAMMETT

IN EARLY JANUARY of 1936 a *Black Mask* dinner was arranged in Los Angeles, and Joe Shaw talked Hammett into attending. Since Hammett's departure from the magazine in 1930, Raymond Chandler had taken over as the star of *Black Mask,* and this occasion marked the only time these two influential talents would meet. Eight other writers were there, including Horace McCoy (who would become known for his brilliant short novel, *They Shoot Horses, Don't They?*).

The photographer gathered them at the table for a group portrait; flanking the group, only Hammett and Chandler remained somber; they seemed pensive and withdrawn from their smiling fellow writers.

The Hammett-Chandler conversation was not recorded, but when Chandler was asked, at a later date, to give his impression of their meeting, he commented on Hammett's "fearful capacity for Scotch," adding that he liked him "very much." In 1945 he wrote: "Hammett was one of the many guys who couldn't take Hollywood without trying to push God out of the high seat."

Feeling ill, Hammett returned to New York a few days after

the *Black Mask* evening and entered Lenox Hill Hospital for "a little rest." He remained there until early February.

Blanche Knopf wrote Hammett while he was in the hospital, reminding him of his promise to deliver a new novel by Christmas. He assured her that he had one under way but that film work had been cutting into his writing time. He planned to work on the novel in the summer.

That same year, 1936, marked the conversion of *Secret Agent X-9* into a Universal serial, while Warners made a second attempt at bringing *The Maltese Falcon* to the screen. In this ill-conceived version, Sam Spade was rewritten into lawyer Ted Shayne (as played by Warren William), while Bette Davis, in a loose approximation of Brigid, played Valerie Purvis. A hefty Alison Skipworth was ineptly cast as a female version of Gutman.

William Dieterle directed and Brown Holmes wrote the screenplay, which replaced the falcon with a jeweled French horn and had Shayne marrying his secretary. There were several prerelease titles, including "Men on Her Mind" and "Hard Luck Dame." The film reached theaters as *Satan Met a Lady,* and Bette Davis later pronounced it "one of the worst turkeys I ever made." It fizzled at the box office, and Hammett's credit line "from a story by" did not carry the title of his original novel.

Again, Hammett and Hellman were separated. Early that spring she'd left New York for a small industrial town, near Cleveland, to research her new play, *Days to Come.* She remained there a month, gathering background material, then headed for a vacation in Cuba, where she started on her second major writing project.

The theme tied directly into the political climate of 1936. (No fewer than thirty-one plays centering on social or political issues were staged on Broadway that season.) Hellman's new drama dealt with a strike by starving workers at a brush factory in a backwater Ohio town. Mobsters and toughs are called in to break up the strike, and the town is torn apart (shades of *Red Harvest*!). The attempt to organize a union fails, and the defeated workers are forced to resume their jobs at the factory.

In the manuscript's first draft Hellman's characters were mere symbols, not flesh and blood, and the political message was unsubtle and heavy-handed. In Havana, wrestling with these problems, she was depressed, uncertain of her ability to bring the play into proper focus.

She returned to New York at the end of June and rented a cottage for the summer in Connecticut, on Tavern Island, off the South Norwalk coast. Hammett went with her and they spent the remainder of that season working on *Days to Come*. It went slowly, and to Hellman's mind, the playscript retained serious flaws. But Hammett told her he liked the final draft and not to worry; the play *would* be successful. Hellman retained strong doubts.

In November, when *Days to Come* began rehearsals in New York, Hammett was in Princeton, New Jersey, attempting to start another novel. He had leased the spacious, richly furnished house of a wealthy college professor—and the place was often visited by students eager for Hammett's advice on writing. He granted an interview to one from *The Daily Princetonian:* Was he working on a book? Yes, "but it's not a mystery. I really don't like writing detective stories anyway."

Hadn't he just finished working on a Nick-and-Nora detective film in Hollywood? Yes, but he didn't take such work seriously. "Before they started monkeying around with the plot it was a logical follow-up to *The Thin Man*—but now its own mother wouldn't recognize it."

He claimed that the studio bosses were difficult. "They're screwy—but they've got tons of money to be screwy with."

Hammett was not happy as a mystery writer, and expressed annoyance at having his work considered "artificial." He hoped that his current novel would put him in a new category. The interviewer asked about the plot.

"It's about a family of a dozen children out on an island. All I ever do with *any* story is put some characters together and let them get in each other's way. And let me tell you, twelve kids can sure get in each other's way!"

This novel never got written, and no parts of it survive among the Hammett manuscripts in Texas.

On December 15, 1936, *Days to Come* opened at the Vanderbilt in New York. Hammett was there, sitting glumly through the stage action as Hellman got sick in the aisle on brandy. Hammett refused to sit near her at any play, claiming that her "fidgeting and foot tapping" ruined his concentration.

Within ten minutes, Hellman knew the play was "a disaster." William Randolph Hearst and his entire party walked out during the first act.

Joining her in the lobby after the final curtain, Hammett was grim. "I told you it was a good play," he said to Hellman. "I was wrong. It is *not* a good play."

The critics agreed—and *Days to Come* closed after just seven performances.

This failure almost destroyed Hellman's theatrical career; she was crushed, feeling that she would never write again.

Hammett calmly returned to Princeton, assuring her that no one succeeds 100 percent of the time, and that she would turn out many more plays, including a lot of good ones. All she needed to do was to quit feeling sorry for herself.

Having decided not to continue his involvement in MGM's *Thin Man* series, Hammett sold the studio film rights to the Nick and Nora characters early in 1937 for $40,000. He was still at Princeton, that March, when French novelist André Malraux lectured to the students there. The two writers met after the lecture, and Malraux insisted that Hammett was "the technical link between Dreiser and Hemingway." As Hammett reported the incident to Hellman: "I suggested that *he* might be the French O'Flaherty but he didn't seem to know what I meant!"

In order to stimulate his own creativity, he was now reading classics, and wrote Hellman to tell her he'd just finished *Don Quixote* and that, regrettably, he had "missed a lot of things in that San Francisco Public Library."

Hammett was not eager to return to Hollywood. While at Princeton he turned down a script job for Sam Goldwyn ("Sam's nice, but he's also crazy") and he rejected a $50,000 offer from William Randolph Hearst to write an original screen story for Marion Davies. ("The money tempted me, but the assignment didn't.")

However, by July of 1937, he was back in the film world with Hellman. They were invited to the home of actor Fredric March for a showing of a new pro-Loyalist documentary, *The Spanish Earth*. Earlier in the year, following the outbreak of the Spanish Civil War, Hellman had joined Ernest Hemingway, John Dos Passos, and Archibald MacLeish in a group called Contemporary Historians. Their purpose was to fund this documentary on the plight of the Spanish Republic in its battle against the Fascist troops of Francisco Franco. Hemingway had returned from Madrid with a print of the film, and had agreed to present it, with his narration, at the March home in Hollywood as a fund raiser for Spanish war relief.

Hellman arrived with F. Scott Fitzgerald, joining Hammett, Dorothy Parker, and her husband, Alan Campbell. Two dozen other film luminaries were also on hand for this private screening.

The film paid stirring tribute to the bravery of the Loyalists, and the evening's contributions funded twenty ambulances for the Republic. Later, Dorothy Parker invited several of the guests to her place for "a nightcap or two."

Hemingway was tense and nervous (since he never liked speaking to groups), and Hellman recalled his smashing a glass against Parker's stone fireplace. This upset Fitzgerald; he prepared to bolt the party. Hellman asked Hammett to talk to Fitzgerald and calm him, but Hammett ignored the problem, drunkenly repeating that Hemingway could never write real women: "He only puts them in his books to admire him."

Dashiell Hammett and Ernest Hemingway have often been linked by critics as masters of objective realism—but the analysis has not always been complimentary to Hammett, nor has

it always been entirely fair. Several of these critics have un-
justly dismissed him as a "pulp extension" of Hemingway.
This charge merits examination.

Hemingway did not publish a book in the United States
until late 1925 (*In Our Time,* from Liveright). By then Hammett had been writing professionally for three years. As a
near-starving Hemingway labored in a Paris loft during 1922–
23, carving out the lean, muscular prose that was to change
the face of mainstream writing, so labored a near-starving
Hammett in a San Francisco hotel room, in these same years,
carving out the tough, stripped, objective prose that was to
change the course of popular crime fiction. They might be
compared to a pair of scientists, an ocean apart, working on
the same experiment, each solving it independently.

In linking the two writers, essayist Walter Blair finds a common emotional background: "Wounded by the war, and unhappy in the postwar world, contemptuous of many
pre–World War I standards, both were battered by disillusionment and cynicism, and both created worlds and characters justifying their attitude."

Later, as each read the other's works, a cross-influence may
have developed. André Gide was to say of Hammett: "His
dialogues can be compared only with the best in Hemingway." Widespread circulation of "The Killers," printed in
1927, may have had an influence on Hammett's fiction—yet
it is equally reasonable to conjecture that 1929's *Red Harvest*
might well have helped shape Hemingway's *To Have and Have
Not,* published in 1937.

Certainly, Hemingway was a Hammett buff. In *Death in the
Afternoon,* he declared: "My eyes were too bad to read, and my
wife was reading Dashiell Hammett's bloodiest to date, *The
Dain Curse,* out loud. . . ." Apparently, if Hemingway could not
read Hammett, he wanted Hammett read to him.*

---

*Inventories of Hemingway's library show that he ordered a copy of *The Glass Key*
and that he also owned copies of *The Thin Man* and *Blood Money.* (No EH library
record exists of *The Maltese Falcon,* advertised by Knopf as "Better Than Hemingway!")

Novelist Rex Stout, in reviewing *The Glass Key,* stated that "the things that were bothering Hammett's hero were exactly the same things that bothered Hemingway all his life."

During the summer of 1937 Hellman received a cable from the U.S.S.R. inviting her to a theater festival in Moscow. She wanted Hammett to go with her, but he refused, saying he had no love for the theatrical world and would not enjoy the trip. He expressed what Hellman called "an amused contempt for Russian bureaucracy." Trotting around Moscow, to Hammett, was a waste of time and energy. "You go, and I'll be here when you get back," he told her.

Dorothy Parker and her husband agreed to accompany Hellman, and they sailed for Europe at the end of August.

Through the years since he had lived in San Francisco, Hammett kept in occasional touch with his wife and daughters, but they all knew that there was no hope of any kind for a close relationship. Late that same month, from California, Jose informed him that she had mailed a set of divorce papers to Nogales, Mexico, in the hope that a Mexican decree would end their marriage. However, the decree had no legality in the United States and their marriage remained binding.

Once again, Hammett was out of money, and that September, when MGM offered him $40,000 to write an original outline for their third *Thin Man* film, he reluctantly said yes. Upon his return to California, Hammett, in typical fashion, rented a six-bedroom penthouse suite at the Beverly Wilshire Hotel. The tab was $2,000 a month—to which was added the cost of a valet and a chauffeured limousine. Hammett's pattern was consistent: when the money is there, spend it; when it isn't there, earn more, and then spend that. Money was a tool, a means of enjoyment, nothing more.

Bill Sibilia, now a barber in San Francisco, recalled that Hammett paid him thirty dollars for a shave each morning. He'd show up at Hammett's suite, shave him, and leave with the money. "It was more in a morning than I made all week at my shop," he said.

Hammett often drank alone in his suite, becoming sullen by late afternoon. It was during one of these depressed afternoons that a producer showed up with an "ideal project" for Hammett to write. He had wanted to pitch it personally, and Hammett's agent had set up the appointment. The producer was shown into the main living room of the suite by Hammett's houseboy and told to wait. He waited. And waited. And waited. Finally, an inner door opened and Hammett appeared in a yellow silk robe, a scarf at his neck, a drink in his hand. He stood unmoving, cool-eyed, silent.

The producer began his pitch, gesturing wildly, pacing the carpet, presenting his plot in glowing words. At the conclusion of the pitch, as the producer waited for his reaction, Hammett remained totally silent. The silence lengthened. Then Hammett said one word: "No." And abruptly closed the door.

The dazed producer was shown out.

As Hammett began work on the third *Thin Man* story, he soon grew depressed with this new "potboiling assignment." He missed several story conferences, argued heatedly with Hunt Stromberg over plot points—and wrote letters to Hellman about his struggle to create a bright, comedic mystery when all he really wanted to do was stay drunk. His "only joys" were gambling at the Santa Anita race track and listening to Gershwin concerts on the radio.

He also told Hellman that her trip to see plays in Moscow was probably a waste of time since, in his estimation, she didn't like the theater except when she was in a room getting a new play written.

He was right; by her own admission, she did not enjoy the theatrical experience in Moscow. However, she very much enjoyed touring the bistros of Paris with Dorothy Parker; she later went on to Madrid, joining Hemingway for an on-the-scene view of the Spanish Civil War.

In a letter to Hellman late in December 1937, Hammett referred with bitterness to his "charming fable of how Nick loved Nora and Nora loved Nick and everything was just one

big laugh in the midst of other people's trials and tribula-
tions. . . ." His closing words reflect the depth of self-disgust:
"Nobody ever invented a more insufferably smug pair of characters."

The sparkling, empty chatter of Nick and Nora Charles had
become intolerable to Dashiell Hammett, but he would finish
the job MGM was paying him for; he was a professional. And
pros don't quit.

16

A STAGE OF FOXES

The happiest years for Hammett were at
Hardscrabble Farm.

—RICHARD MOODY

HAMMETT CONTINUED TO consider himself a serious novelist. In 1938 he broke with Alfred Knopf and contacted Bennett Cerf at Random House, proposing a book to be called
"There Was a Young Man." Cerf recalled his excitement at
the chance to publish a new Hammett novel. However, he did
not want Knopf to feel that Random was stealing one of his
writers.

"I phoned Alfred," recalled Cerf. "He told me to go ahead,
warning me 'you'll have nothing but trouble with Hammett.
He is a terrible man and I want nothing more to do with him.'
When Alfred Knopf had a fight with somebody, it meant curtains. He later threw out Irving Wallace and Harold Rob-
bins."

Cerf immediately set up a contract with Hammett, who
accepted an advance of $5,000 against future royalties. He
told Cerf that he was confident he could deliver a finished
manuscript "within the next twelve months."

Although Hammett had not published a new work in over
four years, his reputation as a novelist had not suffered. Mystery authority Howard Haycraft, in the *Wilson Library Bulletin*
(February 1938), praised him as the "founder of the modern,
hard-boiled, high-speed school of detective writing." Hammett's reaction was mixed; he was pleased to be singled out

as a leading influence in the genre, but disliked being tied to the genre itself.

His spirits were lifted early in 1938 when Hellman wired that she was going to visit him in Hollywood, after a brief stopover in New Orleans.

One of Hammett's diversions, while waiting for Hellman's return, was hunting. William Faulkner was also writing for the studios during this period, and he and Hammett enjoyed several days together hunting wild boar on Catalina Island, off the Southern California coast. Although excellent shots when sober, the writers spent more time drinking than hunting, and brought home few trophies.

When Hellman finally arrived at Hammett's Beverly Wilshire suite in late February, their reunion was intense, launching a round of all-night parties. But the fun was cut short in March, when Hellman returned to New York. She was eager to begin work on her third play, *The Little Foxes* (a title suggested to her by Dorothy Parker).

Hammett felt abandoned. Obliged to remain in Hollywood in order to complete the final draft of the outline on his *Thin Man* assignment, he chafed under his MGM contract. Politically, he was becoming more active, and had accepted chairmanship of the Motion Picture Artists Committee, a liberal group that raised enough money that year to supply eighteen ambulances for the embattled Loyalists in Spain.

His energy was ebbing. Alcohol had weakened him, and his old problem, lack of sleep, aggravated the condition. By the time his final 144-page screen outline for *Another Thin Man* had been okayed by MGM, in the early summer of 1938, Hammett was very sick. He had gambled away his studio earnings on the races at Santa Anita and had run up a liquor bill at a local pharmacy that totaled $1,300. His limo service was also threatening another court action for nonpayment. And, topping all this, he owed almost six months' rent on his penthouse suite at the Beverly Wilshire.

Hammett's good friend, film producer Charles Brackett, came to his rescue. Brackett was known for generous aid to hard-drinking pals, and he had nursed both Scott Fitzgerald and Dotty Parker through more than one alcoholic bout. He told Hammett that he would lend him enough to pay off all of his outstanding bills if Hammett would agree to leave town immediately. Brackett then phoned Lillian Hellman, telling her that Hammett was being put on a plane to New York, and to meet him at the airport.

"Dash is a very sick guy," said Brackett. "He'll need some caring for. Can you handle it?"

She agreed to try, and took Hammett to the Connecticut cottage on Tavern Island for recuperation. He slowly regained strength there. His life again had a focus—the shaping of Hellman's new play.

Lillian Hellman credits Hammett with major help on *The Little Foxes.* As she said in *Pentimento:* "I knew he was working so hard for me because [the failure of] *Days to Come* had scared me and scared him for my future."

The action in *The Little Foxes* centered on the Hubbards— a thinly disguised portrait of the Newhouse side of Hellman's family. Her father's family, the Hellmans, were not well-off, while the Newhouse clan, her mother's people, were rich and spoiled, full of contempt for social inferiors—and this included the Hellmans.

Lillian loved her mother, Julia, but also pitied her. Hellman had no love or pity for her domineering grandmother, Sophie Newhouse, or for Sophie's equally formidable brother, Jake. She based the power-and-money-obsessed characters of Regina and Ben Hubbard in *The Little Foxes* on Sophie and Jake Newhouse. The sensitive, victimized Birdie was an affectionate portrait of her mother. Hellman also wrote a version of her younger self into the play, as sixteen-year-old Alexandra, who sides with the ineffectual Birdie against Regina and Ben—just as young Lillian had sided with her mother against Sophie and Jake.

The play was set in a deep-South town during 1900, with the industrial revolution as a backdrop. Tension and drama build with the Hubbards' attempt to obtain control of a new cotton mill, led by the ruthless, scheming Regina. The Hubbards were the "despoiling foxes," destroying the South with their power games. The play was envisioned as a drama of passion and high intensity, and Hellman wasn't sure she could bring it off.

Hammett urged her on; he worked painstakingly with her, questioning motivation and character, assaulting weak logic, throwing out ineffectual dialogue—page by slow page. Tough and unrelenting in his criticism of each scene, Hammett refused to placate her or render false encouragement, sending her back to the typewriter for "another draft, and another and another" until, at one point, she considered walking into the sea to end the "torment."

When she threatened to quit, to throw the play out entirely, he told her to go ahead, that "no one but us gives a damn if it gets finished or not."

Hellman admitted: "At that moment, I never hated anybody so much in my life." But later she realized that it took "bravery and great affection to say such things." Hammett's criticism was based on what she termed "the most carefully guarded honesty I have ever known."

His blunt talk made her determined to show him, and the world, that she *could* come back from theatrical failure to write another hit play.

She kept on with *The Little Foxes*, digging deeply and painfully into her past—and with each new draft the play improved, became taut, hard, uncompromising. The characters progressed from pale symbols of corruption into breathing, three-dimensional people. The dialogue crackled with menace and human greed.

When producer Herman Shumlin read the final manuscript that November (actually Hellman's *ninth* draft), he was greatly impressed and marked the script for immediate preproduction. The choice role of Regina, the leading "fox," went to an actress known for her intensity and passion, Tallulah Bankhead. She was ideal, and her portrayal of Regina Hubbard became the high point of Bankhead's career.

Having exhausted himself on Hellman's play, Hammett
found that he could not progress beyond the opening pages
of his new novel, which he was now calling "My Brother
Felix." He abandoned it in mid-September of 1938 after seventeen pages.* He very much envied Pep West's accomplishment in completing his superb novel of Hollywood, *The Day
of the Locust,* and agreed to provide a promotional blurb at
publication, admitting to West that "you've created the god-
damndest set of characters ever!"

Frustrated at his inability to move forward on the novel,
Hammett plunged back into the New York nightclub round.
At the Stork Club he found himself in direct confrontation
with Ernest Hemingway. Hellman documented the scene in
An Unfinished Woman. Commanding a table at the club, Hemingway was in a truculent mood, jabbing at what he called
"the safe New York crowd" who had not experienced war on
the Spanish front. Stung by his insults, several people in the
group left Hemingway's table, until only Hellman, Hammett,
and the German writer Gustav Regler remained with him.

Hammett lowered his head into his hands, and Hemingway
demanded to know what was wrong. Hammett told him that
he didn't enjoy lectures. Hemingway scowled, and the talk
lapsed into a tense silence. Hellman and Regler attempted to
lighten the mood, but Hemingway ignored them. Glaring at
Hammett, he picked up a metal tablespoon and placed it
between the muscles of his upper and lower right arm. Slowly,
he drew up his arm—and the spoon collapsed under elbow
pressure. Hemingway nodded toward an unbent spoon in
front of Hammett, challenging him to match the performance.

Hammett shook his head. "Let's go," he said to Hellman.

Hemingway suddenly gripped his arm, demanding that he
attempt the spoon trick. Calmly, Hammett asked why Hemingway didn't stick to bullying poor Scott Fitzgerald. The big

*In a letter in August of that year regarding this novel, Hammett bragged about
having passed the 160-page mark, but there is no evidence to support this claim.

man's face reddened, and again he *demanded* that Hammett bend the spoon.

Hammett stood up. He looked down coldly at Hemingway. "I don't think I could bend the spoon. But when I did things like that I did them for Pinkerton money."

And he walked out.

Another New York nightclub incident was more amusing. Hammett's dealings with producers were often erratic, and columnist Leonard Lyons recalled the evening Hammett met producer Dudley Murphy at the 21 Club. "They discussed a film project Murphy wanted Hammett to write. Shook hands on it. Then Murphy scrawled out the contract on the back of a menu," said Lyons. "The next year Dash wrote to Murphy, asking for a similar deal on a new story, and enclosed a fresh 21 Club menu!"

On February 2, 1939, *The Little Foxes* began its trial run in Baltimore. Hellman's play was enthusiastically received. Success was in the air, and the opening-night party was wild and strident. Dorothy Parker argued with Tallulah Bankhead; Sara and Gerald Murphy nostalgically recounted some Riviera antics of Scott and Zelda Fitzgerald; Hellman experimented with exotic food-and-drink combinations, stirring whiskey sours and dry martinis into a plate of baked Maryland crabmeat, while Hammett conducted what Hellman termed "his usual alcoholic literary discussion" with a confused post office clerk who had innocently wandered into the party.

Bankhead, who had been brilliant that evening as Regina Hubbard, was in an exuberant mood. She approached a young black waiter and loudly offered to sleep with him, insisting on a passionate kiss. Hellman came to the boy's rescue, allowing him to make a hurried exit. Angry and frustrated, Bankhead glowered at Hellman, threatening to bash her with a plate. Hammett stepped between them, and Tallulah broke into a smile, saying she could never be aggressive around a handsome man. Would he like to share some cocaine with her?

Hammett said no thanks, that he didn't much like being mixed up with a "doper" and that when he was a detective the most dangerous and unpredictable people he'd been forced to deal with had been addicts.

This angered Bankhead, and Hellman recalled her shouted words: "You don't know what the hell you're talking about, Hammett! Cocaine isn't habit-forming. I *know*—because I've been taking it for years!"

A month after that Baltimore opening, in March of 1939, Hammett returned to Hollywood for yet another shot at some studio money. His contract with MGM had expired, and he was taking on "polish jobs" for various producers, uncredited work which paid well but gave him no creative control on the projects to which he was assigned. He soon earned enough to pay off his loan from Charlie Brackett in full. Hammett prided himself on repaying every personal debt, but he seldom received the same treatment from those friends who asked him for emergency money. During his long tenure in Hollywood he handed out many thousands in loans that were never repaid.

The Little Foxes opened in New York to rave reviews, and Hellman wrote to Hammett regarding her mixed feelings of "terror and delight." Success frightened her, she admitted; she was uncertain how to handle it, afraid of what it did to people. On the other hand, she was delighted at the new play's reception.

Hammett told her that success was like anything else; you just live with it, and make sure never to believe what other people say about you. For example, he had just seen a trade-paper item written by columnist Dorothy Kilgallen describing him as "a fiction writer's version of a hard-boiled Dream Prince." Flattering, but meaningless. She was not to worry about success; just worry about doing another play as good as *Foxes*. It was the work that counted, not what critics said about it.

Orson Welles remembers a bizarre encounter with Hammett that year. Welles had just finished adapting and directing a radio version of Hammett's *The Glass Key* for *Campbell*

Playhouse—and when the two met one evening over drinks, Welles asked him if he knew of anyone, through his theatrical contacts, who would be willing to invest some cash in *Five Kings*, a Shakespearean project foundering for lack of funds. Welles told Hammett that he desperately needed $15,000 to save the production.

"I'll get it for you," Hammett assured him. "I know just the guy to ask. I'll set things up for tomorrow morning."

A meeting was arranged with a Texas millionaire who was, according to Hammett, "very anxious" to finance important theatrical properties.

"Just leave everything to me, Orson," said Hammett. "Now, let's have another drink."

The next morning Hammett marched Welles in to meet the Texas moneyman. Mellowed by a long night of alcoholic pleasure, Hammett hailed the prospective backer with the ill-chosen words "Hello, sucker!"

That did it.

"Hammett's greeting," Welles asserted, "cost me seven thousand five hundred dollars a word."

Later, reflecting on that incident with Welles, Hammett acknowledged: "I do odd things when I drink. For instance, one night down in Florida with Nunnally, I decided to attack a department store." He referred to the time when he and screenwriter pal Nunnally Johnson, who was then living in Miami Beach, set out for a hard night's drinking. Jack Kofoed, who was involved, told the story: "When those two boys were on the town, they drank it dry. After midnight, on this particular evening, they found themselves standing in front of Burdines Department Store. Some street construction had been under way, and considerable rubble lay around.

"Hammett looked up at the store's big plate-glass windows with alcoholic repugnance. 'I don't like them,' he growled—and began hurling chunks of concrete, cheering wildly as the big panes shattered. The police arrived and arrested Hammett, carting him off to jail. They let Nunnally go since he had not participated in the destruction.

"The inebriated Johnson immediately set out to raise bail

money for his pal. By then it was four in the morning. Johnson began a boozy house-to-house canvas of his home neighborhood, pounding on doors and asking his sleep-frazzled neighbors for 'whatever cash you've got around the place. I assure you it will be used to free America's finest mystery writer, an authentic genius of letters, from the local hoosegow.' Beyond getting a lot of doors slammed in his face, he actually raised enough to spring Hammett. I was among the lenders; Nunnally came by our house at 4:30 and hit me for eighty-three bucks—but I got it back from him the next afternoon."

Johnson had met Hammett in the *Black Mask* days of the twenties, and they remained friends for more than three decades. Hammett admired what Alistair Cooke called "Johnson's wry, uninhibited humor." Also, Nunnally Johnson (author of more than half a hundred screenplays, including *The Grapes of Wrath*) knew everyone in Hollywood, and Hammett could always count on Nunnally's having invitations to all the best parties in town. "We emptied a lot of Scotch bottles together," Hammett once said.

According to Johnson, the most remarkable thing about his friend was Hammett's disregard for the future: "Here was a man who had no expectation of being alive much beyond Thursday—which is why he spent himself and his money with such recklessness."

With royalties flowing in from her plays, Lillian Hellman searched for a quiet retreat beyond the clamor of New York, but within commuting distance of the theatrical world. She found what she'd been looking for in Westchester County in May of 1939—an estate she was to call Hardscrabble Farm. It was a 130-acre tract of woods and open fields near Pleasantville, New York, on Hardscrabble Road, between the Saw Mill River and Bronx River parkways. It had its own lake, a six-room caretaker's cottage, twin guesthouses, a large main residence, barns, stables, gardens, and a vineyard. There were horses to ride and a boat for fishing the lake.

Hammett was delighted—he had always loved the country—

and looked forward to spending time at the farm with Hell-man. For the moment, however, he was "stuck" in Holly-wood, adapting one of his old pulp stories into a screenplay and making the usual round of Hollywood parties. The third Nick-and-Nora film, *Another Thin Man,* had been released by MGM and was reaping a rich box-office harvest. The title of this third series film refers to Nick and Nora's son, who would grow up to become "another Thin Man." Its final storyline was a combination of original material by Hammett and a reworking of his *Black Mask* Continental Op story, "The Fare-well Murder." The case revolved around an elderly munitions manufacturer who is murdered on his Long Island estate. Goodrich and Hackett again provided the screenplay based on Hammett's detailed outline.

Despite the film's success, Hammett felt detached from his own creation. There would be three more films in the series, but he would have nothing to do with any of them. Something else was on his mind. The thirties were over, and America was entering the wartime forties. For Hammett, an era of intense commitment was beginning.

17

FROM FASCISM TO FALCONS

[Hollywood is] a slack, soft *place. . . .*
Everywhere there is . . . either corruption or
indifference. The heroes are the great corruptionists
or the supremely indifferent—by whom I mean the
spoiled writers, Hecht, Nunnally Johnson, Dotty
[Parker], Dash Hammett. . . .

—F. Scott Fitzgerald,
in a 1940 letter

By the summer of 1940 Europe had been plunged into war
and Britain was fighting for survival. Hammett spent the summer with Hellman at Hardscrabble Farm, troubled by the
atmosphere of war, but enjoying country life.

Hellman had employed an experienced farmer, Fred Herr-
mann, to help her run the place. Together, they would raise
and sell poodles, stock the lake with bass and pickerel, make
butter and cheese, sell pigs and cross-breed ducks. There
were chickens to feed, horses to curry and stable, and three
thousand asparagus plants to be cared for. Cook and
housekeeper Helen Anderson did most of the indoor chores,
leaving Hellman free for writing.

Again, Hammett was editing, criticizing, and helping shape
her latest play, *Watch on the Rhine,* which concerned the impact
of anti-Fascism on the lives of an American family in Washington, D.C. Hellman had begun the play at Hardscrabble the
previous August and was now fully involved with it.

One of the chores at the farm she attended to herself was

174

milking the cows. She'd rise at 4 A.M. to do this, then help
Helen prepare breakfast, write until lunchtime, eat again,
then write three more hours until it was time to help Helen
fix the evening meal.

Hammett tramped the woods and fished while she worked
on the play. He had suspected that there might be snapping
turtles in the lake—and when one of the farm dogs got bitten
by a snapper, Hammett determined to set traps and rid the
lake of them. The initial stage was preparation, and in this
Hammett was extremely thorough, sending away for books on
the life and habits of the snapping turtle, how to handle them,
how to cut them up for soup, and what to use for catching
them. Government turtle pamphlets, boxes of special
fishhooks, and wire-mesh cages arrived in the mail.

After a month of this Hellman grew bored, as she often did
with Hammett's "slow precision." But finally he was ready.
Carrying a variety of fishhooks and cages to the lake, Hammett and Hellman set up their turtle traps.

According to Hellman's account in *Pentimento,* they hooked
a giant snapper with a three-foot-round shell. In boating him,
Hammett slipped backward. Immediately, Hellman was there
with an outstretched oar to support him in the boat. She
recorded the cryptic warning he gave her on this occasion.

"Remind me," he said.

"Remind you of what?"

"Never to save me," he said. "I've been meaning to tell you
for a long time."

Hammett's unyielding pride was echoed in this remark; he
didn't want anyone to "save" him from anything—and he
knew that Hellman was concerned about his drinking, his
unhappiness with Hollywood, his inability to finish another
novel. They did not argue about these things, yet Hammett's
attitude was clear: he would solve these problems for himself,
or they would not be solved at all. His stubborn pride demanded that he do things alone, and in *his* fashion. Even his
love for Hellman, his trust and closeness to her, did not alter
this requirement.

Back at the main house, following the pamphlets' instructions, Hammett tried to chop off the turtle's head, without success. The big snapper was dangerous; a single bite from its strong jaws could sever a finger. When the turtle lunged for Hellman's hand, Hammett told her to "go inside and lie down." But she stayed with the turtle as he got a rifle from the house. If he couldn't chop off the snapper's head, he would shoot it off.

Hellman watched Hammett place his first shot directly behind the creature's eyes; he then used the ax for a finishing blow, dragging the turtle into the kitchen by its tail.

"Tomorrow we'll make soup out of it," he told Hellman.

But the turtle had other ideas. The next morning they were shocked to discover that the creature was gone. They found it outside the house. It had crawled into the rock garden and finally expired there.

As Hammett dragged it back into the kitchen, Hellman told him she felt this particular turtle had earned the right to be buried instead of being turned into soup. Hammett thought that was a very silly idea, but told her to go ahead and bury it if that's what she wanted to do. He then retired to his room.

Angry and determined, Hellman returned to the kitchen, tied a rope to the snapper's tail, hauled it out to the car, drove to the lake, dug a hole on the bank, and buried the creature.

The next day Hammett was out catching more turtles. "What would you like to do with them?" he asked her.

"Make soup," Hellman said.

She told Hammett that he and the first turtle had something basic in common.

"And what's that?" he asked her.

"The turtle was a survivor," she said. "And so are you."

Scott Fitzgerald considered Hammett to be "a spoiled writer"—and Hammett might well have agreed with this estimate since he had written nothing that pleased him for over six years and had, in fact, returned to Bennett Cerf the Random House advance on his unwritten novel. Nevertheless, he received an immense amount of satisfaction in working with Hellman, sublimating his own creative drive in furthering her expanding theatrical career. Lillian Hellman's success was, in a way, his own. Each of her plays benefited from Hammett's tough, unrelenting criticism, and she often commented on this: "Nobody ever gave more aid to anybody than he gave to me. . . . It was more than friendship. It was the care and sacrifice of a scholarly, warm-hearted man who knew about writing, who wanted it to be good, and who was generous enough to help. . . . He was generous to all writers who came to him—because writing was something he respected very deeply."

Increasingly disturbed over what he perceived as "a rising tide of anti-Semitism and Fascism," Hammett turned to the Communist Party, whose members claimed to be actively concerned about such issues. In 1940 Hammett vigorously supported their political slate and, as chairman of the 1940 Committee on Election Rights, he conducted a spirited campaign that year to get Communist Party candidates on state ballots across the nation.

In an October letter to *The New Republic,* Hammett declared that "election rights have been violated by ruling minority parties off the ballot on flimsy charges, through terror, intimidation and arrest of ordinary citizens."

Richard Layman, in his study of Hammett, revealed that "the FBI took a special interest in his active role in Communist Party affairs." They assigned agents to follow Hammett, often without success since their shadow tactics were obvious to a former master of the art. "On at least one occasion," Layman reported, "they apparently broke into Lillian Hellman's home in Pleasantville."

The FBI dossier on Hammett was expanding each month, but as one friend of that period observed: "Dash wasn't worried. He never promoted violence or revolution, remained rigidly loyal to his own strict moral code of personal conduct, and felt he was doing no wrong, that he had the legal right, as an American citizen, to express his political beliefs as he

chose. Dash acted openly and honestly—and although it is my
personal opinion that he was misled by the Communist Party,
he continued to endorse and work for many leftist causes.
And one thing was surely true of him: he was deeply committed to helping others. There was no attempt at power-build-
ing or self gain. Mistaken or not, his political views were
selfless and utterly sincere."

Hammett's name appeared five times that year in the pages
of *New Masses* and the *Daily Worker,* as a co-signer in support
of anti-Fascist causes. The Communist press seemed to be
confused about him; they wanted to include Hammett in their
ranks, but he maintained an outside, independent stance.
They could count on his support only if he believed in a
particular cause.

Responding to the climate of the country, Hellman built
her new play, *Watch on the Rhine,* on a political base. It made
a statement regarding the evils of Fascism, pitting a
Rumanian pro-Nazi against a victim of German oppression.
The villain was modeled on a nobleman Hellman had met in
Europe, who had been an international gambler. Hellman,
like Hammett, had a passion for gambling, and in Hollywood
she had been a regular at the Clover Club, favoring high-
stakes chemin de fer. Friends recall the night she won $21,000
at this game—returning the next evening to lose $19,000 of
it. Hammett admired her gambler's nerve and her ability
to take heavy losses without complaint or regret. She was
tough-minded, and Hammett appreciated a tough-minded
woman.

When *Watch on the Rhine* opened as a hit, in April of 1941,
Warner Brothers quickly purchased film rights, assigning
Hammett to write the screen version. It was a "dream assignment," one of the few projects he'd ever been enthusiastic
about. He began working on it that summer at Hardscrabble,
with the intention of retaining as much of Hellman's dialogue
as possible. His main contribution would consist of "opening
up" the action, carrying several of the key scenes beyond the

stage into the streets of Washington. Fidelity to the spirit of the play was Hammett's chief concern.

Watch on the Rhine won the New York Drama Critics Circle Award for 1941, competing against such heavyweight dramas as Maxwell Anderson's *Key Largo,* Hemingway's *The Fifth Column,* and Robert Sherwood's *There Shall Be No Night.* Beyond doubt, Lillian Hellman had another major success.

Hammett achieved his own kind of success that year with Warners' final version of *The Maltese Falcon,* starring Humphrey Bogart as Spade.

Screen historian Allen Rivkin tells an amusing story of how Hammett's novel came to be filmed for the third time. Young John Huston had never directed films, but he *had* directed his actor-father, Walter Huston, the previous year on the New York stage. "Johnny had some good credits as a writer, but wanted to get into film directing," said Rivkin. "So he asked me to work with him as screenwriter on a new version of *Falcon,* telling me, 'Christ, Al, the book's never been done right!' He thought we could get an assignment out of it."

Studio head Jack Warner said he'd go along with another remake *if* the script was right. Rivkin reported his reaction.

"Great!" said Huston. "I'll have my secretary set up the book in basic shots, and then we can get started on the script."

The secretary did as Huston instructed, using the novel as a word-for-word guide—and this working copy somehow reached Jack Warner, who was delighted with the manner in which the novel had been "adapted." He phoned Huston. "You've got my okay, Johnny. It's a great script!"

Rivkin knew he was out of a job. Huston ended up trimming the secretary's copy a bit, adding a line here and there—but, basically, he was "shooting the book." It was almost entirely Hammett's novel.

"Dashiell Hammett remains the real author of the film without ever having worked on it," wrote critic Allen Eyles. "Huston . . . imposed no viewpoint of his own, but sought to realize on film the atmosphere of the book, merging precisely into the aloof position Hammett adopts in his writing. Hammett's

Above, William Powell and Myrna Loy as Nick and Nora Charles, of the *Thin Man* films. Below, the stars of *The Maltese Falcon*: Humphrey Bogart, Peter Lorre, Mary Astor, and Sydney Greenstreet.

Lillian Hellman, circa 1941. Below, a dinner for *Black Mask* writers, 1936. Seated left to right: Arthur Barnes, John K. Butler, Tod Ballard, Horace McCoy, Norbert Davis. Standing: unknown, Raymond Chandler (wearing glasses), Herbert Stinson, Dwight Babcock, Eric Taylor, Dashiell Hammett.

style is tersely descriptive, involving no explanation of any of his characters, and is entirely concerned in conveying a situation by its externals, letting events speak for themselves."

Although the film retains the novel's dialogue, almost word for word in many scenes, there are deletions. Huston eliminated a minor character (Gutman's daughter) and dropped the Flitcraft parable; he also toned down the homosexual aspects of the Cairo-Cook relationship. And the final exchange, between the cop and Spade, is Huston's—when Sam is asked what the falcon is: "It's the stuff that dreams are made of." This is a brilliant final touch on a remarkably faithful film.

Jack Warner wanted actor George Raft to play the role of Sam Spade, but Raft refused; he did not trust Huston, an untested director, with a property that had already bombed twice at the box office.

"Guess you'll have to settle for Bogie," Warner told Huston. Humphrey Bogart was forty-two; he'd been in films for over a decade, and he was just weathered enough and tough enough to look the part (one critic remarking on "the face that seems to have been eroded and battered by harsh words and blunt instruments").

The other main cast members were equally effective: Mary Astor was perfect as Brigid, playing the role in her mid-thirties and projecting just the proper blend of sensuality and nervous innocence. Gutman was superbly played by Sydney Greenstreet. At sixty-one, weighing in at 285 pounds, he'd been picked by Huston from the New York stage, where he had specialized in portraying butlers; *Falcon* was his first film. Peter Lorre was shrewdly chosen for the perfumed rogue, Joel Cairo. The boy gunsel, Wilmer, was nastily acted by Elisha Cook, soft-voiced and menacing.

Even the supporting players were ideally cast—and each became memorable: Barton MacLane as Dundy, the tough cop; Ward Bond as Polhaus; Jerome Cowan as Spade's murdered partner, Miles Archer; Lee Patrick as the faithful Effie; quavery Gladys George as Archer's widow, Iva. And Walter Huston, young John's celebrated actor-father, accepted an uncredited bit part "for luck"—playing the mortally wounded Captain Jacobi, who staggers into Spade's office, drops the falcon, and expires.

Deftly imitating the voice of the film's producer, Hal Wallis, John phoned his father the evening after the Jacobi scene had been shot and told him that he was "terrible" in it and that he must come back to the studio in the morning so they could reshoot the entire sequence. Walter was furious, but agreed to the retake, having fallen for his son's practical joke. John twitted him about it for years.

Jack Warner wanted to call the finished film "The Gent from Frisco," but the novel's original title was restored just prior to release in 1941. Production had been completed in two months, at a total cost of $300,000. Hammett got no additional money, since Warners had made an "all rights" buy at the time of the original sale—but the ultimate satisfaction was his. He was pleased that the film "had finally been done right." And, again, his name was in the public eye.

London's *Sunday Times* named *The Maltese Falcon* "the most interesting and imaginative detective film to come out of America, or anywhere else, since the first *Thin Man*. It is, of course, not irrelevant that both stories have the same author, Dashiell Hammett."

Six pages were devoted to Hammett in Howard Haycraft's history of crime fiction, *Murder for Pleasure*, published in 1941:

> They [his novels] established new standards of realism in the genre. . . . Commercial in conception, they miss being Literature, if at all, by the narrowest of margins. [His] prose is economical, astringent and muscular. . . . Hammett's lean, dynamic, unsentimental narratives created a definitely *American* style, quite separate and distinct from the accepted English pattern . . . and no other author of modern times—certainly no other American—has so basically changed and influenced the form. [Hammett] has given the American detective story a nationality of its own.

Hammett's reputation as a writer was at its peak, but the man himself was directing more and more of his energy toward social and political activism; his time was taken up not by detective fiction but by work on the editorial board of *Jewish Survey,* by his presidency of the League of American Writers, and by his involvement with the Fourth Writers Congress, to which he delivered a speech that summer. One reporter covering the event (also attended by writers Theodore Dreiser, Richard Wright, and Donald Ogden Stewart) reported that Hammett "spoke, sarcastically, of our national defense effort against civil liberties."

When he sold film rights to Nick and Nora Charles, Hammett had retained the broadcast rights, and now they paid off. He signed a two-year contract with the NBC network for a radio series, "The Adventures of the Thin Man," which made its debut on July 2, 1941. Les Damon played Nick, Claudia Morgan was Nora, and Himan Brown produced and directed. Hammett did not actually write any of the scripts. In fact, he insisted on a contractual clause that completely separated him from the series—no personal involvement. He was paid $500 a week simply for the use of his name and characters; he refused to supervise scripts or even discuss the show with its head of production.

However, Hammett's by-line did appear on one radio "scenario" in *Click* that year, "The Thin Man and the Flack," presented as a group of story-captioned photos. The writing may well have been Hammett's; the style is tough-funny, on the unsubtle level of the *X-9* strip: "I was minding my own business, my own wife, and my own drink at Barney's. Al Thornton was sitting at the next table with Sonia Bellkoff, the Russian lollypop Monarch signed up. Al was Sonia's flack."

Such writing was no more than game playing, but now, for Hammett, the games were ending. By year's end the United States had entered World War II. Hammett would soon be a part of it.

18

TO THE END OF THE WORLD

*The wind blows west on one side and east on the
other. The rain falls in Siberia and hits the
Islands sideways, at sixty miles an hour! A man
can't survive more than thirty minutes in the
Bering Sea.*

—ROBERT COLODNY

IN 1942, WITH Knopf's publication of *The Complete Dashiell
Hammett,* all five of Hammett's major novels, from *Red Harvest*
through *The Thin Man,* were available in one volume. For
Warner Brothers, he had completed the final revisions on
*Watch on the Rhine.** Radio's *Suspense* aired one of his short
stories, while "The Adventures of the Thin Man" continued
to pick up listeners for NBC.

Another Hammett book reached the screen that year, with
Paramount's remake of *The Glass Key.* This new version featured pint-sized tough guy Alan Ladd, fresh from his starring
role in *This Gun for Hire.* He was teamed with blond Veronica
Lake, described in studio ads as "Little Miss Dynamite." The
film was blurbed as a "Battle of the Sexes."

Behind the hoopla was an intelligent script, the work of
mystery novelist Jonathan Latimer. He had restored the
novel's original ending, and his dialogue retained the tart
Hammett flavor. Still, Alan Ladd was unable to inject much
life into his portrayal of Ned Beaumont, and the film was no
match for Huston's classic *Falcon.*

---

*Hammett won an Academy Award nomination for his screenplay.

With NBC royalty checks arriving regularly, Hammett was financially secure enough to turn his back on film work. After twelve years of sporadic screen jobs, on dozens of projects, most of them bringing him neither credit nor satisfaction, he was fed up. It was time to get out of Hollywood.

Hammett returned to New York, and Hellman recalled that he "vanished for several days" that September. When he saw her again and she asked where he'd been, he said he'd gone to the dentist.

The dental visit hardly explained his absence. Hammett had gone to the Whitehall Street induction center in New York and had tried to enlist in the service. Hellman was stunned when he told her. He was a disabled veteran with damaged lungs. He was rail-thin. He drank. He was overage. Surely, he'd been rejected?

Yes, he admitted, he *had* been turned down. The old tuberculosis scars showed up on his X-rays. But he'd convinced the medics that his lung troubles were over. They rejected him anyway—for having rotten teeth. But he had gone to the dentist and had the worst of his teeth pulled. Now he was sure they'd accept him.

And, to Hellman's amazement, they did. On September 17, 1942, at the age of forty-eight, Samuel Dashiell Hammett was accepted into the U.S. Army Signal Corps.

Hammett never revealed the reason for his enlistment, but Al Weisman, who knew him in the army, offered this explanation: "The reason he joined up had to do with his personal campaign to fight Fascism, a fight he'd been engaged in since 1937, and to which he'd devoted most of his time and money."

After a week at the reception center at Camp Upton, Long Island, Hammett was sent to Fort Monmouth, New Jersey, for basic training as a communications instructor, and he wrote Hellman that it was fun to be called "Sam" again—although, he said, many of the young officers had a hard time not calling him "Mr. Hammett." He slept in a tent, was up at dawn, and was "off the booze." He reported that army manners had changed for the better since he was in "back in '18." But even in the service he couldn't escape being tagged as a writer; the army soon had him revising Lesson Plans. His job was "trying to correct, rewrite, coordinate, de-shit and otherwise make sense of three divergent courses in what they call 'Army Organization.' "

Hammett was promoted to the rank of corporal in mid-May of 1943 and by July had been sent to Camp Shenango in Pennsylvania, which was described as "a containment center for members of the service considered to be subversive."

First lady Eleanor Roosevelt was shocked that members of the nation's armed forces should be politically segregated and raised the subject with her husband. President Roosevelt subsequently ordered the Camp Shenango troops dispersed, and Hammett ended up at Fort Lawton, near Tacoma, Washington.

Having, as he put it, "gone nowhere in the last war," Hammett told Hellman that he had volunteered for overseas duty. He didn't know where they'd send him, and he didn't care. He just wanted to *go.*

Hammett went. To the end of the world. That's what many GIs called the wind-blasted string of rock-ribbed volcanic islands stretching for a thousand miles across the desolate North Pacific, from Alaska to the threshold of Japan. The Aleutians: Unalaska, Atka, Adak, Amchitka, Kiska, Attu. . . . The battle for these strategic islands had been under way since June of 1942, when Japan had attacked Dutch Harbor on Unalaska; soon thereafter the vital base of Kiska had fallen to the Japanese. But by August of 1943, when Hammett was sent to the Aleutians, Kiska had been won back by American troops—and B-25s from the Eleventh Air Force were bombing the Japanese bases along "the road to Tokyo."

Hammett was first assigned to the cryptanalysis code division on the island of Umnak, directly west of Unalaska. But his stateside reputation as a radical apparently still worried the military, and in early September he was hastily transferred to Adak, a key island base east of Kiska, which had been under

American occupation since August of 1942. (John Huston, who arrived on Adak ahead of Hammett, had filmed his noted documentary, *Report From the Aleutians,* in the same area.)

Hammett's new job was to help compile a two-year history of the Aleutian Campaign under supervision of the Intelligence Section on Adak. His partner was another corporal, Robert Colodny, who wrote a first draft as well as captions for the maps and sketches. Hammett left the captions alone, but totally rewrote the 4,000-word text, feeling that Colodny had not made it direct enough for the average soldier.

By the end of October *The Battle of the Aleutians* had been completed.

In this pamphlet Hammett described the ragged chain of islands "where modern armies had never fought before. . . . We could borrow no knowledge from the past. We would have to learn as we went along, how to live and fight and win in this new land, the least known part of our America."

Back on the home front, another Hammett book was printed. Fred Dannay, co-editor of the new *Ellery Queen's Mystery Magazine,* had contacted Joe Shaw and arranged for publication of two 1927 *Black Mask* novelettes under the title *$106,000 Blood Money.* These linked stories formed a complete short novel, the first "new" Hammett book published in nine years.

Dannay had written to Hammett, telling him he wanted to edit a series of original paperbacks composed of Hammett's old, uncollected *Black Mask* stories. They would be "Edited and Introduced by Ellery Queen," the pen name Dannay shared with Manfred B. Lee. Hammett agreed to the plan, and this first book, under the publishing imprint of Lawrence E. Spivak, was on newsstands by the summer of 1943. (World issued the only hardcover edition as *Blood Money* that October.)

Hammett's name continued to be prominent while he was on Adak. *Watch on the Rhine* had been released with his screenplay credit, and both *Glass Key* and *Maltese Falcon* had been adapted for network broadcasting (the latter for *Lux Radio*

Theatre), while his "Thin Man" series continued its steady run on NBC.

Lillian Hellman had finished a new play, *The Searching Wind*, and was experiencing her usual preproduction jitters. She was not sure, for one thing, that the title was right. From the Aleutians, Hammett wrote to encourage her on the project, telling her that he *liked* the title, "so don't let's have anymore dilly dallying about it."

The play displayed Hellman's strong anti-Fascist stand, and concerned the "inaction of bystanders" who had compromised with Fascism, characters who wanted "peace at any price" and refused to face the evil surrounding them. Unhappily, as with *Days to Come*, genuine human drama was sacrificed for a moral message—and *The Searching Wind* became Hellman's weakest play. Critic Stark Young called it "more windy than searching."

Had Hammett been able to work with her on the playscript, lending his sharp critical eye to each page, *The Searching Wind* might have been a critical success. Without him, it failed.

In a New Year's letter dated January 1, 1944, Hammett reported that he was "fooling around with training programs again," and joked about his influence, declaring that "the Hammett-trained soldier will win the war."

One of the men who served on Adak with him, E. E. Spitzer, recalled that the commanding officer, Brigadier General Harry Thompson, wanted to establish an island newspaper to serve the Aleutians. A mystery buff, he chose Hammett to edit it.

"I'll want a free hand," said Hammett. "No restrictions."

"No restrictions," agreed Thompson.

"And I'll need some men to help."

"How many?"

"Five at least, plus cartoonists, to liven up the thing."

"Okay, you've got it. Pick your staff."

Thus, *The Adakian* was born in January 1944, edited and written in a Quonset hut on Adak by Corporal Hammett and his staff of five "assistant journalists," plus three cartoonists. Two of Hammett's chosen group were black. Biographer Richard Layman has observed: "He broke the official racial barriers quietly and nonchalantly."

"Ours was a Special Service outfit," his friend Spitzer said. "It contained a newspaper unit, and Hammett got his men from this unit. They really had no experience with a newspaper beyond reading one—but at least they knew how to type and run a mimeo machine."

Hammett had his own ideas about what should go into a service publication. He devoted the first two pages of this four-page daily to war news, followed by a rundown of sports and entertainment, and he included one or two cartoons in each issue. He wrote many of the captions to these, and Bernard Kalb (now a professional news correspondent, who was then part of the *Adakian* staff) fondly recalled one of Hammett's captions, having to do with the utter, unbroken bleakness of the terrain: "The cartoon shows a G.I. pointing out the 'sights' to a newcomer. Hammett's line was, 'There's nothing over there, too.' I always liked that one."

For the men who served on Adak, the duty was harsh and depressing. Strong winds continually battered the island. The fierce wind known as the Willawaw could reach 140 miles an hour and reduce the temperature to forty degrees below zero. The sky was always overcast, and the wind-whipped Pacific, merged with the Bering Sea, crashed hard into the rocks, sending curtains of iced spray over the land, turning the black volcanic soil into swampy gumbo. As one GI declared, "You had to mud-crawl to the latrines because if you stood up the wind would take you to Siberia."

Hammett, however, found it "stimulating" and "starkly beautiful." He would set out on long walks across the high tundra, his gaunt frame bent against a raging Willawaw, enjoying the ruggedness of the mountains. When Spitzer complained about the muck and the freezing gray dampness, Hammett suggested that he raise his eyes from the mud to take in the sight of snow-topped Mount Moffit, rising "clean and lovely against the sky."

Spitzer shook his head. "Sam, I gotta tell you," he said. "You're full of shit."

Hellman, too, was surprised at Hammett's repeated references to the beauty of the Aleutians. (After the war, on several occasions, he seriously proposed that they go there to live; Hellman was horrified at the thought.) She was baffled by his attitude of "pleasure and acceptance" in living the austere life of a soldier. No elegant parties. No flashy gambling. No women. What did he get out of all this?

She had her theories. She believed that the army served as a test for Hammett, that he gained pride from the fact that he could pull his weight with soldiers less than half his age; he won not only their respect but their affection as well. They wanted "Pop" to like them.

The story is told of the time several of Hammett's bunkmates in the hut were bemoaning their womanless existence. Hammett listened patiently, then said, "Look, a woman *would* be nice, but not getting any doesn't cause your hair to fall out—and if you kiddies don't stop this stuff I'm going to move."

They shut up. (As one declared, "We didn't want to lose him!")

Hammett enjoyed his role as "Pop," lending them money, giving advice, listening to their letters from home. He gave one young soldier enough cash to pay for a honeymoon when the GI went off on leave to get married. It gave Hammett satisfaction, being able to help. One GI recalled the time "a guy from the outfit ran up a scary bar bill in Nome. Pop paid it—and told us that if any of the brass asked about it to say the bill was his."

The Adakian, with a maximum circulation of 6,000 copies, quickly became "the Bible of the Aleutians." A new issue was put together each night, with Hammett and his staff working till dawn. Kalb described this killing routine: "It meant that we were on the job from before midnight to breakfast, assembling the incoming news, monitoring shortwave broadcasts, typing our copy, cutting cartoon stencils—and running six thousand copies through the mimeo machine." Kalb was intrigued with Hammett, describing him as "more hermit than handshaker . . . a bayonet of a man, with the constant glint of a bemused smile. . . . He was a good listener, and preferred silence to small talk. When he *did* talk he sounded like his characters, using words economically, and to the point."

Writing a friend in early March, Hammett reported that he had received a letter from his brother, Richard—"the first I've heard from him in well over fifteen years."

Hammett was curious about Hellman's new play. (Despite the critics, *The Searching Wind* ran for 318 performances.) He couldn't send her *The Adakian,* since copies were not permitted to be mailed to the mainland, but he would sometimes quote from his editorials. One of these signed editorials, from the May 5, 1944, issue, was headed "Don't Let 'Em Kid You into Buying War Bonds." This piece raised a few eyebrows, but Hammett saw bonds as a "wrong investment" for GIs and didn't hesitate to say just that. (In fact, he considered this editorial so important that he reprinted it in *The Adakian* seven months later.)

On May 27, 1944, Hammett turned fifty—and Kalb recalled that the *Adakian* staff arranged a special present: "We ran off a private edition of the paper that day, with the headline reading 'Hammett Hits Half-Century.' Pop was delighted."

During his tenure on Adak, Hammett continued to stay on the wagon, but as Spitzer reported, "his fall was spectacular." It began when heavyweight champ Joe Lewis arrived on Adak to kick off a boxing tournament. "The winners on each of the Aleutian Islands would compete with one another," Spitzer wrote, "and the finalists would be flown to heaven—namely Anchorage, Alaska—where they would box the mainland winners."

The thorough boxing coverage by *The Adakian* was due to

Hammett's long-time knowledge of the sport. Therefore, as Spitzer recounted, when it was time for the boxing team to leave Adak, Hammett was assigned to accompany them "so that the whole Alaskan Department would have the advantage of his expert reporting."

The main street in Anchorage boasted a large number of bars, and Hammett made it his business to hit each of them. His boisterous journey through Anchorage became the stuff of legend, and Spitzer observed that "off the wagon, he was as effusive as he was withdrawn when sober. He wanted company for his drinking. Anybody's company. Finally, he was talking nonsense . . . He yelled, he shouted four-letter words . . . ran the whole gamut, including weeping. It was one hell of a performance!"

Having been ejected from several bars, and "fat with cash," Hammett decided to purchase a drinking establishment in Anchorage. He proceeded to buy out the owners of the Carolina Moon, hiring a black woman to manage it for him.

Another friend recalled: "After the war, Dash just up and signed the bar over to her, as a gift, for running it."

During this period, Hammett met Jean Potter, an attractive young writing student who was then attending the University of Alaska in Anchorage. She had been working on a manuscript, *The Flying North,* dealing with Alaskan bush pilots, and Hammett not only gave her editorial help with the book but arranged for its acceptance by Macmillan. It was published in 1946, dedicated to Hammett.

Hammett was now staying sober, having been assigned a job he felt was important; he would head a team of four men scheduled to tour the entire Aleutian chain for the purpose of education and morale-boosting. It was dubbed the "Why We Fight" campaign.

"That was a subject Sam took seriously," said Spitzer. "So he went back on the wagon."

19

THE THIN MAN COMES HOME

Dashiell Hammett, America's leading detective
fiction writer and creator of Sam Spade . . . and
William Spier, radio's outstanding director of
mystery and crime drama, join their talents to
make your hair stand on end with THE
ADVENTURES OF SAM SPADE—presented by
Wildroot Cream Oil!

—On-the-air radio
lead-in, from ABC

In September 1944, Lillian Hellman flew to Fairbanks, Alaska, then across Siberia into Moscow. She was on an unofficial "cultural mission" from Washington as an invited guest of the U.S.S.R. Two of her plays were about to open in Moscow, and she had written a pro-Soviet film, *The North Star,* which guaranteed her a warm reception. She stayed for the remainder of that year with her Russian hosts, spending her final two weeks on the Warsaw front (in January of 1945) interviewing Soviet troops for *Collier's.*

During this same period, Hammett was touring the long Aleutian chain, making "an island jump every five or six days when the weather lets us."

He was now Sergeant Hammett (having attained this rank in late August 1944), and joked about the promotion: "In only two years I've already worked myself up to the rank I held twenty-six years ago."

Hammett was also much amused by the fact that after he had joined the service the FBI had totally lost track of him, and that when FBI agents were informed, in 1944, that Hammett had been seen in an army uniform, they had planned to arrest him for impersonating an American officer. ("It took them almost two years to establish that I was actually *in* the army. I don't think these fellows would have lasted too long working for Pinkerton.")

In a mid-December letter from Whittier, Alaska, Hammett estimated that he had logged almost ten thousand miles of island-hopping since August, "flying from spot to spot in a territory roughly bounded by Attu, Kodiak, Fairbanks and Nome," and that he was eager to get back to Adak, calling it "my island home."

That same month, Hammett achieved major critical attention in the pages of *Atlantic Monthly.* In an essay on crime fiction, "The Simple Art of Murder," Raymond Chandler dismissed the formal detective novel as "arid . . . and superficial." He named Hammett as the genre's revolutionary realist, the "ace performer," claiming that he "took murder out of the Venetian vase and dropped it into the alley. . . . Hammett gave murder back to the kind of people that commit it for reasons, not just to provide a corpse. . . . He did over and over again what only the best writers can do . . . he wrote scenes that seemed never to have been written before." Chandler added: "And there are people around who say that Hammett did not write detective stories at all—merely hard-boiled chronicles of mean streets with a perfunctory mystery element dropped in like the olive in a Martini."

Reading these words that Christmas in the snow-blasted wilds of Alaska, Hammett must have been somewhat depressed by the fact that everything Chandler said about him was phrased in the past tense, as if he had died long ago after conducting his one-man revolution in the mystery field.

Hammett had by no means given up in his attempt to write another novel and was even then making plans for a new book he hoped to begin upon leaving the service. He described it as "about a guy who comes home and doesn't like his family." His tentative title was "The Valley Sheep Are Fatter," and he filled several file cards with character and plot notes.

The new year of 1945 began, for Hammett, back on his island base as he happily resumed editorship of *The Adakian.* In letters he talked about "fumbling around with rosy nebulae, which I hope will presently merge to form my novel . . . for which I've got a kind of feel, if not exactly any very clear idea."

In mid-March his political interests were stimulated when he "happened across" a copy of Lenin's *Theoretical Principles of Marxism.* He told Hellman he was "looking forward to a fine time with it."

He continued to assert his individuality with *The Adakian,* and when the base chaplain phoned him to complain about an appearance of the phrase "God damn," Hammett politely told him that with the paper shortage "It's lucky God gets his name in the paper at all."

His connection with *The Adakian* ended in late summer when he was given a new assignment: editing a monthly publication, *Army Up North* (for the Alaskan Department's Information and Education section), at Fort Richardson in Anchorage. Before leaving Adak he helped compile a pamphlet of cartoons, *Windblown and Dripping,* containing the best work of his three staff cartoonists. In the introduction Hammett wrote: "There is, in man, a need to see himself, to have his pursuits and environment expressed." With these cartoons from *The Adakian,* the unique environment of the Aleutians had been expressed. Hammett would always remember his years on Adak with a wry fondness; it had been a "real haven" for him.

Away from Adak, he quickly tired of army life, and when he toured Edmonton, in Alberta, Canada, that August in his newly earned rank of master sergeant, Hammett gratefully savored the comforts of a big city: hot baths, room service, and fine food. He was fifty-one, and his lungs were acting up again; the years of heavy smoking had given him emphysema. It was time to go home.

"Ten days later Sam returned to Anchorage," said Al Weisman, "and surprised everyone by putting in for his discharge on the age ruling."

In September 1945, after three full years of army service, Hammett the soldier officially became Hammett the civilian.* Lillian Hellman was happy to have him back in New York, and they celebrated his safe return with a round of parties.

Prior to her Russian trip, Hellman had bought one of New York's more modest mansions, a neo-Georgian house at 63 East Eighty-second Street, and Hammett now divided his time between the farm in Pleasantville and the Manhattan residence. He also maintained a small New York apartment.

Reader response to *Blood Money* was good, and by the end of 1945 Fred Dannay had edited three more Hammett paperback collections: *The Adventures of Sam Spade* (which included the three Spade short stories, as well as other fiction), *The Continental Op,* and *The Return of the Continental Op.* In appreciation, Hammett inscribed a first edition of *The Maltese Falcon:* "For Fred Dannay, with all due thanks for his help in keeping the stuff from dying on the vine."

In late November of 1945 he received a letter from his old *Black Mask* editor, Joe Shaw, who wanted permission from Hammett to include one of his stories in a *Black Mask* anthology he was editing for Simon and Schuster. As a final choice, Shaw had settled on "Fly Paper," which became the only story in *The Hard-Boiled Omnibus* representing the twenties. The other eleven stories in the book dated from 1930 into 1936 (when Shaw had been replaced as editor).

An examination of Shaw's correspondence relating to this anthology reveals that he very much wanted to include Erle Stanley Gardner in the book. Gardner turned Shaw down, declaring that he did not think that editor Phil Cody was getting the credit he deserved in the formation of the *Black Mask* school of writing.

---

*Richard Layman summed up Hammett's service: "He was authorized to wear the Asiatic-Pacific Service Medal, four Overseas Bars, and a Good Conduct Medal. He received a Letter of Commendation for his organization of *The Adakian.*"

"Cody was the first man to appreciate the real genius of Dashiell Hammett," Gardner stated. "And he was editor . . . when Hammett developed his 'Continental Op.'" Gardner would not allow his work to appear in a book which made it seem as if *Black Mask* had achieved its style exclusively under Shaw's ten years of editorship.

Radio drama again moved into the forefront of Hammett's career. CBS had taken over the "Thin Man" series and, among other shows, *The Mollé Mystery Theatre* was successfully adapting Hammett works. Since he couldn't get moving on his novel, Hammett decided to cash in on this network potential—and created a brand new detective series for ABC, "The Fat Man," which debuted in late January of 1946.

This show dealt not, as one might suspect, with Casper Gutman, but with a crime chaser named Brad Runyon—a combination of sophisticated Nick Charles and the hard-headed, practical Continental Op. ABC's lead-in was distinctive: "There he goes now," the breathless announcer declared, "into the drugstore. He's stepping on the scale. Weight? Two hundred thirty-nine pounds! Fortune? Danger! Whooooooo is it? The Fat Man!" The radio star and Hammett's title character were ideally matched. J. Scott Smart, who portrayed Runyon, actually outweighed him—tipping the scale at 270.

Radio historian John Dunning described Hammett's new character: "Brad Runyon was unique . . . and it had a lot to do with the tough way he had of dealing with difficult people. This was a direct gift from the master of the hard-boiled school, Hammett himself. . . . Runyon was urbane and slick, with a sense of humor rooted deeply in the grotesque. . . . [He] bore the unmistakable Hammett influence. It came through even on radio. . . . Although he created the character and . . . set the mold, Hammett left the writing to others."

Hammett's radio career continued to soar during 1946. *Academy Award* presented "The Maltese Falcon" (with Bogart, Astor, and Greenstreet repeating their original screen roles), and two separate network versions of *The Glass Key* were aired that year, on *Hollywood Players* and *Hour of Mystery*. Hammett's biggest advance came during the summer, in July, when ABC launched its new radio series, "The Adventures of Sam Spade," starring Howard Duff in the title role.

Duff was brash, hard, wise, and humorous as Spade—but he was not Bogart, and he was not the Spade of Hammett's novel or Huston's film. Director William Spier kept the show fast and funny, using the wisecrack as Spade's trademark.

Radio critic Jim Harmon called the show "outright satire ... played not so much for drama as for comedy. . . . [The scripts] by Bob Tallman and Gil Doud were wild parodies of the taut, often grim Hammett novels of the thirties."

The shift in dramatic emphasis did not concern Spade's creator. Network drama, by its very nature, could never be creatively satisfying for Hammett; he never involved himself with any of his shows and refused to comment on their quality or content. They paid very well—up to $6,000 each month— and millions of people listened to them. That was enough.

A curious aspect of the Spade show concerned the fact that several of the early episodes were based directly on Continental Op stories from *Black Mask*. Spade's comedic persona, as presented on radio, was totally alien to the hard, no-nonsense Op, yet Hammett's basic plots, in terms of theme, characters, and situation, seemed to work well in the new format. Thus, listeners heard Sam solving such ex-Op cases as "The Fly Paper Chase," "The Blood Money Caper," and "The Farewell Murders."

E. E. Spitzer, the former *Adakian* staffer, wrote: "After World War II there was a brouhaha about building a new world. . . . The temper of the times [indicated] that the downtrodden of the world needed a more ballsy version of the American Civil Liberties Union. It was called the Civil Rights Congress (CRC), and all it lacked was a name that could attract public support, such as Dashiell Hammett." Members of the new organization, including Spitzer, approached Hammett early that summer and obtained his support, electing him president of the CRC during their meeting at the Diplomat Hotel on June 5, 1946.

The FBI kept a close watch on Hammett's activities for the CRC, a group cited as subversive by the attorney general. The FBI noted that as president of the CRC, Hammett had demanded that New York City's Mayor O'Dwyer cease police brutalities against blacks.

Beyond politics, Hammett's creative concern that summer centered on Lillian Hellman's new drama, *Another Part of the Forest,* conceived as the second play (following *The Little Foxes*) in a projected trilogy about the Hubbards. (Hellman never got around to writing the third.) This second Hubbard saga was set in 1880, a generation before *Foxes,* and involved a bitter conflict between father and son. Lillian Hellman was undergoing analysis during this period of her life, and claimed she wrote the play as a form of therapy, as a root examination of evil. She referred to the Hubbards as "my nest of diamondback rattlers," and she wanted to explore the reasons behind their abhorrent behavior. She dedicated the new play to her psychoanalyst, Gregory Zilboorg.

(Hammett refused to submit to analysis. Years later, when Hellman was asked what she got out of her sessions with Dr. Zilboorg, she said they had helped with her drinking problem, but that "Hammett used to say he learned more about himself through my analysis than I learned about myself.")

Because she felt that no one else really understood the Hubbard characters, Hellman insisted on directing the play herself. She was amused by the fact that Hammett, master of the hard-boiled school, sternly warned her about the play's excess of violence. ("Dash always thought I used too much of it in my stuff.")* Certainly, *Another Part of the Forest* was a violent stage presentation. Critic Brooks Atkinson called it "a witch's brew of blackmail, insanity, cruelty, theft, torture, in-

---

*Screenwriter Dennis O'Flaherty commented on this, claiming that Hammett was "caught up in the conflict between a fascination with violence and a revulsion toward it."

sult, and drunkenness, with . . . incest thrown in for good measure."

Max Hellman, Lillian's father, attended the play's opening performance in November 1946. When the curtain came down on act one, he stood up from his seat to announce, "My daughter wrote this play. It gets better." At the cast party, Dr. Zilboorg told Hellman that her father was senile.

Earlier that fall, at Hardscrabble Farm in September, Hammett attempted to revive "The Valley Sheep Are Fatter." But instead of working on his novel, he spent many hours each day in the woods, reading, fishing, hiking, learning to handle a bow and arrow, studying the animals and insects. One of his pet projects that fall involved a Zenith hearing aid; he took the device apart, rewiring it "to see if there's a practicable way of stepping up reception of insect, bird and animal sounds in the woods."

Dashiell Hammett's commitment to liberal causes was combined with his love of literature when he became an instructor in mystery writing at the Jefferson School of Social Science in New York—described by one observer as "a radical institution devoted to left wing social studies, housed in a crummy building in lower Manhattan with a beat-up classroom on the second floor."

The purpose of the school, according to its catalogue, was to educate students "in the spirit of democracy, peace and socialism. It teaches Marxism as the philosophy and social science of the working class."

Hammett met with his students each Thursday evening; his class was described as being "devoted to the history of the mystery story, the relationship between the detective story and the general novel, and the possibility of the detective story as a progressive medium in literature."

By this point, Hammett's drinking had become a severe and desperate problem. One of his students at Jefferson recalled that "he'd come in glassy-eyed, his hair all tangled, looking pretty bad. It was obvious he'd been hitting the bottle before class. But he pulled himself together for us. He taught us that tempo is the vital thing in fiction, that you've got to keep things moving, and that character can be drawn *within* the action. . . . He was very serious, very intense when he talked about writing."

By the close of that year, Dannay (as Queen) had edited another collection of early fiction, *Hammett Homicides,* which included the two linked "Silver Eyes" *Black Mask* novelettes from 1924, as well as magazine work from *Collier's* and *Sunset.* (Dannay's plan for a Hammett trilogy was now, he announced, expanded to a pentalogy. The fifth collection, *Dead Yellow Women,* would be out in 1947.)

E. E. Spitzer, Hammett's *Adakian* army buddy, visited New York that Christmas with his wife, and Hammett arranged for dinner at the Stork Club. Spitzer had known "Pop" as a sober, quiet-voiced soldier and was unprepared for this loquacious, hard-drinking civilian. "We reminisced and we drank and I got a little smashed," Spitzer recalled. "Sam got a *lot* smashed. After a while, he didn't make much sense."

Spitzer's final comment on that evening summed up Hammett's rootless, postwar existence: "It seemed to me as if he felt a lack of interest in his life."

20

"I JUST CAN'T DO IT ANYMORE"

This hard-boiled stuff is a menace.

—HAMMETT, 1950

THE ALWAYS VOLATILE relationship between Hammett and Lillian Hellman was severely strained in 1947 by his heavy drinking.

As a mutual friend observed: "Dash could get pretty damn mean when he was juiced up. He and Lillian would get into hot and heavy arguments over his boozing and his womanizing. They'd be together, then break up for a while, then be together again. Basically, they needed each other . . . there was this invisible steel cable that was never broken between them . . . but their relationship was sure no bed of roses. The thorns were there in abundance!"

In her memoirs Hellman recalled a particularly unsettling argument that year. She was loudly protesting Hammett's cruelty, his carelessness, his implacable insistence that their life be played by *his* rules. Hellman was striding the room, delivering her angry tirade, her back to him. When she walked around his chair to face him she was shocked into instant silence: Hammett was pressing the lighted end of a cigarette into his cheek. Horrified, she demanded to know why he was *doing* such a thing?

"Keeping myself from doing it to you," he said.

Hammett's popular reputation was maintained with publication of *Dead Yellow Women,* with the continuation of all three of his radio series, and by the release, from MGM, of the sixth (and final) Nick-and-Nora adventure, *Song of the Thin Man*. (In it, a grown-up Nick Jr. has inherited his father's talent for nabbing crooks, and the film could just as easily have been called *Son of the Thin Man*.)

Hammett was still trying to activate a major creative project. Putting aside plans for his novel, he filled fifteen file cards with notes on a projected three-act play, "The Good Meal." And crime was part of the plot: it concerned the murder of a certain Howard Dublin, whose daughter was having an affair with a character named Bostell. Among the other characters was a sex-hungry woman named Charlotte who, according to one of Hammett's notes, "laid everybody in sight."

Only eight pages survive of the typescript, and it is impossible to judge Hammett's promise as a playwright. Certainly he possessed an amazing ear for dialogue, and many of his best stories adapt easily into a stage format. (*The Maltese Falcon* was adapted as a stage play, but never produced; Hammett had nothing to do with the adaptation.) There is no doubt that he learned much about the art of writing for the stage during his years with Hellman, when he acted as chief critic on her manuscripts. Had he completed "The Good Meal," the New York stage might have been the richer for it.

In the winter of 1947 Hammett rented a duplex apartment in Greenwich Village at 28 West Tenth Street. He asked the manager of the building where he could find a good housekeeper.

"There's this woman Rose Evans," the manager said, "but you may not want to hire her."

"Why not? Is she a lousy housekeeper?"

"Oh, no, she's quite good . . . but . . . she's colored."

"I don't care if she's navy blue," snapped Hammett, angered by the racial slur. "Just give me her phone number."

Rose Evans became one of the vital people in Hammett's

life. She worked days for him, Monday through Friday, quickly winning his trust and respect.

On many weekends, Hammett entertained what Rose called "gold digger ladies" at his apartment—and it was not uncommon for him to awaken from a weekend binge with his wallet empty.

Rose grew increasingly concerned over this constant financial drain and on one occasion intervened: "Mr. Hammett had withdrawn three thousand dollars in cash one Friday for a party he was planning," she recalled. "Then he began drinking just before I left and I knew, for sure and certain, that if he kept that cash around over the weekend some lady of his would up and grab it—so I just took it home in my purse and brought it back to him Monday morning. Mr. Hammett was sober by then, and seemed real glad that I did what I did."

During 1947 Hammett continued to be politically active, and his name appeared six times that year in the *Daily Worker* in support of radical causes. He was a member of Contemporary Writers, described by the FBI as "a militant group of Marxist and anti-Fascist authors." Hammett was also on the editorial board of *Soviet Russia Today* and served on the magazine's Advisory Committee.

The Hammett paperback flow had not ended. In February of 1948, under Dannay's editorship, a new collection was released, *Nightmare Town*, containing the 1924 title novelette from *Argosy All-Story*, two Op tales from 1925, and Hammett's 1933 short from *Esquire*. Dannay (writing as Ellery Queen) informed the reader: "This time we say positively [that] this is the last in our series of Hammett short stories."

Of course it was not; three more volumes were eventually published in this Queen/Spivak series. Aside from the money he received from these collections of his early fiction, Hammett had nothing to do with them. He did not revise the works as they went into book form, seeing "no real permanence" to the stories. He was not ashamed of the work, but it was all in his past. If Dannay and Spivak wished to dig it up, story by story, he would happily spend the money they paid him.*

In a 1948 review of *Nightmare Town,* critic Anthony Boucher declared that "no writer has suffered more from his imitators than has Hammett. The pygmies have aped his tough terseness without realizing that, in Hammett, the key scenes are not the spectacular bloodlettings but the quiet, tense interplays of character in dialogue."

As he approached his midfifties, Hammett's rigid attitude regarding his father had softened and his bitterness had lessened considerably. Hammett's sister Reba now informed him that their father, in his late eighties and suffering from diabetes, was living at a cheap hotel in Berkeley Springs, Virginia.

"My mother had died by then," said Hammett. "Pop was alone and sick down there in Virginia, so I figured I ought to see him."

When they met, Hammett found that one of his father's legs had been amputated. "I bought him an artificial limb from a medical store down there, and he showed it off to some old cronies around the hotel. Seemed real proud of it—but he died that March without ever walking on it."

After two decades, Hammett also reestablished contact with his brother, Richard, and they began meeting in New York for occasional dinners.

In April 1948, *PM,* a liberal newspaper, reported: "Dashiell Hammett was among sixty-five prominent Americans who signed a petition questioning the legality of tactics employed by the House Un-American Activities Committee."

This report disturbed Hammett's brother, a political conservative. At dinner, Richard said: "I have to know something."

"What is it?"

"I want to ask you a very personal question."

"Go ahead."

---

*After Hammett's death, two "permanent" hardcover collections of the best of these early stories were published to excellent reviews: *The Big Knockover,* in 1966, and *The Continental Op,* in 1974. Both remain in print in paperback editions.

"Are you a Communist?"

Hammett looked at him steadily. "I'm a Marxist," he said. And they never discussed the matter again.

Dashiell Hammett faced a costly lawsuit from Warner Brothers that May. They claimed that neither he nor the CBS network had the legal right to use the character of Sam Spade for commercial radio—that all of the characters in *The Maltese Falcon* belonged to the studio as a result of their purchase of Hammett's novel.

He said no, that he had sold only the novel to Warners, and not future rights to the characters. The plot of *Falcon* was theirs; Spade was his. It took over three years to resolve the case in Hammett's favor. Meantime, the Sam Spade show remained on the air.

In June 1948, because the money was too good to turn down, Hammett agreed to become script supervisor on "The New Adventures of the Thin Man" for NBC. Attempting to edit these "brainless" radio scripts soon depressed him, and his drinking increased. It was not party drinking now or bar drinking; it was the solitary drinking of a desperate man.

After a period of two months during which she had neither seen nor spoken to Hammett, Lillian Hellman received a late-night call from Rose Evans. She was phoning from his apartment. "It's about Mr. Dash," she said, her voice strained. "I think you'd better come see him."

Hellman declared that she didn't *want* to see him and he didn't want to see her. (Their last quarrel had been a bitter one.)

"You'd better come anyway, Miss Hellman. You'd better."

She did—finding Hammett barely conscious, weak from alcohol and lack of food. She took him back to her place, helping him into bed. He could barely speak; his face was drawn and without color. That night he convulsed, thrashed, and twisted, crying out in shocked agony. Hammett was suffering delirium tremens, and by morning Hellman had him in a hospital.

"If you go on drinking after you leave here," the doctor warned, "you'll be dead within six months. That's a fact, Mr. Hammett. Now, what are you going to do?"

Hammett sat quietly for a long moment, staring hard at the doctor. "I'll quit drinking," he finally said. "You've got my word on it."

The doctor didn't believe him. At fifty-four Hammett was too far gone; the long years of alcoholism had eroded his system, his will. He could never stop.

But he did.

"I gave my word," said Hammett, "and I keep my word when I give it."

While Hammett slowly regained his strength in New York that October, Hellman flew to Belgrade, Yugoslavia, for an interview with Marshal Tito. She then journeyed on to France, where she saw the Paris stage version of Emmanuel Robles's *Montserrat,* a "philosophical examination of the nature of freedom." Backed by Kermit Bloomgarden, who had produced *Another Part of the Forest,* Hellman commissioned a translation of the play and agreed to adapt it for an American production. Again, as with *Another Part of the Forest,* Hellman would direct, with Bloomgarden producing.

The first serious analysis of Hammett's politics, "Dashiell Hammett's 'Private Eye'," appeared in the May 1949 issue of *Commentary.* The author, David T. Bazelon, accused Hammett of creative bankruptcy and of misguided political beliefs: "The kind of mind that is able to construct commercial myths [detective stories] without believing in them is the same kind of mind that needs to construct one great myth in which it can believe, whether it is the myth of Abraham Lincoln–Walt Whitman–John Henry, or the myth of the Socialist Fatherland, or some incongruous mixture of the two." He claimed that Hammett had taken "a joy ride on the Hollywood gravy train," and was ready for political "religion," that his heavy drinking was symptomatic of his ultimate defeat as a creative writer. "Literal drunkenness becomes a symbol of that more fundamental drunkenness that submerges the individual in commercialized culture and formularized 'progressive' politics."

It was a public blow to Hammett that he accepted without comment, knowing that a printed rebuttal would only rouse dissent and animosity. His politics were his own and, to his mind, needed no defense.

An idealist and a visionary, an activist in the cause of human rights and social justice, Hammett chose what seemed to him the best (and only) means at hand with which to pursue this vision. He never wavered from his humanistic philosophy which, in large part, differed radically from the "party line" to which he was connected.

As Lillian Hellman observed, "He was highly critical of many Marxist doctrines." She stated that although he was "a committed Marxist," he was often "contemptuous of the Soviet Union," and could be "witty and bitingly sharp about the American Communist Party. A great deal about Communism worried him." She added: "Unlike many radicals, whatever Dash believed in . . . came from reading and thinking. He took time to find out what he thought."

Political analyst Garry Wills wrote that Hammett was a radical trying "to uphold a private kind of honor in a rotten world. . . . Hammett wielded that most self-wounding of human instruments, irony; and ironists make terrible crusaders. The worst thing one could have wished on the mousy world of Communist ideologues in America was a dozen more Hammetts."

During the summer of 1949, preceding the fall opening of *Montserrat*, Hammett and Hellman were happily occupied at Hardscrabble, raising pups, taking in stray cats, caring for pigs and chickens, tending asparagus, picking berries in the woods, curing ham, making sausage, planting, swimming, and fishing.

It was a good summer, free of alcohol and arguments; Hammett was regaining his health and enthusiasm for life.

Kermit Bloomgarden sought his advice in early October regarding a possible stage production of O'Casey's *Purple Dust* and received a four-page letter from Hammett outlining "what I think ought to be done." As a play doctor, having worked so closely with Hellman, he was able to pinpoint structural problems with accuracy, and Bloomgarden valued his criticism.

Hammett accompanied Hellman to Philadelphia that same month for a tryout of *Montserrat*. She was having some problems directing the actors, and before the play opened in New York (on October 29), major cast replacements were made. Even with these out-of-town improvements the drama was unsuccessful. Audiences found it ponderous—"one of those Gallic seminars," said a critic, "in which a moral question is talked to death."

As a result, Hellman vowed never to direct again; writing was difficult enough. She determined to avoid the trials and nervous tension connected with the direction of a stage play, and felt "lucky to have survived this last one."

Having fired himself up to write again, Hammett hired a secretary, Muriel Alexander, purchased a Dictaphone and a new IBM Executive typewriter, and set up an office in the lower floor of his Tenth Street duplex.

He told friends that he was starting a new novel he would call "The Hunting Boy," but no pages emerged. Instead, he dictated notes on a never-completed article dealing with life in the U.S.A.

Like Rose Evans (who was still his housekeeper), Muriel Alexander proved to be loyal and devoted. Richard Layman described their close relationship: "He would ask Alexander to come downstairs to sit with him, in his living room/bedroom. . . . There was a fireplace in that room, faced by his wing-back chair on one side and an armchair on the other. He sat in one chair, she in the other, silent, for hours at a time. In the winter the apartment was always kept cold because, Hammett said, it reminded him of the Aleutians.

"Alexander's duties consisted of helping Hammett answer

his mail, keeping track of his finances, buying his apparel at Abercrombie & Fitch and Brooks Brothers, and purchasing gifts for his friends. On her own she undertook an inventory of his published works and recorded copyright information. She also fetched him books from the public library and local used-book dealers."

Hammett had long since given up the idea of working in Hollywood. He had done no screen writing for almost eight years, and (during this period) had rejected several offers: to provide a new film vehicle for William Powell, to adapt one of his early short stories for José Ferrer, and to write a script on the life of General "Black Jack" Pershing for Fox. He had made it known that screen work no longer interested him.

Therefore, Hammett was surprised, late in 1949, to receive a call from director William Wyler, asking him if he'd be willing to adapt the hit play *Detective Story* as a film for Paramount. The plot concerned a stubborn New York precinct detective who functions as a one-man judge and jury, ignoring the policies of modern police work. The detective's career and his marriage are in trouble over his refusal to face reality. Sidney Kingsley was the author, and the play had enjoyed a very successful Broadway run.

"This is a high-quality project, Dash, and you're the only writer I know who can do it justice."

Hammett thought it over. "Well . . . I suppose I could give it a try."

"Great!" said Wyler. "Come out right away. I'll arrange everything."

When Hammett arrived in Hollywood, Wyler had reserved a suite of rooms for him at his old stomping ground, the Beverly Wilshire Hotel.

"I hear you're on the wagon," said Wyler when they met.

"You hear right," nodded Hammett.

"Well, that's terrific. I can promise that you'll have no problems with the play, Dash. It's a beaut."

Wyler was wrong. Hammett did have problems. For him,

the play refused to fit into a satisfactory screen format, but he kept trying. In a letter of February 8, 1950, Hammett admitted to Hellman that he was suffering sleepless nights over the project. "The work still goes too slowly, so I'm punishing myself in the name of industry by not going to Santa Anita [for the races] this week."

At night, when he couldn't sleep, he would aimlessly wander the city. Since he no longer drank, Hammett did not enjoy making "the usual round of drunken parties they have out here." Mainly, he was alone.

Hellman worried about him and called Arthur Kober, telling him to "take Dash out to dinner."

When Kober located him at the Beverly Wilshire, Hammett was amused. "Did Lily order you to entertain me?"

"More or less," admitted Kober. "When Lillian tells you to do something, you do it."

"Absolutely," agreed Hammett. "So let's go entertain me."

They drove to Mike Romanoff's and had a quiet dinner there.

Finally, over dessert, Hammett said: "Lily bought me a big desk. I'm supposed to sit at this desk and write things."

"That's funny," mused Kober. "When I was married to Lillian she bought *me* a big desk to help *me* write."

"Mine's an expensive antique," said Hammett.

Kober nodded. "So was mine."

A moment of silence between them.

"Lily thinks it's all in having the right desk," said Hammett. Then he asked: "Did you write anything when you had your desk?"

"No. Have you?"

"No."

Another silence. At that point they were joined by a magazine writer, Betty Buchanan, who was a friend of Kober's. She was young and attractive, and Hammett visibly brightened in her presence. She asked him to tell her something about his Pinkerton days.

"Okay," he said. "There was this time the office sent me out to a bank in town. A bomb was supposed to have been planted there. I went in, looked around for the bomb, and asked myself what I'd do with it if I found it."

"What did you decide?"

"I decided to take it over to the teller's window and deposit it."

Smiles all around.

"What do you think of the radio shows they've made from your books?" Betty asked.

"I liked the title of one," he said. " 'The Fat Man.' "

"Why that one?"

"Because every time they said those three words, I got paid. They took them out of *The Maltese Falcon,* and gave me a lot of money for them. So that's what I call a good radio show."

The talk shifted to friends who had solved drinking problems and who were now on the wagon. Hammett's face began to darken.

"I know ex-drunks who should have stayed drunk," he growled. "Before they quit drinking they got pointed at and people would say, 'Ah, if only he could sober up, what a great writer he'd be. What a genius we've lost to the bottle!' Well— these guys sober up and turn out to be the biggest bores in town. They should have stayed drunk, so they don't wake up to find out they haven't any talent."

Hammett stood, tossing some money on the table. "Let's get out of here, Arthur. I have to hit the Wyler thing again early in the morning and I need some sleep."

The evening had ended on a sour note. Years later, in recalling it, Betty Buchanan admitted: "At the time I didn't realize he was talking about himself."

Hammett wrote Hellman to tell her that he had lunched with his agent and that there was "talk of a future Hitchcock picture with a piece of the take." The Hitchcock project never materialized, and the problems with *Detective Story* remained unsolved. Every few days Wyler would stop by Hammett's suite to see how the script was coming, and each time

Hammett would stall him. After three weeks of this, he met Wyler at the door with a cashier's check for $10,000 in his hand. "Here's your advance back, Willy," he said.

"But I don't want the money, I want your script!"

Hammett shook his head. "I can't do it. I just can't do it anymore." And he handed Wyler the check. "I'm sorry."

He had found that he could no longer adjust himself to the formula of screen writing, and *Detective Story* proved to be Dashiell Hammett's last film assignment.

Before leaving Hollywood for New York, Hammett decided he would visit Jose and his daughter Josephine, who were living in the Mar Vista area of Los Angeles in a house he had purchased for them. He ended up spending several more months in California, visiting them frequently, talking about "the old days" when they'd struggled together in San Francisco, and taking his daughter to the races at Santa Anita. Hammett knew that he had failed as a father and husband, but Jose and Josephine weren't bitter. For those months in 1950 in California, the three of them became a real family again, and Hammett greatly enjoyed the time he spent there.

In early June, Hammett had been approached by a Los Angeles reporter and asked about the current proliferation of hard-boiled novels and films. Hammett told the reporter that he didn't approve: "It went all right in the twenties, in the bootleg era . . . the racketeering days. Now the racketeers are nice, refined people. They belong to country clubs."

Who was his favorite crime writer?

"The best one today is a Belgian who writes in French— Georges Simenon. He's intelligent. There's something of Poe about him."

The piece was headlined, "Hammett Has Hard Words for Tough Stuff He Used to Write."

Hammett story collections from Dannay continued to appear under the Spivak imprint, with a 1950 edition of *The Creeping Siamese* and a final pair of announced books, *Woman in the Dark* and *A Man Named Thin.*

Back at Hardscrabble Farm, he was looking forward to

reading Hellman's new play. Hammett had no idea, at that moment, how deeply he'd be drawn into *The Autumn Garden*, how personal it would become for him. Its theme was lost chances, lost dreams.

21

THE PRICE OF PERSONAL DEMOCRACY

*Honor . . . was conformity to a code of rules
which he himself invented, a means of
demonstrating his own worth against the world.*

—OSCAR HANDLIN

BY JANUARY OF 1950 the FBI had compiled a detailed report
on Hammett covering his political activities over a four-year
period and linking him to thirty-five Communist-front organizations. The Soviet press continued to use his name in connection with stories in the *Daily Worker,* including "100
Notables Urge Talks by U.S., U.S.S.R. on Korean War" and
"33 American Writers Offer to Go Anywhere to Discuss
Peace." Hammett also wrote the introduction to George Mar-
ion's book *The Communist Trial,* published in 1950.

He was well aware that his highly visible political profile
made him vulnerable to attack and that many Americans
might label him a fanatic and extremist. But Hammett was
acting out of deeply held beliefs and was prepared to stand
behind his public statements and convictions. He had proven
his love of country by service in two wars; now he refused to
remain silent about what he felt was politically corrupt in the
society around him. To Hammett, silence in the face of what
he perceived to be injustice was moral hypocrisy, and he
refused to compromise his view of political morality.

Lillian Hellman shared an equally passionate commitment
to social action, lending her name and active support to many

of the same causes. She and Hammett, however, did not always agree. Hellman, for example, campaigned for Progressive party presidential candidate Henry Wallace in 1948;
Hammett was against Wallace and refused to support his
candidacy. Each maintained a sharply individualistic approach to current political issues.

Beyond politics, they were also concerned with the problems of middle age. Hammett was now in his midfifties, Hellman her midforties. Her new play was constructed around the
theme of advancing years; its characters were webbed in the
guilt of unfulfilled hopes and bypassed opportunities.

The Autumn Garden was in first draft when Hammett read it
during that summer of 1950 at Hardscrabble. Hellman was
shocked by his savage response. He reminded her that she
had started as a serious writer. "That's what I worked for,"
he said. "I don't know what's happened, but tear this up and
throw it away. It's worse than bad—it's half good."

Hurt and angry, she left the farm for a week to be alone in
New York. Was Hammett right? Had she betrayed her own
talent? The days in New York were agonizing. Finally, she
concluded that Hammett's judgment was correct; she returned, tore up the draft, and began afresh.

The summer turned out to be one of their best together.
They hiked in the woods, tended the gardens, hunted rabbits,
talked late into the nights. Hardscrabble was a world in minia-
ture, with its own special citizens: Gus and Betty Benson
helped run the farm; there was a housemaid and Helen Anderson, the cook; there were the livestock and the growing
pups.

Occasionally, Hellman and Hammett would visit friends
nearby. Later she wrote of one country breakfast when Hammett was teasing her about having "no sense of direction."
She protested, telling him that, if she wanted to, she could spit
directly in his eye from across the table.

He laughed, shaking his head, and said he'd bet his rare and
treasured set of Japanese prints that she couldn't. The wager
was agreed upon—and the guests at the table were shocked

as Hellman leaned forward and spat directly into Hammett's left eye.

Grinning, he faced the stunned guests: "That's my girl," he said. "Some of the time the kid kicks through."

While Hellman worked on *The Autumn Garden,* Hammett indulged his lifelong passion for reading. He would devour almost any book he could lay hands on. His favorites were on mathematics and baseball, but he also read works on how to tie knots, on how to play chess in your head, on German gun makers, and on the shore life of the Atlantic, true crime, poisonous plants, and the language of bees. "And Dash remembered what he read," said a friend. "Ask him about the history of Indian religion, or about New Orleans jazz, Greek architecture, glassmaking, topology or plasma physics. He could talk on any of these subjects." Hellman recalled an entire season during which Hammett read about the retina of the eye. In another period he delved into Icelandic sagas, and once he spent a month reading about the cross-pollination of corn. His curiosity was endless.

At summer's end, having worked long hours each day to finish the new version, Hellman gave her rewritten playscript to Hammett. As he read it, she fell asleep on the couch. She woke with Hammett gently patting her head, grinning down at her. "It's good, Lily," he told her. "In fact, it's the best play anybody's written in a long time."

Numbed and happy, she started for a walk, wanting to savor this unexpected praise, but he stopped her. There was still work to be done, he said, and she'd better get at it—the character of Ben Griggs needed some sharpening.

The setting of *The Autumn Garden* was a summer house, based on one Hellman remembered from her childhood. In her play, the place had been converted by a strong-minded southern lady, Constance Tuckerman, from a family home into a boardinghouse. General Ben Griggs and his weak, pathetic wife, Rose, were among the boarders. Others included a middle-aged alcoholic, Ned Crossman,* once romantically involved with Constance, and also Nick and Nina Denery. Nick was once a brilliant artist, but has not been able to complete a painting in twelve years. (Richard Layman sees Nick and Nina as "a sort of tragic version of Nick and Nora Charles.") The drama revolves around Griggs and his failure to achieve the goals he had sought as a young man. He refers to his lost life in a major speech, and it was this speech that Hammett kept insisting was "not right."

Hellman, exhausted, said she was going to bed and that if Hammett didn't like the speech, maybe he could improve it. Hammett did just that, and the final words from Ben Griggs are Hammett's words. They reveal his own frustration and guilt about his life. He speaks of the "turning point" in a career, when you are able to "wipe out your past mistakes, do the work you'd never done, think the way you'd never thought, have what you'd never had. . . ." A man is either ready for the moment, has trained himself for it, or "you've let it all run past you and frittered yourself away." He ends the speech by admitting, "I've frittered myself away."

In early March 1951, when *The Autumn Garden* opened at the Coronet Theatre in New York, Hammett was there to applaud it. Of all Hellman's plays he had the largest emotional investment in this one. A critic commented: "Sometime in the middle years every man is awakened to what might have been, and struggles to give his dream a last chance. . . . Hellman's people are captured in their own pasts, obsessed with these dreams . . . yet bound to the present and the small comforts that provide an illusion of escape." Hammett felt, acutely, this passage of time, and remarked often in letters to friends that he was "growing old." He had abandoned his latest attempt at a novel, "December 1," after just two pages.

In April Hammett spent a week in Los Angeles, visiting his

---

*One critic saw Crossman as a disguised portrait of Hammett. In a television interview years later, Hellman admitted: "There's some of Hammett, some form of him, in almost every character I ever wrote."

daughter, Josephine, and his young grandchild, Ann. Savoring his role as grandfather, he took Ann home to New York with him that same month. "We had two great weeks of farm life together at Hardscrabble," he wrote a friend. When he returned to Los Angeles in May with his granddaughter, he told Josephine he very much enjoyed being with the child and that his chief regret, in returning to New York, was that he'd miss "playing grandpa."

"I'll try to get back here soon," he told her. "But I can't make any promises." He did not return. It had been his final trip to Los Angeles.

After Hammett had become president of the Civil Rights Congress in 1946, a CRC fund was set up to be used by its trustees to provide bail for defendants arrested for political reasons. Hammett was elected chairman of this bail fund, which totaled almost $800,000 by the end of 1950. The CRC decided not to divulge the names of fund contributors.

In the summer of 1951 four Communist leaders—Gus Hall, Henry Winston, Robert Thompson, and Gilbert Green—were convicted on charges of criminal conspiracy. Scheduled to begin serving jail sentences, they jumped bail and vanished. The U.S. District Court in New York wanted CRC bail fund information in order to aid authorities in tracing the fugitives. (CRC bail money, in the amount of $80,000, had been forfeited when the four men failed to appear.) In July subpoenas were served on all five of the bail fund trustees, including Hammett.

The secretary of the fund, Frederick Field, took refuge in the Fifth Amendment and refused to provide CRC information. He was sentenced to a six-month prison term for contempt of court.

Hammett was the next CRC member to testify, and he told Hellman that he would not violate his trust as chairman of the fund in order to avoid a jail sentence. "I have my own ideas about democracy," he said. "And I don't let cops or judges tell me what democracy is."

Hammett was questioned by District Attorney Irving Saypol (called, by *Time*, "the nation's number one hunter of top Communists") before Judge Sylvester Ryan of the United States District Court of New York on July 9, 1951. On more than eighty occasions during his testimony Hammett invoked the Fifth Amendment, stating: "I decline to answer on the ground that the answer might tend to incriminate me." Judge Ryan repeatedly told Hammett, "I *direct* you to answer," and each time Hammett replied, "I decline to answer for the reason given."

Ryan told the witness: "Mr. Hammett, you are thwarting the processes of this court . . . your claim of immunity has neither legal basis nor factual foundation. . . ."

As chairman of the bail fund, Hammett was asked to produce records of the CRC which listed fund contributors; the assumption was that some of these contributors might be providing shelter to the four fugitives. Again, Hammett invoked the Fifth Amendment, refusing to produce the documents. Several times, he was shown CRC documents bearing his initials, but he refused to identify these or comment on them.

Judge Ryan ultimately lost patience with the witness: "Mr. Hammett, I find you guilty of contempt of court for your failure and refusal to comply with the directions of the court, to make answer to questions asked of you, and to produce books, documents and records of the bail fund of the Civil Rights Congress of New York." On the evening of the same day Judge Ryan sentenced Hammett to six months in federal prison.

When Hammett's attorney protested the sentence, Judge Ryan told him: "I was inclined, counselor, at first, to impose a longer sentence upon him because he had seen an example of what happened to Mr. Field and he knew what was going to happen. . . . He occupies the important position of chairman of this fund and . . . I felt that his claim of privilege was especially unwarranted and unjustified, either in law or in fact. . . . I feel that I have dealt with him extremely leniently."

Bail was set at $10,000, but when Muriel Alexander arrived with the money, the bail ruling was canceled and the court refused to release him.* A news photo showed Hammett, in handcuffs, being led toward a police van. His false teeth had been removed and his suit was rumpled; at fifty-seven, heading for prison, he looked much older.

On July 10 Hammett was booked into the Federal House of Detention, a seedy holding facility on West Street in New York, where he was to await transfer to a federal penitentiary.

V. J. Jerome, a leading Communist theoretician (who had once attempted to talk Hellman into joining the American Communist party), was also at the West Street facility. At the rooftop recreational area, Hammett and Jerome were partnered in a game of table tennis against two other prisoners, one of whom, a tall, burly-looking fellow, was there for murdering a federal agent. Jerome accused the big man of cheating. Hammett took Jerome aside after the game and told him that he should not count on honest behavior from a murderer. Jerome launched into a lecture based on his socialist belief in the reform of all mankind.

Another game began. When Jerome again accused the condemned murderer of cheating, the enraged man threw a knife. Hammett saved Jerome's life by pushing him to the floor. He assured the angry killer that Mr. Jerome was mentally ill and did not realize what he was saying. As a peace gesture the murderer ended up with two packs of Jerome's cigarettes.

Lillian Hellman's lawyer brought her a message from Hammett: he wanted Lily to get out of New York. He didn't need proof that she loved him, and he didn't want it. He knew she was a worrier, and he did not want her hanging around town worrying about him.

She took Hammett's advice and fled to London. During the trip, she met Richard Crossman, a member of Parliament and editor for *New Statesman and Nation*. He told her that it was a

---

*Demonstrating her devotion to Hammett, his housekeeper, Rose Evans, had offered her life savings to help him post bail.

"disgrace" that not one American intellectual had come to Hammett's aid. If such a gross miscarriage of justice had taken place in London, Crossman assured her, he, and many others like him, would have lodged vigorous objections.

She tried. Over Hammett's stern protests and without his cooperation, Hellman's lawyers attempted to obtain a reversal from the U.S. Court of Appeals, but that body denied the motion to reverse Judge Ryan's original decision—and the Supreme Court refused to review the case. Late in September, Hammett was sent to the Federal Correctional Institute at Ashland, Kentucky, to serve the remainder of his sentence.

Since Hammett was allowed to write only to relatives, Hellman received no letters from him while she was in Europe, but one personal message from him somehow did reach her that summer. Jail, he reported, reminded him of the army, because the guards called him "sir." His prison job was to keep the bathroom clean, and he wanted her to know that he was doing very well at this job, cleaning toilets better than she had ever done.

This mordant humor was typical of Hammett during difficult periods, but Lillian Hellman did not find anything amusing about the grim situation. She returned from Europe just before his release that winter. His six-month sentence had been shortened by thirty days for good behavior, and he was freed on December 9, 1951.

Walking the streets of the Kentucky town in which he had been released, waiting for his plane back to New York, Hammett encountered a moonshiner who had also served time. The man was broke and jobless. Hammett gave him all the money he had, arriving back in New York weak from hunger, having kept no money for food. Hellman was there when he got off the plane; he stumbled coming down the steps, gripping the rail tightly. His gaunt body, always thin, had lost even more weight, and his smile was tight and strained.

She was distressed by his condition, but Hammett assured her he'd be fine again once he had some "decent grub" and a little time to rest.

True to his prediction, after a week of sleep and fresh food,

Hammett was much improved. He laughed about his jail experience, shrugging off the long months of imprisonment as "not really so bad." He joked about the convicts, saying that their conversation was no worse than he'd endured at most New York cocktail parties.

"Hammett's form of humor," Hellman wrote, "was always to make fun of trouble or pain." He believed in taking whatever life handed him without complaint, and he had no patience with "public suffering." (Hellman noted that when he ran into fellow writer Howard Fast, who was bemoaning a pending jail sentence, Hammett told him, "It'll be easier for you, Howard, if you take off the crown of thorns.")

Hammett went to court again that year in his extended battle with Warner Brothers over ownership of the characters from *The Maltese Falcon*. He won a final court decision on December 28, 1951, giving him the legal right to use the character of Sam Spade "in whatever commercial manner." His victory, however, was an empty one; NBC had chosen to cancel the Spade radio series, the last of his three network shows. NBC's response to Hammett's imprisonment was not unique. Universal removed his name from the source credits of their 1951 film version of *The Fat Man,* and Spivak quietly stopped publication of *A Man Named Thin.* (*Woman in the Dark,* out in June 1951, was the last book to see print in Hammett's lifetime.)*

Hammett was blacklisted in Hollywood. Then the Internal Revenue Service began what they announced as "a careful investigation of Mr. Hammett's tax forms." (After this investigation, the IRS billed him for $111,000 in back taxes and attached all of his royalties.)

As one friend put it, "The hounds were snapping at his heels, but Dash refused to run. He walked proud. He lost a lot—but he never lost his nerve or his pride."

---

*Ironically, during this same dark year, *Black Mask* ceased publication, having printed a total of 340 issues during its thirty-one-year history. Joe Shaw was to die the following year.

22

McCARTHYISM AND THE LOSS OF HARDSCRABBLE

Nothing lasts. You can't count on anything but yourself.

—HAMMETT

BACKED BY PRESIDENT Harry Truman, the House Un-American Activities Committee (HUAC) began gathering strength in 1947. International events perceived as setbacks for America swelled its power. In 1949 Chiang Kai-shek and his Nationalist forces retreated to Taiwan, abandoning the whole of mainland China to Communist rule under Mao Tse-tung. The Korean War broke out in June 1950. Then the Soviets began testing nuclear bombs. A nervous and apprehensive nation was ready for the dark era of McCarthyism, named for Joseph Raymond McCarthy, the ruthless, bombastic senator from Wisconsin. By 1952, when he was reelected to the Senate, McCarthy had chosen anti-Communism as the ideal crusade on which to build his career. His Senate Investigating Committee was fueled by information supplied by HUAC; this gave McCarthy the base he needed, and he made full use of it.

When Hammett was jailed, Lillian Hellman knew it was only a matter of time before she too would face an investigation—and was not surprised when she was served with a HUAC subpoena in late February of 1952. Armed with legal advice, she worked on a plan in which she would agree not to plead the Fifth Amendment and *would* answer all questions

223

relating to her own political actions, so long as she was not asked to name anyone else during her testimony. It was a gamble she was willing to take.

Things got worse. Hellman was hit with an unexpected tax bill of $175,000 from the IRS, based on what they called "nonacceptable deductions." The money was due immediately. She did not have enough to pay such a bill, and knew that the only way to raise the money was to sell Hardscrabble. It was the most painful decision of her life; the farm was her refuge from the world. In April of 1952 Hardscrabble was put up for sale.

Hammett and Hellman talked about the future, planning their lives together when this "dirty business" was over. She could write films in Europe, free of the blacklist. He could work on his novel. There would be time for sailing, for extended fishing trips. Hammett spoke of buying a small house on the Maryland shore, near his birthplace. He liked the country there.

But all this was idle dreaming. They'd stay where they were and fight clear of the trouble.

On May 21, while Hammett remained in New York, Hellman faced the HUAC questioners at a closed session in Washington. The Committee refused to abide by her terms, forcing her to plead the Fifth Amendment, as Hammett had done. Technically, she could be held in contempt and sentenced to prison.

But she won. The Committee decided to accept her testimony as she gave it, without legal penalty. There was little doubt that their decision had been influenced by the fact that copies of a letter she'd sent to HUAC had been distributed to the press. In the letter, she had offered to testify openly, on a no-names basis. Thus the Committee would have lost face in jailing her. She'd won a narrow victory. She emerged from the session pale and shaken.

The farm sold that same month, for the incredibly low price of $67,000. The sale was emotionally devastating. Hammett and Hellman moved in a sad, numbed silence through the house, packing books and possessions, marking things for sale and storage.

Shortly thereafter, Hammett left for New York. They had agreed it would be too painful to leave together.

Hellman's final act at Hardscrabble was to sell the animals and special farm equipment to her Westchester neighbors. Over the next few days she disposed of ducks, chickens, milk cows, horses, and eleven poodles, as well as canning machinery and kitchen items.

Hellman once described Hammett as "never believing in any kind of permanence." Therefore, for him, the loss of the farm was simply part of life's moving current. She took the loss much harder. Somehow, she had expected Hardscrabble to last through her lifetime, but now, in the summer of 1952, she was forced to leave it. Locking the door behind her for that final time was one of the saddest acts of her life.

In New York, unable to concentrate on another play, Hellman again picked up *The Children's Hour*. Its theme of lives being ruined by scandal was very timely in this McCarthy era, and the play was successfully revived for Broadway. The money it earned allowed Hellman to maintain her Georgian house on Eighty-second Street.

Hammett did not wish to stay there. He said that it was now time "to get a book going," and maybe if he lived alone for a while he could do that. Nineteen long years had passed since *The Thin Man*, and his repeated attempts at a new novel had all ended in failure. In desperation, spurred by the bitter self-examination he had written into *The Autumn Garden*, he determined to "stick with this new one until it's finished."

He didn't have a title. All he knew was the novel was going to be about a man who couldn't finish a novel. Facing this truth about himself, perhaps he could write his way past the mental block that had forced him to put aside all of the unfinished manuscripts since *The Thin Man*. "I've taken a place far enough out of New York to keep me from being tempted— and just big enough for me and my books." He had

Above, Corporal Hammett and staff on Adak, in the Aleutians. Below, Hammett and Hellman at the 21 Club in 1945. Opposite, Hammett during his testimony before the Senate Internal Security Subcommittee, March 1953.

responded to the hospitality of a political friend, Dr. Samuel Rosen, who offered him, rent free, a four-room gatekeeper's cottage on the grounds of his estate in Katonah, New York, some twenty miles north of Manhattan. This was a long step down from the luxury of his penthouse suites in Beverly Hills, but with the IRS freeze on his income Hammett could no longer afford to pay rent. He gratefully accepted Rosen's offer.

In 1953 Hammett was still teaching part-time at the Jefferson School and this worried Hellman. She felt that the school's radical reputation might lead him into trouble with the forces of McCarthyism. Joseph McCarthy had mounted his circus on television, playing ringmaster for an audience of millions, and rumors were circulating that Hammett might be called in for testimony. If so, couldn't his connection with the school do him harm?

Hellman recalled voicing this fear to him one afternoon as they were walking down Fifty-second Street. Hammett listened impassively, then stopped to face her. He told Hellman she must realize, surely she ought to *know* by now, that he had to go his own way no matter what the risk. If his troubles had become a burden to her, then he would not blame her for saying good-bye. But if not, if she wanted their friendship to continue, "we must never have this kind of conversation again." They would walk to the corner and each go a separate way if that's how it had to be.

At the next corner she hesitated, beginning to cry. He smiled, touched her shoulder in a gesture of farewell, and walked off. He was almost out of sight before she caught up with him.

In March of that year McCarthy *did* call in Dashiell Hammett to testify before his Senate Internal Security Subcommittee. The hearings were televised, and McCarthy's smear tactics drew a large viewing audience. Anguished, Hellman watched on her home TV set as Hammett faced the senator and his two aides, Roy Cohn and David Schine. Among the other five members of the Committee, only Senator John McClellan was participating on that afternoon of March 26.

To the expected questions regarding his political affiliations, Hammett pleaded the Fifth—but when asked if he had been involved in any form of espionage against the United States, Hammett responded with a firm "No."

McCarthy followed up the question. "Have you ever engaged in sabotage?"

Hammett, firmly: "No, sir."

"Do you believe that Communism, as practiced in Russia today, is superior to our form of government?"

Hammett shook his head. "I don't think Russian Communism is better for the United States."

McCarthy kept pressing the point: "Then, do you think that American Communism would be a good system to adopt in this country . . . that it is superior to our form of government?"

"Theoretical Communism is *no* form of government . . . there *is* no government."

"I repeat, sir, *would* you favor the adoption of Communism in this country?"

"No," said Hammett. "For one thing, it would seem to me impractical if most people didn't want it."

The testimony ended with a widely quoted exchange between Hammett and the senator:

"Mr. Hammett, if you were spending, as we are, over a hundred million dollars a year on an information program allegedly for the purpose of fighting Communism, and if you were in charge of that program to fight Communism, would you purchase the works of some seventy-five Communist authors and distribute their works throughout the world, placing our official stamp of approval upon those works?"

Hammett replied, "Well, I think—of course I don't know— if I were fighting Communism, I don't think I would do it by giving people any books at all."

As a self-appointed book censor, McCarthy had been combing the files of the overseas U.S. Information Service libraries

in order to "root out books by Communist sympathizers."
Three hundred copies of Hammett's novels had been
removed from the shelves, and it took an order from President Eisenhower (who did not agree with McCarthy) to get
them returned.

In the small gatehouse at Katonah, Hammett worked slowly
on the manuscript of his novel. He was fighting "the old
familiar doubts" about being able to finish it, and he would
come into New York once each week to see Hellman. She was
concerned about him, but he assured her that he had what he
needed; he would survive.

Actually, Dashiell Hammett had nothing left but his talent.
For the novel now called "Tulip," he hoped it would be
enough.

23

OFF THE EDGE

His detective is a man . . . who may not re-order
the world, but who tries rather to maintain in that
world his own track of integrity, professional
fidelity, and . . . his own sort of gallantry.

DONALD PHELPS,
National Review

A PLAY CALLED *The Lark* kept Lillian Hellman busy during the last months of 1954. It was an adaptation of *L'Alouette,* the French drama by Jean Anouilh, and tailored for the actress Julie Harris, who starred as the play's doomed heroine, Joan of Arc. Again, Kermit Bloomgarden produced, and the play, which opened in 1955, was a satisfying success.

The fresh influx of money from *Lark* allowed Hellman to purchase a comfortable summer home on the island of Martha's Vineyard, off the Massachusetts coast. It was a Yankee farmhouse dating back to the Revolutionary War. Its bright, yellow-shingled exterior was covered with climbing roses, and from its site atop a high sandbank, overlooking the beach at Vineyard Haven, one could watch the Nantucket ferries as they steamed in and out of the harbor.

Hammett agreed to come and stay at the house which was large enough to accommodate all of Hellman's weekend guests, yet still provide the seclusion she and Hammett required for themselves. Beyond the boxlike cluster of main rooms, at the east end of the house, stood a tower built from the shell of an old Cape Cod windmill. This was Hammett's

229

"private escape hatch," and he often remained out of sight there for an entire party weekend. He disliked, or was bored by, many of Hellman's guests, and avoided contact with nearly all of them.

Oil painting had been a longtime hobby for Hammett, a form of relaxation, and he spent many afternoons in the tower at work on his paintings. He kept them safely out of sight, and very few of Hammett's friends knew about them. That suited him fine.

Early in 1955 Hammett was once again required to testify, this time before the New York State Joint Legislative Committee, then conducting an investigation of various Communist-linked groups. During his testimony, Hammett again refused to confirm or deny that he was a member of the party, but he did declare that he was "working for the advance of mankind," and that "Communism, to me, is not a dirty word." The committee, after considering his testimony, dismissed him without penalty.

He remained on the board of trustees at the Jefferson School and continued to conduct a writing class there until the mid-1950s, when his health no longer permitted him to go on teaching. During his final year at the school Hammett noted that his class enrollment had increased, and he attributed this to the faithful attendance by FBI agents, monitoring him for subversive political statements.

Without warning, in August of 1955, Hammett suffered a major heart attack. Although he survived it, Hammett's doctor warned him that other attacks might follow. The doctor asked if he was under any particular stress. Hammett said, yes, that he had been trying to finish a novel.

He referred to "Tulip." Clearly an autobiographical work, "Tulip" is thinly disguised as fiction. The protagonist is Hammett himself, an ex-drunk called "Pop," living in a house in the woods, trying "to get a book started." The title character is an old friend from World War II, a lieutenant colonel Hammett had known on Kiska; he comes to Pop and tells him that he wants Pop to write his life story. Pop says that he has been trying for many years to write his *own* story. Tulip insists that his is the more interesting of the two, but Pop does not agree. To prove his point, he tells Tulip about some adventures during his tuberculosis cure at a hospital near San Diego, and about the early days when he began to write in San Francisco.

Throughout the narrative, Hammett keeps returning to Pop's problem: that he cannot write about the things that happened to him beyond his early years. "I've never [been able to write] about any of these things. Why? All I can say is they're not for me. I used to try now and then, but they never came out meaning very much."* At the end of "Tulip," Hammett declares: "If you are tired, you ought to rest, I think, and not try to fool yourself and your customers with colored bubbles."

Hammett's 17,000-word unfinished manuscript stops there; he had written himself to a standstill, as Pop is at a standstill in the novel itself. There was nowhere for Hammett to go from this point in the book, and he knew it, accepted it—and put the work aside.

"Tulip" is gracefully written, demonstrating that Hammett had retained his skill with images and dialogue; it describes, with knowledge and precision, the woods, lakes, terrain, and the other characters who live with Pop at the house. A faithfully rendered segment of Hammett's life at Hardscrabble, it contains a superb, neatly dialogued duck-hunting sequence. But, in the final analysis, it is little more than a novelist's cry: I can't write! Why can't I write?

Tulip gave Pop no answer, just as the novel gave its creator

---

*Among the unpublished manuscripts in the Hammett Papers at the University of Texas are three stories obviously based on Hammett's early life. One is set at the hospital in Tacoma, Washington, another involves migratory workers in a cannery near Baltimore, and a third concerns a railroad ticket agent.

no answer. A final impasse had been reached in Dashiell Hammett's career; his desperate effort to break down his self-built wall of silence had failed.

Except for the island summers on Martha's Vineyard, Hammett continued to live at the cramped little cottage in Katonah. Hellman's visits there depressed her. She noted "the many signs of sickness"—the phonograph, dusty and unplayed; books stacked everywhere in sagging piles; the unwashed dishes in the sink; sun-faded newspapers littering the floor; the unopened mail spilling across Hammett's desk. On two occasions, at night, shots had been fired through the windows of the cottage from a passing car. Hammett refused to phone the police. If people who didn't like his politics wanted to shoot at him, then let them. Calling the police wouldn't help.

The IRS had now filed a tax judgment of $140,800 against him, and the New York State Tax Commission had billed him for an additional $16,000. They were sniping at him with bills instead of bullets, but he ignored these harassments as he ignored the shattered windows.

Two FBI agents visited him in Katonah. They came to ask him about "past Communist activities." Hammett calmly refused to discuss his politics with them. He assured them he was no threat to the country. Would they please just leave him alone?

In March of 1957 Hammett was interviewed at the cottage by James Cooper of the London *Daily Express,* who headed his story "Lean Years for the Thin Man." Cooper noticed three dusty typewriters lined up on a table. "I keep them to remind myself I was once a writer," Hammett said.

The journalist described Hammett as being "in pajamas at noon . . . gazing listlessly over the lonely countryside from his isolated cottage."

How did he feel about his past works?

"I was never too enthusiastic about my detective stories," he said. *"The Thin Man* always bored me. . . . I stopped writing because I found I was repeating myself. It is the beginning of the end when you discover you have style."*

They talked about his health, and Hammett smiled without humor: "I'm learning to be a hypochondriac."

Again, the talk shifted back to his writing.

"I'll tell you the thing that ruined me," stated Hammett. "The writing of the last third of *The Glass Key* in one thirty-hour sitting."

But how could one long work session on a book written so many years ago have ruined him?

"Because, ever since then, I've told myself I could do it again if I had to. And, of course"—he hesitated, staring out the window—"I couldn't."

That same month, the FBI called Hammett into their New York office for a "friendly talk." They were seeking reasons for his nonpayment of back taxes. Hammett declared that he was totally unable to make any further payment on his $140,-000 tax debt, that he owned no property, no stocks or bonds, and had no bank account or safe deposit box, nor was he physically able to work. All overseas royalties from his books went directly to the IRS.

"Beyond the overseas royalties, I made thirty dollars last year," he declared. "That was my percentage of a play I once invested in."

An agent asked him what his plans were.

"To keep breathing," said Hammett. "That's my main job these days."

During the winter months of 1956, with her adaptation of *The Lark* a critical and box-office success, Hellman had accepted an offer to fashion a musical version of Voltaire's *Candide*; it was scheduled to open that December. She was under such pressure that she failed to visit Katonah. When she finally did get out to Hammett's cottage, she found him barely

---

*This is similar to a remark by Raymond Chandler: "Everything a writer learns about the art or craft of fiction takes just a little away from his need or drive to write at all. In the end he knows all the tricks and has nothing to say."

able to walk. "I can't live alone anymore, Lily," he told her. "I've been falling. But I'll be okay. I'm going to a VA hospital."

Hellman refused to allow it; tearfully, she convinced him that he should move in with her. When she was out, she said, her secretary would be there in case he needed help of any kind. Helen Anderson was also on hand. "We'll all look after you," Hellman said, "better than any hospital."

He hated being "looked after." But Hammett was realist enough to know that his health would not improve. His years of independent living were over, whether he liked it or not. He finally agreed to her plan: winters at the Eighty-second Street mansion, summers at the house in Vineyard Haven.

Hellman was creatively frustrated, eager to turn away from adaptations and work on a new play of her own. Walking along the beach with Hammett in the summer of 1957, she listened to an idea of his for a play: "There's this man . . . other people say they love him, want him to make good, be rich. So he does, he gets rich—but then they don't like him that way. He comes out worse than before. Think about it." She did. Hammett's idea supplied the basic plot for *Toys in the Attic*, which Hellman finished in first draft a year later.

The action centers around Julian Bernier, who brings his young bride, Lily, home to his two devoted maiden sisters in New Orleans. (Hellman had her aunts in mind and in the early draft used their real names, Hannah and Jenny. She later changed them to Anna and Carrie.) The three women *seem* to want Julian to succeed. In truth, they want him to fail; when he seems on the verge of success, they sabotage him. At the play's climax he is a beaten man who will always remain in their power.

Ironically, by the time Hellman had completed *Toys in the Attic*, Hammett was himself powerless and completely dependent on three women (Hellman, her cook, and her secretary); "Tulip" was an abandoned failure—and real success was so far behind him that it seemed an illusion.

Upon application, in April of 1959, Hammett was granted

a monthly pension of $131 by the Veterans Administration. He complained of "severe and continual shortness of breath."

Hammett's last trip out of New York was to Boston, for the pre-Broadway opening of *Toys*. In the years since the IRS had cut off his income, he had spent nothing on himself beyond the bare necessities. His stubborn pride did not allow him to accept more than a bare minimum of money from Hellman. However, for this Boston opening, Hammett allowed himself the luxury of a new suit, his first in ten years.

The trip was rewarding. Hammett and Hellman joked together, toured historic sites, visited Paul Revere's house and the Old South Meeting Hall, wandered through Concord, ate leisurely meals at old Boston restaurants.

"For a while I was able to forget how sick Dash was," Hellman recalled. "For the first time in years, he seemed better." But he was not better. The trip back to New York exhausted him; his reserves were rapidly running out.

Under Arthur Penn's superb direction, and starring Jason Robards (who would later portray Hammett himself in a film version of Hellman's *Julia*, in 1978), *Toys in the Attic* was a financial and critical triumph when it opened in New York during late February of 1960.

That final summer at Martha's Vineyard was sad and difficult. Hammett could no longer walk the beach; the simple act of eating wearied him, and his emphysema was severe. Shortness of breath made climbing the stairs a panting agony. By the fall, he was telling Hellman about "pain in my gun shoulder." He had diagnosed it as rheumatism, caused by the early years of hunting in cold woods. She suspected something more serious, and after her November return from the British opening of *Toys* in London, she insisted that Hammett submit to a full physical exam. The results were grim; Hellman learned that his shoulder pain was caused by cancer of the lungs—and that the disease had already progressed to an inoperable stage.

She decided to keep the truth from Hammett, telling him the tests had revealed increased liver and heart damage, which was true. She did not mention the lung cancer.

In his struggle with emphysema, sleep became almost impossible as Hammett fought to breathe. Some nights were worse than others, but, as Hellman declared, "they were all bad." She would sleep in two-hour intervals, then wake to sit with him in his room. During one of these long nights she found him with tears in his eyes. She knew the pain must be intense.

"Do you want to talk about it?" she asked.

Hammett shook his head. "No. My only chance is *not* to talk about it."

His suffering was a "private matter," and there was to be no invasion of it. Hammett's code forbade any yielding to weakness or pain. As he had sat so many years ago in San Francisco, silently fighting the head wound he had received as a Pinkerton, he sat now in his New York bedroom, stolid and uncomplaining, fighting the pains of his dying body.

Hellman hired a nurse to remain with Hammett that New Year's Eve; he had insisted she accept a dinner invitation with friends. The dinner, for Hellman, was strained; she felt guilt and apprehension. The nurse phoned. Mr. Hammett was "acting very odd." What should she do? "I'll be right there," Hellman told her.

When she walked into Hammett's bedroom, he smiled vacantly at her. He had his favorite book of Japanese prints on his lap—but didn't seem to realize that the book was upside down. He was mumbling, grinning foolishly, and Hellman could see that he was irrational. She had been warned that this might occur; the emphysema was depriving his brain of oxygen. She found it "a terrible thing," seeing "a man who had such respect for thinking no longer *able* to think."

The next morning Hammett was under intensive care in Lenox Hill Hospital. Before this collapse they had been making plans to move to Cambridge; Hellman was under contract to teach at Harvard. She had flown there and found a nursing home for Hammett, but she now knew he'd never live to reach it. And he didn't. He went into a coma and, at 7 P.M. on

January 10, 1961, Dashiell Hammett died of the cancer that had lodged in his right lung. The medical examiner reported that his death was "further complicated by emphysema and pneumonia, in addition to a diseased heart, liver, kidneys, spleen and prostate gland."

He was sixty-six at his death, and weighed 118 pounds.

Some three hundred people attended the memorial service two days later at the Campbell Funeral Home on Madison Avenue. The mourners included Arthur Kober, Quentin Reynolds, Bennett Cerf, Dorothy Parker, Leonard Bernstein, Kermit Bloomgarden, Muriel Alexander, and Rose Evans.

Lillian Hellman delivered the eulogy. She praised Hammett's honor and bravery. "He would not have wanted many words today," she said. "He was a man who respected words in books, but *suspected* words in life. He believed they often took the place of thought. . . . He had the greatest respect for knowledge of anybody I have ever known. He believed in the salvation of intelligence. . . . He didn't always think very well of the society we live in, and yet when it punished him he made no complaint against it, and had no anger about the punishment."

Hellman ran her gaze across the solemn faces; her voice was steady: "Never, in all the years, did he play anybody's game but his own. He never lied. He never faked. He never stooped." Her voice faltered; the last words were spoken slowly, softly: "He seemed to me a great man."

As requested in his will, Hammett's body was buried in Arlington National Cemetery. Hellman attended the service, and so did his sister, Reba, and two cousins.

The ravaged thin man was finally at rest.

NOTES AND SOURCES

1 THE BEGINNING OF THE HUNT

p. 3 *Epigraph:* James H. Moynahan, "Dashiell Hammett Confesses!," various newspapers, as syndicated by King Features in 1936. (Interview with DH.)

p. 4 *Hammett family background:* A major portion of the data on the Hammett family is based on research conducted in St. Mary's County, Maryland, by Josiah Thompson in an unpublished report dated 16 August 1977. Also, as Richard Layman notes in his *Shadow Man: The Life of Dashiell Hammett* (New York: Harcourt Brace Jovanovich, 1981), p. 263, the Saint Mary's County Historical Society has gathered extensive data relating to Hammett genealogy.

p. 4 *DH's birthplace:* "Three Favorites," *Black Mask*, November 1924, p. 128. (DH letter.)

p. 4 *DH learning to shoot:* Based on research conducted by Joe Gores for his novel *Hammett* (New York: Putnam, 1975). See p. 202.

p. 4 *DH's father's political ambitions:* Richard T. Hammett, "Mystery Writer Was Enigmatic Throughout His Life," *Baltimore News-American,* 19 August 1973. (DH was his uncle.)

p. 6 *DH's early taste in books:* Fred Worden, "Gooseberries and Dashiell Hammett," *Baltimore Sunday Sun Magazine,* 11 June 1978, p. 26.

p. 6 *DH's early jobs:* "Three Favorites," *Black Mask*, p. 128.

p. 6 *DH fired for being late:* Lillian Hellman, introduction to the Hammett collection she edited, *The Big Knockover* (New York: Random House, 1966), p. xvii.

p. 7 *DH's difficulty with figures:* Hammett related this story under the heading "Dashiell Hammett" on the dust jacket of *The Maltese Falcon* (New York: Knopf, 1930).

p. 7 *Statistics for apprehension: The Pinkerton Story* by James D. Horan and Howard Swiggett (New York: Putnam, 1951), p. 357.

p. 8 *Agency dictum:* Allan Pinkerton, *General Principles and Rules of Pinkerton National Police Agency,* as quoted in *Sleuths, Inc.* by Hugh Eames (Philadelphia and New York: Lippincott, 1978), p. 104.

p. 8 *Kidnapping:* Eames, *Sleuths, Inc.,* p. 104.

p. 8   *Pinkerton on deception:* Ibid., p. 99.

p. 8   *Pinkerton training operatives:* Ibid.

p. 9   *Ferris wheel theft:* Joseph Harrington, "Hammett Solves Big Crime, Finds Ferris Wheel," *New York Evening Journal,* n.d. 1934. (Interview with DH.)

p. 10   *One-armed suspect:* "From the Memoirs of a Private Detective," *The Smart Set,* March 1923, p. 89.

p. 10   *Disguise:* Ibid.

p. 11   *Gun thrown in DH's lap:* Moynahan interview, King Features, 1936.

p. 11   *DH's leg injury:* Ibid.

p. 11   *DH's injuries:* Hellman, *The Big Knockover,* p. x.

p. 11   *Shadowing suspects:* "From the Author of 'Zigzags of Treachery,' " *Black Mask,* 1 March 1924, p. 127. (DH letter.)

p. 12   *Jewel theft:* S. J. Perelman, *The Last Laugh* (New York: Simon and Schuster, 1981), pp. 34–35.

p. 13   *DH on pickpockets:* "From the Memoirs of a Private Detective," *Smart Set,* p. 89.

p. 13   *DH on criminal character:* Ibid., p. 88.

p. 13   *DH on denial as best defense:* Ibid., p. 89.

p. 13   *DH on house burglary:* Ibid., p. 88.

p. 13   *DH on fingerprints:* Ibid., p. 89.

p. 13   *DH on unsolved mysteries:* Ibid., p. 90.

p. 13   *Union strike:* DH to Mary Jane Hammett Miller. See *City of San Francisco,* 4 November 1975, p. 38.

p. 14   *Origins of DH's radicalism:* Lillian Hellman, *Scoundrel Time* (Boston: Little, Brown, 1976), pp. 47–48.

p. 15   *Driving accident:* Josephine Dolan Hammett, during an interview with David Fechheimer (conducted 12 October 1975), *City of San Francisco,* 4 November 1975, p. 36. (Mary Jane Hammett Miller, Hammett's elder daughter, was also interviewed by Fechheimer at this same time.)

p. 15   *Discovery of tuberculosis and disablement pension:* DH hospitalization data recorded in Veterans Administration files.

p. 16   *Pleasure of manhunting:* Joe Gores writes about this aspect of the profession in "Hammett the Writer," *Xenophile,* March–April 1978, pp. 5–10.

p. 16   *Shadowing Fanny Brice:* Leonard Lyons, "Tales About Hammett Told," *Hollywood Citizen-News,* 19 January 1961.

p. 16   *Recurrence of tuberculosis:* "Tulip," in *The Big Knockover,* 1966, p. 263. (Although written as fiction, this unfinished work is clearly autobiographical, detailing Hammett's early experiences at hospitals in Tacoma, Washington, and Camp Kearny, California, near San Diego.)

p. 17   *Lending blackjack to Whitey:* Ibid.

p. 18   *Jose's first impression of DH:* Fechheimer interview with the Hammetts, *City,* p. 36.

p. 18 *Early courtship:* Ibid.
p. 18 *DH on early relationship with Jose:* "Women Are a Lot of Fun, Too," a typed, seven-page unpublished story, with the Hammett manuscripts at the Humanities Research Center (HRC), University of Texas at Austin. (For an extensive listing of the DH material at HRC, see Nolan, "Revisiting the Revisited Hammett Checklist," *The Armchair Detective,* October 1976, pp. 292–94.)
p. 19 *DH's attitude toward discussing emotions:* Peter Wolfe, *Beams Falling: The Art of Dashiell Hammett* (Bowling Green, Ohio: Bowling Green University Popular Press, 1980), p. 41.
p. 20 *Tuberculosis improves:* Veterans Administration file on DH, 1921.
p. 20 *Move to San Francisco:* W.F.N. interview with Luther Norris, April 1969. (Norris knew DH in the service during WW II.)

2 A PINK IN SAN FRANCISCO

p. 21 *Epigraph:* Fechheimer interview with Hammetts, *City,* p. 39.
p. 21 *Jose on marriage ceremony:* Ibid., p. 38.
p. 21 *First apartment:* Ibid.
p. 22 *Pinkerton Agency advertising:* The San Francisco City Directory, 1921.
p. 23 *DH's head injury:* Fechheimer interview with Hammetts, *City,* p. 38.
p. 24 *Lehrman on Arbuckle:* Paul Sann, *The Lawless Decade* (New York: Crown, 1957), p. 69.
p. 25 *DH's shadowing tricks:* "We Never Sleep," Fechheimer interview with Phil Haultain, *City,* 4 November 1975, p. 34.
p. 25 *DH and Geauque as team:* Ibid.
p. 25 *DH's contempt for publicity in Arbuckle case:* Elizabeth Sanderson, "Ex-Detective Hammett," *The Bookman,* January–February 1932, p. 517. (Interview with DH.)
p. 26 *Arbuckle glaring at DH:* "Seven Pages," as quoted in "Revisiting the Revisited Hammett Checklist," *Armchair Detective,* p. 292. (This DH manuscript is at HRC.)
p. 26 *Carrying weapons:* Fechheimer interview with Haultain, *City,* p. 34.
p. 27 *Sharpshooter story:* "From the Memoirs of a Private Detective, *Smart Set,* p. 89.
p. 27 *Carrying concealed weapons:* "We Never Sleep," Fechheimer interview with Jack Knight, *City,* 4 November 1975, p. 35.
p. 27 *DH a star performer:* Ibid.
p. 27 *Kaber murder case:* Ibid.
p. 28 *San Francisco's bad weather:* W.F.N. interview with Norris, 1969.
p. 28 *Stolen gold on ocean liner:* Ibid.
p. 29 *DH misses trip to Australia:* Ibid.
p. 30 *Shadowing "Gloomy Gus" Schaefer:* This case reported as "Hammett Traps Gem Holdup Suspects," *San Francisco Call-Bulletin,* 26 January 1934, p. 7.

p. 31 *DH resigns from Pinkerton:* This is the date given by David Fechheimer after extensive research into Hammett's San Francisco
years. During a public lecture on 22 October 1977 (Scene of the
Crime DH Tour), Fechheimer stated that "a relapse in his health
caused Hammett to leave his job with Pinkerton on February 15,
1922."

3 PULPS AND THE PRIVATE EYE

p. 32 *Epigraph:* "Our Own Short Story Course," *Black Mask,* August
1924, p. 127. (DH letter.)

p. 34 *Description of Nathan and Mencken:* Burton Rascoe, in his introduction, "Smart Set History," *The Smart Set Anthology,* co-edited with
Groff Conklin (New York: Reynal & Hitchcock, 1934), p. xxxiii.

p. 34 *First known story:* "The Parthian Shot," *The Smart Set,* October 1922,
p. 82.

p. 35 *Mencken writing to Boyd:* Ron Goulart, *Cheap Thrills: An Informal History of the Pulp Magazines* (New Rochelle, N.Y.: Arlington House,
1972), p. 115.

p. 35 *Origin of* Black Mask's *title and trademark:* Ibid., p. 116.

p. 36 *Mencken to Boyd on reading manuscripts:* Ibid.

p. 37 *Early* Black Mask *style:* Schuyler Hamilton, "The Silvered Sentinel," *Black Mask,* May 1920, p. 65.

p. 37 *F. Jackson Melville-Smith summing up case:* Hamilton Craigie, "According to Specifications," *Black Mask,* May 1920, pp. 102–103.

p. 37 *DH's detective Hagedorn incorruptible:* "The Road Home," *Black Mask,*
December 1922. (As "Peter Collinson.")

p. 38 *San Francisco in 1920s:* Herb Caen, "Nights of Old," *San Francisco
Chronicle,* 26 November 1967.

p. 39 *DH selling stories and ads:* Josephine Hammett to Fechheimer, October 1975.

p. 40 *Daly's criminal research:* W.F.N. interview with Frank Gruber, 1970.

p. 41 *Example of Daly's style:* Carroll John Daly, "Three Gun Terry," *Black
Mask,* 15 May 1923, p. 5.

p. 41 *Daly's "instant" clichés:* Ibid.

p. 41 *Daly's "instant" clichés:* Ibid., p. 19.

p. 41 *Daly's "instant" clichés:* Ibid., p. 23.

p. 42 *Daly's "instant" clichés:* Ibid., p. 26.

p. 42 *Daly's "instant" clichés:* Ibid., p. 14.

p. 42 *First Race Williams story:* Daly, "Knights of the Open Palm," *Black
Mask,* 1 June 1923, p. 33.

p. 43 *Description of Race Williams:* Daly, "Getting Personal," *Black Mask,*
April 1927, p. 127. (Daly interview.)

p. 43 *Total of Race Williams stories:* For a complete checklist of Race Williams stories in various pulp magazines from 1923 into 1955, see

"There's No Sex in Crime: The Two-Fisted Homilies of Race Williams," by Michael S. Barson, *Clues*, Fall–Winter 1981, pp. 103–12.

p. 43 *Description of Daly:* Daly, "Getting Personal," *Black Mask*, p. 127.

p. 44 *Daly as owner of moving picture theater:* Frank Gruber, *The Pulp Jungle* (Los Angeles: Sherbourne Press, 1967), p. 110.

p. 44 *Daly writing for comic books:* Ibid., p. 141.

p. 44 *Daly's death:* For a full profile of Daly's career, see Nolan, "Pulp Pioneer of the Private Eye," *Mike Shayne Mystery Magazine*, October 1980, pp. 58–68.

4 ON THE JOB WITH CONTINENTAL

p. 45 *Epigraph:* From the dust jacket of *The Maltese Falcon*, 1930.

p. 45 *DH a detective writing fiction:* Gores, *Xenophile*, p. 7.

p. 46 *DH on clues:* "From the Memoirs of a Private Detective," *Smart Set*, p. 90.

p. 46 *Fictionalization of Pinkerton as Continental Detective Agency:* "Who Killed Bob Teal?" *True Detective*, November 1924. (Beyond *Black Mask*, only one other magazine printed a Continental Op story: "This King Business," *Mystery Stories*, January 1928.)

p. 47 *DH on detectives:* "From the Author of 'Arson Plus,' " *Black Mask*, 1 October 1923, p. 127. (DH letter.)

p. 48 *The Op's lack of background:* Wolfe, *Beams Falling*, p. 53.

p. 48 *Changing fingerprints with gelatin:* "From the Author of 'Slippery Fingers,' " *Black Mask*, 15 October 1923, p. 127. (DH letter.)

p. 49 *"The Old Man" as automaton:* William Ruehlmann, *Saint with a Gun* (New York: New York University Press, 1974), p. 61.

p. 49 *DH on basis for characters in fiction:* "From the Author of 'The Vicious Circle,' " *Black Mask*, 15 June 1923, p. 126. (DH letter.)

p. 49 *Characters based totally on real people:* Harrington interview, *New York Evening Journal*, 1934.

p. 49 *Friends becoming blackmailers:* "From the Author of 'The Vicious Circle,' " *Black Mask*, p. 126. (DH letter.)

p. 50 *Phil Cody becomes editor of* Black Mask: Erle Stanley Gardner, "The Case of the Early Beginning," *The Art of the Mystery Story*, ed. Howard Haycraft (New York: Simon and Schuster, 1946).

p. 50 *Elvira prototype for Brigid O'Shaughnessy:* "The House in Turk Street," *Black Mask*, 15 April 1924, p. 13.

p. 51 *Original for Porky Grout:* "The Girl With the Silver Eyes," *Black Mask*, June 1924, p. 127. (DH letter.)

p. 51 *DH on stool pigeons:* Ibid.

p. 51 *Prototype for McCloor:* Moynahan interview, King Features, 1936.

p. 52 *DH to Cody and North acknowledging his sloppy work:* "Our Own Short Story Course," *Black Mask*, p. 127.

p. 52 *DH's use of jargon:* Frederick H. Gardner, "Return of the Continental Op," *Nation*, 31 October 1966.

p. 53 *DH on the role of the gumshoe:* "Finger-Prints," *Black Mask*, June 1925, p. 128. (DH letter.)

p. 53 *DH on the job of the writer:* From a speech delivered in June 1937 at the Third Writers Congress, "The Need for Tempo in the Contemporary Novel," as collected in *Fighting Words*, ed. Donald Ogden Stewart (New York: Harcourt, Brace, 1940), pp. 53–57.

p. 54 *DH transcends genre writing:* Wolfe, *Beams Falling*, p. 27.

p. 54 *San Francisco as locale for stories:* For a complete listing of these San Francisco stories, see "A Hammett Bibliography," *City*, 4 November 1975, p. 49.

p. 54 *Op stories viewed as literature:* Ruehlmann, *Saint with a Gun*, p. 65.

5 "ACTION, MORE ACTION!"

p. 56 *Epigraph:* Goulart, *Cheap Thrills*, p. 32.

p. 56 *Recurrence of tuberculosis and separation from family:* Fechheimer interview with Hammetts, *City*, p. 39.

p. 57 *DH on sex in writing:* "In Defense of the Sex Story," *Writer's Digest*, June 1924, p. 7.

p. 57 *DH on writing fiction:* "Genius Made Easy," *The Forum*, August 1925, p. 316.

p. 58 *Total action on printed page:* "Nightmare Town," *Argosy All-Story Weekly*, 27 December 1924, p. 525.

p. 60 *DH on Chinatown:* "Tulip," in *The Big Knockover*, p. 252.

p. 61 *"The Gutting of Couffignal" as rehearsal for* The Maltese Falcon: "The Gutting of Couffignal," *Black Mask*, December 1925.

p. 61 *Cody tries to get more stories for* Black Mask: Dorothy B. Hughes, *Erle Stanley Gardner: The Case of the Real Perry Mason* (New York: Morrow, 1978).

p. 63 *DH as copywriter:* W.F.N. interview with Albert S. Samuels, December 1967. (This is the only interview Samuels is known to have given regarding his association with DH.)

p. 63 *DH's use of understatement in ads:* San Francisco Examiner, 6 June 1926, p. 12 ff.

p. 64 *DH's views on prose:* "The Advertisement IS Literature," *Western Advertising*, October 1926, pp. 35–36.

6 LEADING THE *BLACK MASK* BOYS

p. 66 *Epigraph:* "Hammett (Samuel), Dashiell," by Ay. B. (Anthony Boucher), *Encyclopaedia Britannica*, Vol. 11 (Chicago: Wm. Benton, 1966).

p. 67 *DH's position in genre recognized by Shaw:* Joseph T. Shaw on DH from various sources, including an unpublished preface he wrote on Hammett (in the Shaw Collection, UCLA), and commentary from Shaw's introduction to his edited anthology, *The Hard-Boiled Omnibus* (New York: Simon and Schuster, 1946).

p. 67   *DH to Shaw on writing at greater length:* Shaw, introduction, *The Hard-Boiled Omnibus*, 1946. (DH letter.)

p. 68   *Return of the Op:* Shaw, editorial blurb on "The Big Knock-Over," *Black Mask*, February 1927, p. 7.

p. 69   *Roll call of the dead "savage poetry":* "The Big Knock-Over," *Black Mask*, pp. 17–19.

p. 69   *Animalistic violence:* Ibid., p. 26.

p. 70   *DH writes "poetry of violence":* Philip Durham, "Hammett: Profiler of Hard-Boiled Yeggs," *Calendar, Los Angeles Times,* 21 November 1965.

p. 70   *Wright's decision to write detective stories:* Jon Tuska, *The Detective in Hollywood* (New York: Doubleday, 1978), p. 24.

p. 71   *DH as caustic critic:* "Poor Scotland Yard!" *Saturday Review of Literature,* 15 January 1927, p. 510. (Review of *The Benson Murder Case.*)

p. 72   *Character of Elfinstone in unfinished novel "The Secret Emperor":* "Revisiting the Revisited Hammett Checklist," *Armchair Detective,* p. 292.

p. 73   *Evenings with Mary Jane:* Fechheimer interview with Hammetts, *City,* p. 38.

p. 73   *Shaw visits Hammetts:* Ibid., p. 39.

7 OF CORRUPTION AND COMPASSION

p. 75   *Epigraph:* Marguerite Tazelaar, "Film Personalities," *New York Herald Tribune,* 12 November 1933. (Interview with DH.)

p. 75   *Pinkerton in Mariola:* Allan Pinkerton, *The Model Town and the Detectives* (New York: G. W. Carleton, 1876).

p. 76   *DH's portrait of Poisonville:* All quotes from this novel are taken from the DH first edition, *Red Harvest* (New York: Knopf, 1929).

p. 77   *Gide on* Red Harvest: André Gide, "American Writing Today: An Imaginary Interview," *New Republic,* 7 February 1944, p. 186.

p. 78   *Universe seen as the enemy:* John G. Cawelti, *Adventure, Mystery and Romance* (Chicago: University of Chicago Press, 1976), p. 173.

p. 79   *Potential of the crime story:* DH letter, 20 March 1928, *A Catalog of Crime,* by Jacques Barzun and Wendell H. Taylor (New York: Harper & Row, 1971), p. 586.

p. 79   *Review of* Red Harvest: Herbert Asbury, "Red Harvest," *The Bookman,* March 1929, p. 92.

p. 80   *Brooks review of* Red Harvest: W. R. Brooks, *The Outlook,* 13 February 1929, p. 274.

p. 80   *Red Harvest a literary landmark:* Robert Graves, *The Long Week End: A Social History of Great Britain, 1918–1939,* with Alan Hodge (New York: Macmillan, 1941).

p. 80 Red Harvest *takes crime from backroom pulps to bookstores:* Ben Ray Redman, "Decline and Fall of the Whodunit," *Saturday Review of Literature,* 31 May 1952.

p. 80 *Conan Doyle image shattered:* Martin Maloney, "A Grammar of Assassination," *The Use and Misuse of Language,* ed. S. I. Hayakawa (New York: Harper & Row, 1962).

p. 80 *Overdone plot of* Dain Curse: John Bartlow Martin, "Peekaboo Pennington, Private Eye," *Harper's,* May 1946.

p. 81 *DH's dissatisfaction with* The Dain Curse: Sanderson interview, *Bookman,* p. 518.

p. 81 *Gabrielle Dain Leggett's part in plot:* All quotes from this novel are taken from the DH first edition, *The Dain Curse* (New York: Knopf, 1929).

p. 82 *Criticism of the Op going soft:* Philip Durham, "The Black Mask School," in *Tough Guy Writers of the Thirties,* ed. David Madden (Carbondale: Southern Illinois University Press, 1968), p. 69.

p. 84 *DH naming characters:* W.F.N. interview with Samuels, 1967.

8 THE STUFF THAT DREAMS ARE MADE OF

p. 86 *Epigraph:* For a thorough analysis of the DH novels, see "The Problem of Moral Vision in Dashiell Hammett's Detective Novels" by George W. Thompson, in seven issues of *The Armchair Detective,* May, August, November of 1973 and 1974, and February 1975.

p. 87 *Sam Spade on* Miles Archer's *death:* All quotes from this novel are taken from the DH first edition, *The Maltese Falcon* (New York: Knopf, 1930).

p. 87 *Parallels between* Falcon *and* "Who Killed Bob Teal?": Christopher Bentley, "Murder by Client: A Reworked Theme in Dashiell Hammett," *The Armchair Detective,* Winter 1981, p. 79.

p. 88 *Description of the McDonough brothers:* Bob Patterson, "Bailing Out in Style: The McDonough Brothers," *City,* 4 November 1975, p. 46.

p. 88 *Historical basis for the history of the falcon:* Introduction (dated 24 January 1934), *The Maltese Falcon* (New York: Modern Library, 1934), p. vii.

p. 89 *Jeweled falcon DH's creation:* Diane Moore to Hugh Eames, 8 September 1976. See *Sleuths, Inc.,* p. 116.

p. 89 *Possible model for falcon:* Fechheimer interview with Haultain, *City,* p. 35.

p. 90 *Originals for Brigid O'Shaughnessy:* Introduction, *The Maltese Falcon* (New York: Modern Library, 1934), p. viii.

p. 90 *Original for Cairo character:* Ibid., pp. vii–viii.

p. 90 *Original for Polhaus:* Ibid., p. viii.

p. 90 *Sam Spade a dream man of detectives:* Ibid., pp. viii–ix.

p. 91   *Maugham on Sam Spade:* W. Somerset Maugham, "The Decline and Fall of the Detective Story," *The Vagrant Mood* (New York: Doubleday, 1953).

p. 93   *DH on the essence of suspense:* "Tempo" speech, 1937, Third Writers Congress, *Fighting Words,* 1940.

p. 94   *Locations in San Francisco:* Joe Gores, "A Foggy Night," *City,* 4 November 1975, p. 30.

p. 95   *DH's vision of an irrational cosmos:* Cawelti, *Adventure, Mystery and Romance,* p. 166.

p. 96   *Falcon as symbol of falseness and illusion: John Huston's The Maltese Falcon* (a scene-by-scene reconstruction of the 1941 film in 1,400 frame blowup photos), ed. Richard J. Anobile (New York: Avon, 1974), p. 253.

9 THE WINNER TAKES NOTHING

p. 97   *Epigraph:* Ernest Hemingway, *To Have and Have Not* (New York: Scribners, 1937).

p. 97   *Ad for* The Glass Key: *Black Mask* ad in *Liberty,* 22 February 1930. (Written by Shaw.)

p. 98   *Beaumont as antihero:* Wolfe, *Beams Falling,* p. 145.

p. 98   *Beaumont as gambler:* All quotes from this novel are taken from the DH first edition, *The Glass Key* (New York: Knopf, 1931).

p. 99   *DH's own gambling:* "Finger-Prints," *Black Mask,* p. 128.

p. 100   *DH's reasons for drinking:* "Tulip," in *The Big Knockover,* p. 270.

p. 100   *DH's favorite book:* Sanderson interview, *Bookman,* p. 518.

p. 101   *DH not "glorifying crime and criminals":* Joseph T. Shaw, "Dear Editor," *Writer's Digest,* September 1930.

p. 102   *James M. Cain denying influence of DH:* "Tough Guy," an interview with James M. Cain, by Peter Brunette and Gerald Peary, *Film Comment,* May–June 1976, p. 51.

10 AN UNFINISHED DETECTIVE IN NEW YORK

p. 104   *Epigraph:* A. Alvarez, *Beyond All This Fiddle* (New York: Random House, 1969).

p. 105   *DH as reviewer—Green Ice:* "Crime Wave" (column), *New York Evening Post,* 19 July 1930, p. S5. (Review of *Green Ice.*)

p. 105   *Whitfield attacked as Hammett imitator:* Quoted from unlocated clipping in *Judge,* n.d. (From the personal collection of Joseph T. Shaw.)

p. 105   *Review of* Green Ice: Will Cuppy, "Mystery and Adventure" (column), *New York Herald Tribune Books,* 13 July 1930.

p. 105   *Whitfield as aviator:* See Whitfield's autobiographical preface to his story "Delivered Goods," *Black Mask,* November 1926, p. 68.

p. 106 *Whitfield and DH's conversations on fiction:* Shaw, unpublished story preface, Shaw Collection, UCLA.

p. 106 *Number of murders a novel can sustain:* Whitfield story preface, *Ellery Queen's Mystery Magazine,* May 1948.

p. 106 *Umbrella story:* Frederick Nebel to Goulart, *Cheap Thrills,* p. 185.

p. 107 *DH to Herbert Asbury on publication of* The Maltese Falcon: DH to Herbert Asbury. Having written the first major critical review on a DH novel (*Red Harvest*), Asbury became a close friend during Hammett's years in Hollywood.

p. 107 *Review of* The Maltese Falcon: William Curtis, "Some Recent Books," *Town & Country,* 15 February 1930.

p. 107 *DH compared to Hemingway:* Ted Shane, "Judging the Books," *Judge,* 1 March 1930.

p. 107 *DH puts draft of novel aside:* For a facsimile of this holograph DH letter (dated 14 January 1942), see *Mystery & Detection Annual,* ed. Donald Adams (Beverly Hills, Calif.: Adams, 1972), pp. 166–167.

p. 110 *Discussing contract for DH: Memo from David O. Selznick,* ed. Rudy Behlmer (New York: Viking, 1972), pp. 26–27. (Memo dated 18 July 1930.)

11 HOLLYWOOD AND HELLMAN

p. 112 *Epigraph:* Ben Hecht, *A Child of the Century* (New York: Simon and Schuster, 1954).

p. 113 *DH's draft for* City Streets: W.F.N. interview with Rouben Mamoulian, December 1977. Hammett's first draft was a seven-page handwritten story titled "After School." He developed this into an eleven-page typed screen treatment titled "The Kiss-Off." (This manuscript now at HRC.)

p. 114 *Lack of talent in Hollywood among writers:* Hecht, *A Child of the Century.* All quoted material is from the book's section on Ben Hecht's experiences in Hollywood.

p. 114 *Office sex in Hollywood:* Ibid.

p. 114 *The town itself:* Ibid.

p. 115 *Hellman's first impression of DH:* Hellman, *The Big Knockover,* p. viii.

p. 116 *DH's charm for Lillian Hellman:* Richard Moody, *Lillian Hellman Playwright* (New York: Pegasus, 1972), p. 28.

p. 116 *DH lending and borrowing money:* W.F.N. interview with Samuels, 1967.

p. 117 *Screen story for Zanuck:* Louella O. Parsons, "Powell Returning to Role of Sleuth in 'Private Detective,'" *Los Angeles Times,* 28 January 1931.

p. 117 *Cortez playing Sam Spade:* Ron Goulart, "The Private Eye," *P.S.,* August 1966.

p. 118   *DH on werewolves:* "Introduction," *Creeps by Night,* ed. DH (New York: John Day Co., 1931), p. 7.

p. 118   *Reader's letter and DH's reply in* New Yorker: *New Yorker,* 7 March 1931.

p. 119   *Indian panhandler story:* Lillian Hellman, *An Unfinished Woman* (Boston: Little, Brown, 1969), pp. 64–65.

p. 119   *Emptiness for chow mein:* DH to Hellman, *Lillian Hellman Playwright,* p. 29. (Letter dated 4 March 1931.)

p. 120   *DH pumping Hellman's friends for information on her conduct:* Ibid., p. 30. (Letter dated 30 April 1931.)

p. 120   *DH's ambition to finish last detective novel:* Ibid.

p. 120   *Review of* The Glass Key: Dorothy Parker, "Reading and Writing," *New Yorker,* 25 April 1931, p. 91.

p. 120   *Dorothy Parker writes fan letter to DH:* Dorothy Parker to DH, n.d. (From the personal collection of Joseph T. Shaw.)

p. 121   *Dorothy Parker meeting DH:* Hellman, *An Unfinished Woman,* p. 212.

p. 121   *DH and Faulkner drunk at the Knopfs':* Joseph Blotner, *Faulkner: A Biography* (New York: Random House, 1974), pp. 740–43.

12 THIN MAN IN A BLIND CORNER

p. 124   *Epigraph:* A Question of Quality, ed. Louis Filler (Bowling Green, Ohio: Bowling Green University Popular Press, 1976), p. 114.

p. 124   *Criticism of Spade short stories:* Wolfe, *Beams Falling,* p. 66.

p. 124   *Editorial explaining DH's absence from* Black Mask: Shaw, *Black Mask,* February 1932.

p. 125   *Description of DH's appearance:* Sanderson interview, *Bookman,* p. 516.

p. 126   *Plans to go to Europe and write a straight novel:* Ibid., p. 518.

p. 126   *Hayward, MacArthur, and Hecht at Turkey Hill:* Ben Hecht devoted a chapter to "Turkey Hill" in his biography of Charles MacArthur, *Charlie* (New York: Harper, 1957), pp. 174–81.

p. 127   *DH and MacArthur drinking:* Ibid., pp. 180–81.

p. 127   *DH's attitude toward money:* W.F.N. interview with W. T. Ballard, 1970.

p. 128   *Drinking with Thurber:* Burton Bernstein, *Thurber: A Biography* (New York: Ballantine, reprint ed., 1976), p. 291.

p. 129   *Nora and Nick:* All quotes from this novel are taken from the DH first edition, *The Thin Man* (New York: Knopf, 1934).

p. 130   *Hellman's German spy story:* Moody, *Lillian Hellman Playwright,* pp. 4–5.

p. 130   *Nick and Nora's repartee:* "A Still Unfinished Woman," *Rolling Stone,* 24 February 1977. (Interview with Hellman by Christine Doudna.)

p. 130   *Famous tenants at the Sutton Club Hotel:* Jay Martin, *Nathanael West: The Art of His Life* (New York: Farrar, Straus and Giroux, 1970), p. 159.

p. 131   *DH and Hellman move to West's hotel:* Ibid., p. 159.

p. 131   *Their life at the hotel:* Moody, *Lillian Hellman Playwright*, p. 31.

p. 131   *DH working in hotel room:* Hellman, *The Big Knockover*, p. xvii.

p. 131   *Hellman and West steaming open envelopes:* Martin, *Nathanael West: The Art of His Life*, p. 166.

p. 132   *Hellman on relationship between Nick and Nora:* Hellman, *The Big Knockover*, p. xvi.

p. 133   *Charles is the first Hammett character . . . :* Hugh Eames, *Sleuths, Inc.*, p. 130.

p. 133   *Moral vision of* The Thin Man: Thompson, "Part VI—The Thin Man," *The Armchair Detective*, November 1974, p. 34.

13   FROM SEX TO SECRET AGENTS

p. 134   *DH and Hellman in Florida:* Hellman, *The Big Knockover*, p. xviii.

p. 135   *Hunting in the woods:* Interview with Hellman, *Paris Review*, Winter–Spring 1965, p. 80.

p. 135   *DH on films:* W.F.N. interview with MGM writer, December 1981. (The writer, friend to both Hammett and Hellman in the Hollywood years, asked not to be identified.)

p. 135   *Dick Tracy's debut:* Ron Goulart, *The Adventurous Decade: Comic Strips in the Thirties* (New Rochelle, N.Y.: Arlington House, 1975), p. 73.

p. 136   *DH working for King Features:* "An Exclusive, Candid Interview with Will Gould," *Graphic Story Magazine*, No. 11 [1970], p. 27. (Gould interview by editor William Spicer.)

p. 136   *Characters in* Secret Agent X-9 *borrowed by DH from own novels:* W.F.N. interview with Ron Goulart, April 1969.

p. 137   *X-9 uses methods of criminals:* Maurice C. Horn, *A History of the Comic Strip* (New York: Crown, 1968), p. 61.

p. 138   *DH's drinking a hobby:* Harrington interview, *New York Evening Journal*, 1934.

p. 139   *Sexual question cut for slick-paper publication:* Edwin Balmer, "Our Literary Nudism," *Esquire*, September 1934.

p. 139   *Possible British reaction to* The Thin Man: Peter Quennell, "Books," *New Statesman and Nation*, 26 May 1934, p. 78.

p. 140   *Unbusinesslike atmosphere:* Gould interview, *Graphic Story Magazine*, p. 29.

p. 140   *DH drunk with slurred speech:* Ibid.

p. 140   *DH encouraging Gould to go to Hollywood:* Ibid., p. 31.

p. 140   *DH unwilling to be wet nurse:* Ibid.

p. 141   *Deterioration of strip:* Bill Blackbeard, "Begins Next Monday!" *City*, 4 November 1975, p. 22.

p. 141   *Choosing the cast for* The Thin Man: Tuska, *The Detective in Hollywood*, pp. 194–95.

p. 142   *Van Dyke's timesaving methods:* Ibid.

p. 142   Plot of *"This Little Pig"*: "This Little Pig," *Collier's,* 24 March 1934, p. 68. (This short story, Hammett's last, has never been collected or anthologized.)

14   LIFE IN THE DREAM FACTORY

p. 144   *Epigraph:* Robert Coughlan, *The Private World of William Faulkner* (New York: Avon, reprint ed., 1954), p. 93.

p. 144   *Lillian Hellman aided by DH:* Lillian Hellman, introduction, *Four Plays* (New York: Random House, 1942).

p. 146   *DH on* After the Thin Man: DH to Hellman, n.d. [October 1934], HRC.

p. 146   *Shall Asta die?:* "Author of Thrillers Is Sorry He Killed His Book Character," *San Francisco Call-Bulletin,* 3 November 1934.

p. 147   *DH's surprise at impact of* The Thin Man: DH to Hellman, *Lillian Hellman Playwright,* p. 36. (Letter dated 5 November 1934.)

p. 148   *Ice-cream parlor story:* Hellman, *Pentimento* (New York: New American Library, reprint ed., 1974), pp. 131–33. (The first edition of this book was issued by Little, Brown in 1973.)

p. 149   *DH drinking at Musso & Frank's:* W.F.N. interview with MGM writer, 1981.

p. 149   *DH's way with kids and sick people:* W.F.N. interview with Howard Benedict, October 1977.

p. 150   *Lillian Hellman's introduction to political activism:* Moody, *Lillian Hellman Playwright,* p. 62.

p. 151   *DH's reaction to Hellman's Uncle Willy:* Lillian Hellman, *Pentimento* (N.A.L. ed.), pp. 78–79.

p. 152   *Stein's high opinion of DH:* Lawrence D. Stewart, "Gertrude Stein and the Vital Dead," *The Mystery & Detection Annual,* 1972, pp. 102–23.

p. 152   *DH as film executive:* W.F.N. interview with MGM writer, 1981.

p. 153   *DH quarrels with West:* Martin, *Nathanael West: The Art of His Life,* p. 268.

15   OF POLITICS AND POTBOILING

p. 155   *Epigraph:* Quoted in ". . . Hammett Flees Night Club Round Succumbing to Rustication in New Jersey," *Daily Princetonian,* 11 November 1936, p. 1. (Interview with DH.)

p. 155   *Chandler's impression of DH:* Raymond Chandler to Charles W. Morton (dated 13 October 1945), *Raymond Chandler Speaking,* ed. Dorothy Gardiner and Kathrine S. Walker (Boston: Houghton Mifflin, 1962), p. 50.

p. 157   *Plot of novel which has not survived: Daily Princetonian,* pp. 1, 7.

p. 158   *DH on Malraux:* DH to Hellman, *The Armchair Detective,* October 1976, p. 294. (Letter dated 13 March 1937.)

p. 159   *Evening with Fitzgerald:* Hellman, *An Unfinished Woman,* pp. 67–69.

p. 160   *DH linked to Hemingway in emotional background:* Walter Blair, "Dashiell Hammett, Themes and Techniques," *Essays on American Literature in Honor of Jay B. Hubbell,* ed. Clarence Gohdes (Durham, N.C.: Duke University Press, 1967), p. 300.

p. 160   *DH's dialogue compared to Hemingway's:* Gide, *New Republic,* p. 186.

p. 160   *Hemingway has* The Dain Curse *read to him:* Ernest Hemingway, *Death in the Afternoon* (New York: Scribners, 1932), p. 228.

p. 160   *Books in Hemingway's library:* See *Hemingway's Reading, 1910–1940,* by Michael S. Reynolds (Princeton, N.J.: Princeton University Press, 1981), p. 134. See also *Hemingway's Library—A Composite Record* by James D. Brasch and Joseph Sigman (New York: Garland, 1981), p. 163. (Hemingway also owned five volumes by Raymond Chandler.)

p. 161   *Stout's review of* The Glass Key: John McAleer, *Rex Stout: A Biography* (New York: Little, Brown, 1977).

p. 161   *Hellman's projected trip to Russia:* Hellman, *An Unfinished Woman,* p. 73.

p. 161   *DH's barber:* W.F.N. interview with David Fechheimer, October 1977.

p. 162   *DH turns down producer: Raymond Chandler Speaking,* p. 50. (RC letter to Charles W. Morton, dated 13 October 1945.)

p. 162   *Hellman's trip to Moscow a waste of time:* DH to Hellman, *An Unfinished Woman,* p. 75.

p. 162   *Bitterness over Nick and Nora Charles:* DH to Hellman, *Lillian Hellman Playwright,* p. 77. (Letter dated 26 December 1937.)

16   A STAGE OF FOXES

p. 164   *Epigraph:* Moody, *Lillian Hellman Playwright,* p. 110.

p. 164   *Phone call to Alfred Knopf:* Bennett Cerf, *At Random* (New York: Random House, 1977), p. 206.

p. 167   *DH's honesty:* Hellman, *Pentimento* (N.A.L. edition), p. 142.

p. 168   *Evening with Hemingway:* Hellman, *An Unfinished Woman,* pp. 69–72.

p. 169   *Contract on 21 Club menu:* Lyons, "Tales About Hammett Told," 1961.

p. 169   *Cocaine not habit-forming:* Lillian Hellman, "The Time of the Foxes," *New York Times,* 22 October 1967.

p. 171   *Hammett's expensive greeting:* Peter Noble, *The Fabulous Orson Welles* (London: Hutchinson, 1956).

p. 171   *Money raised for DH's bail:* Jack Kofoed, "Days of Hammett and Hellman Were Good Old Days Indeed," *Miami Herald,* 23 May 1978.

p. 172   *DH spending self and money recklessly: The Letters of Nunnally Johnson,* ed. Dorris Johnson and Ellen Leventhal (New York: Knopf, 1981), p. 188. (Johnson to Julian Symons, dated 16 January 1961.)

p. 173   *DH's detachment from "Thin Man" films:* In *Shadow Man* (p. 176), Richard Layman claims that "On December 7, 1938, Hammett submitted an eight-page draft of the story for a fourth "Thin Man" movie. . . ." I have a Xerox copy of this eight-page manuscript (from MGM) bearing the notation: "From: Mr. Stromberg. Jan. 8th, 1935" on the title page. Inside, on the first typed page, is the notation: "Copied in Metro Goldwyn Mayer Script Dept. 12/7/38." Obviously, this second *copy* date accounts for the Layman error. Further, both the title page and inside typed page carry the same stamped studio property number, 2193, as well as the same title, "After the Thin Man." Hammett did no work whatever on a fourth "Thin Man" film, or on any of the others in this series beyond *Another Thin Man.*

17   FROM FASCISM TO FALCONS

p. 174   *Epigraph:* Fitzgerald to Gerald Murphy (dated 14 September 1940), *The Letters of F. Scott Fitzgerald,* ed. Andrew Turnbull (New York: Scribners, 1963), pp. 429–30.

p. 175   *The turtle story:* Hellman, *Pentimento* (N.A.L. edition), pp. 223–33.

p. 177   *DH's generosity to writers:* Quoted from two Hellman sources: "A Still Unfinished Woman," *Rolling Stone;* and Hellman's introduction, *Four Plays,* 1942.

p. 177   *DH on violation of election rights:* "Committee on Election Rights," *New Republic,* 21 October 1940, p. 560. (DH letter.)

p. 177   *FBI break into Hellman's house:* Layman, *Shadow Man,* p. 181.

p. 177   *Sincerity of DH's political views:* W.F.N. interview with MGM writer, 1981.

p. 179   *Third filming of* The Maltese Falcon: Allen Rivkin, *Hello, Hollywood!* by Allen Rivkin and Laura Kerr (New York: Doubleday, 1962), pp. 155–56.

p. 179   *DH's terse style:* Allen Eyles, "Great Films of the Century: The Maltese Falcon," *Films and Filming* (London), November 1964, p. 49.

p. 180   *Raft turns down Spade role in* The Maltese Falcon: Tuska, *The Detective in Hollywood,* p. 176.

p. 181   *DH's growing reputation:* Howard Haycraft, *Murder for Pleasure: The Life and Times of the Detective Story* (New York: Appleton-Century, 1941).

p. 182   *DH's by-line on radio scenario:* "The Thin Man and the Flack," *Click,* December 1941, pp. 30–32. (If, indeed, this writing is Hammett's, it is the last new detective story printed during his lifetime.)

18   TO THE END OF THE WORLD

p. 183   *Epigraph: The Battle of the Aleutians,* by Cpl. Dashiell Hammett and Cpl. Robert Colodny (Adak, Alaska: Western Defense Command, 1944), p. 14. (Colodny photo caption.)

p. 184   *DH enlists:* William F. Nolan, *Dashiell Hammett: A Casebook* (Santa Barbara, Calif.: McNally & Loftin, 1969), p. 107.

p. 184   *DH's fight against Fascism:* Al Weisman, "The Thin Man Returns from the Wars," *In Short,* May 1946, p. 52. (Reprinted from *Yank.*)

p. 184   *DH's job in the army:* Moody, *Lillian Hellman Playwright,* p. 138. (DH to LH, letter dated 14 December 1942.)

p. 186   *DH's description of the Aleutian Islands: The Battle of the Aleutians,* p. 7.

p. 187   *DH fooling with training programs:* DH letter, 1 January 1944, HRC.

p. 188   *DH breaks racial barriers:* Layman, *Shadow Man,* p. 191.

p. 188   *DH sets up newspaper:* E. E. Spitzer, "With Corporal Hammett on Adak," *The Nation,* 5 January 1974, p. 8.

p. 188   *DH's cartoon caption:* Bernard Kalb, "Remembering the Dashiell Hammett of 'Julia,'" *New York Times,* 25 September 1977, p. 16.

p. 188   *DH likes Aleutian landscape:* Spitzer, *Nation,* p. 7.

p. 189   *DH on not having a woman around:* From unnamed soldier to Hellman, *The Big Knockover,* p. xix.

p. 189   *DH helping younger soldiers:* Ibid.

p. 190   *Kalb's impression of DH:* Kalb, *New York Times,* p. 15.

p. 190   *DH gets letter from brother:* DH to "Maggie" (Arthur Kober's second wife, Margaret Kober), 5 March 1944, HRC.

p. 190   *DH's fiftieth birthday:* Kalb, *New York Times,* p. 16.

p. 190   *DH starts drinking again:* Spitzer, *Nation,* p. 8.

p. 191   *DH's extrovert behavior when drunk:* Ibid., p. 9.

p. 191   *DH gives away bar:* W.F.N. interview with Norris, 1969.

p. 191   *DH back on the wagon:* Spitzer, *Nation,* p. 9.

19   THE THIN MAN COMES HOME

p. 192   *DH on his promotion:* DH to "Maggie," 30 September 1944, HRC.

p. 193   *DH estimates flying mileage:* DH to "Maggie," 17 December 1944, HRC.

p. 193   *Chandler on DH:* Raymond Chandler, "The Simple Art of Murder," *Atlantic Monthly,* December 1944, p. 58.

p. 194   *DH fumbles with ideas for new novel:* Quoted from two Hammett letters to Hellman, 4 March 1945 and 20 March 1945, HRC.

p. 194   *DH reading Lenin on Marxism: The Armchair Detective,* October 1976, p. 294. (DH to LH, letter dated 18 March 1945.)

p. 194   *DH on need for self-expression:* Introduction (dated 2 April 1945), *Windblown and Dripping: A Book of Aleutian Cartoons* by B. Anastasia, O. Pedigo, and Don L. Miller (privately printed, 1945), p. 3.

p. 194   *DH applies for discharge:* Weisman, *In Short,* p. 52.

p. 195   *DH's medals:* Layman, *Shadow Man,* p. 199.

p. 195   *DH inscribes The Maltese Falcon:* Inscription dated 9 May 1946 in New York. (This copy is at HRC.)

p. 195   *Gardner on Cody:* "Cap Shaw and His 'Great and Regular Fellows,' " by E. R. Hagemann, *Clues,* Fall–Winter 1981, p. 148. (Gardner to Shaw, letter dated 25 January 1946.)

p. 196   *DH creates character for radio program:* John Dunning, *Tune in Yesterday: The Ultimate Encyclopedia of Old-Time Radio* (Englewood Cliffs, N.J.: Prentice-Hall, 1976), pp. 195–96.

p. 197   *Series played for comedy:* Jim Harmon, *The Great Radio Heroes* (New York: Doubleday, 1967), pp. 153–54.

p. 197   *Civil Rights Congress lacks names:* Spitzer, *Nation,* p. 9.

p. 198   *DH and psychoanalysis:* "A Still Unfinished Woman," *Rolling Stone,* p. 55.

p. 198   *DH caught in conflict on violence:* See Tim Hunter, "The Making of 'Hammett'," *New West,* 22 September 1980, p. 46.

p. 199   *Hellman's father's senility:* Moody, *Lillian Hellman Playwright,* p. 179.

p. 199   *DH studying flora and fauna:* DH letter dated 10 September 1946, HRC.

p. 199   *DH as instructor in mystery writing:* Catalogue of the Jefferson School of Social Science, Winter 1965, p. 4.

p. 199   *Student's memory of DH:* W.F.N. interview with Jack Matcha, May 1968.

p. 200   *Soldier from Aleutians on DH's postwar persona:* Spitzer, *Nation,* p. 9.

20   "I JUST CAN'T DO IT ANYMORE"

p. 201   *Epigraph:* "Dashiell Hammett Has Hard Words for Tough Stuff He Used to Write," *Los Angeles Times,* 7 June 1950. (Interview with DH.)

p. 201   *DH's relationship with Hellman:* W.F.N. interview with MGM writer, 1981.

p. 201   *DH puts cigarette in cheek:* Hellman, *An Unfinished Woman,* p. 192.

p. 202   *DH as playwright:* The typed draft and file cards are with Hammett's manuscripts at HRC.

p. 202   *Rose becomes housekeeper to DH:* Layman interview with Rose Evans 22 October 1980. See *Shadow Man* for a full account of the relationship, pp. 205–35.

p. 204   *DH buys father artificial leg:* Based on information supplied to Richard Layman by Fred T. Newbraugh in January 1979.

p. 204   *DH a Marxist:* Layman interview with Mrs. Richard T. Hammett, 1979.

p. 206   *DH gives word to stop drinking:* Hellman, *The Big Knockover,* p. x.

p. 206   *Analysis of DH's politics:* This essay was collected in *Scene Before You,* ed. Chandler Brossard (New York: Rinehart, 1955).

p. 207   *How DH formulated opinions:* Hellman, *The Big Knockover,* p. xii.

p. 207   *DH using irony:* Garry Wills, introduction, *Scoundrel Time,* p. 32.

p. 208   *Muriel Alexander's duties:* Layman, *Shadow Man,* p. 216.

p. 210   *DH's sleepless nights:* DH to Hellman, 8 February 1950, HRC.

p. 210   *DH on drunks who stop drinking (and conversation with Kober):* W.F.N. interview with Betty Buchanan, 1981. (This incident was recorded in her unpublished memoir, "An Evening with Dashiell Hammett.")

p. 211   *Possible Hitchcock picture:* DH to Hellman, 14 February 1950, HRC.

p. 212   *Last film assignment:* Tuska, *The Detective in Hollywood,* p. 364.

p. 212   *DH interviewed in Los Angeles:* Los Angeles Times, 7 June 1950.

21   THE PRICE OF PERSONAL DEMOCRACY

p. 214   *Epigraph:* Oscar Handlin, *Atlantic Monthly,* July 1966, p. 137. (Review of *The Big Knockover.*)

p. 214   *DH linked to Communist front organizations:* For full details of this FBI report, see Layman, *Shadow Man,* pp. 206–12.

p. 215   *DH's unfavorable reaction to* The Autumn Garden: Hellman, *The Big Knockover,* p. xiv.

p. 215   *Hellman spits at DH:* Hellman, *An Unfinished Woman,* p. 197.

p. 216   *DH praises play:* Hellman, *The Big Knockover,* pp. xiv–xv.

p. 217   *Ben Griggs's speech:* "Lillian Hellman: An Interview" by John Phillips and Anne Hollander, *Paris Review,* Winter–Spring 1965, p. 82. (Hellman declared, pp. 81–82, "Dash wrote that speech. I worked on it over and over again, but it never came right. . . . the basic idea was his.")

p. 217   *Review of* The Autumn Garden: Moody, *Lillian Hellman Playwright,* pp. 208, 213.

p. 217   *DH's last visit to Los Angeles:* Hammett wrote three letters to Margaret Kober regarding this visit in April and May of 1951. (The letters are at HRC.)

p. 218   *DH testifying:* Hellman, *The Big Knockover,* p. xi.

p. 219   *DH questioned before Judge Ryan:* For Hammett's full testimony before Judge Ryan, see Layman, *Shadow Man,* pp. 248–62.

p. 220   *Table tennis in jail:* Hellman, *Scoundrel Time,* pp. 90–91.

p. 222   *DH using humor as defense:* Hellman, *The Big Knockover,* p. xii.

p. 222   *Hounds at DH's heels:* W.F.N. interview with Norris, 1969.

22   McCARTHYISM AND THE LOSS OF HARDSCRABBLE

p. 223   *Epigraph:* W.F.N. interview with MGM writer, 1981.

p. 224   *Planning a future:* Hellman, *Scoundrel Time,* p. 62.

p. 224   *Loss of Hardscrabble Farm:* Ibid., pp. 118–19.

p. 225   *DH starts new book, moves to Katonah:* Layman, *Shadow Man,* p. 233.

p. 226   *No money: IRS freezes income:* In *Scoundrel Time,* Hellman writes about the money problems that beset them after she was blacklisted as a screenwriter in Hollywood. She had been earning $140,000 a year; she dropped to $10,000. She speaks of Hammett (p. 134) "living on far too little, never buying anything for himself."

p. 226 *Conversation in Fifty-Second Street:* Hellman, *An Unfinished Woman,* p. 120.

p. 226 *McCarthy hearings:* For Hammett's full testimony before this committee, see Layman, *Shadow Man,* pp. 225–32.

23 OFF THE EDGE

p. 229 *Epigraph:* Donald Phelps, "Dashiell Hammett's Microcosmos," *National Review,* 20 September 1966.

p. 230 *DH's painting:* Hellman, *The Big Knockover,* p. xviii.

p. 230 *DH's testimony:* Layman, *Shadow Man,* p. 233.

p. 231 *Colored bubbles:* "Tulip," in *The Big Knockover,* p. 274.

p. 232 *DH in cottage at Katonah:* Hellman, *The Big Knockover,* p. xxiii.

p. 233 *DH ruined by The Glass Key:* James Cooper, "Lean Years for the Thin Man," *Washington Daily News,* 3 November 1957.

p. 233 *Interview with FBI:* Layman, *Shadow Man,* p. 234, and W.F.N. interview with Fechheimer, 1977.

p. 234 *DH going to hospital:* Hellman, *The Big Knockover,* p. xx.

p. 234 *DH's idea for play:* Hellman, *Pentimento* (N.A.L. edition), p. 170.

p. 235 *DH's last trip out of New York and his apparently improved health:* Ibid.

p. 236 *DH's worsening health and his refusal to talk about it:* Hellman, *The Big Knockover,* p. viii.

p. 236 *DH acting oddly:* Moody, *Lillian Hellman Playwright,* p. 309.

p. 237 *Hellman's eulogy:* "Lillian Hellman Gives Eulogy at Hammett Funeral," *New York Herald Tribune,* 13 January 1961, p. 20.

p. 237 *DH's burial:* For full details on Hammett's will, see Layman, *Shadow Man,* pp. 237–38. Layman states (p. 237): "He divided his estate into four parts: one part to go to his daughter Mary, two parts to his daughter Josephine, and one part to . . . Lillian Hellman." Shortly after Hammett's death, Hellman gained control of all Hammett copyrights and, as Layman further states (p. 238), "his family was left no legal claim to his works."

THE BOOKS OF DASHIELL HAMMETT:
A BASIC CHECKLIST

The one enduring myth about the career of Dashiell Hammett is that after completing his last book, *The Thin Man,* in the spring of 1933, he turned his back on novels and chose to remain "creatively silent" for the remainder of his life. Critics constantly ask the question: Why did Hammett give up creative writing? Even close friends such as Nunnally Johnson declared that "he had no impulse to tell any more stories, no ambition to accomplish more as a writer."

This is not true. After *The Thin Man,* Hammett tried (at intervals for more than twenty years) to finish another novel, progressing through at least a half-dozen aborted attempts: "There Was a Young Man" (1938), "My Brother Felix" (1939), "The Valley Sheep Are Fatter" (1944–1946), "The Hunting Boy" (1949–50), "December 1" (1950), and, finally, "Tulip" (1952–1954).

It was only during the last few years of his life, when he was racked by illness and fighting for breath, that he ceased trying.

Red Harvest (novel). New York: Knopf, 1929
The Dain Curse (novel). Knopf, 1929
The Maltese Falcon (novel). Knopf, 1930
The Glass Key (novel). Knopf, 1931
The Thin Man (novel). Knopf, 1934
Blood Money (novel). Cleveland and New York: World, 1943
The Adventures of Sam Spade (collection). World, 1945
#*The Continental Op* (collection). New York: Spivak, 1945
#*The Return of the Continental Op* (collection). Spivak, 1945

All U.S. hardcover first editions are listed. The symbol # indicates issued *only* in paperback. For full data, see Richard Layman's *Dashiell Hammett: A Descriptive Bibliography* (University of Pittsburgh Press, 1979).

#*Hammett Homicides* (collection). Spivak, 1946
#*Dead Yellow Women* (collection). Spivak, 1947
#*Nightmare Town* (collection). Spivak, 1948
#*The Creeping Siamese* (collection). Spivak, 1950
#*Woman in the Dark* (collection). Spivak, 1951
#*A Man Named Thin* (collection). New York: Ferman, 1962
The Big Knockover (collection). New York: Random House, 1966.
    (Contains the unfinished novel "Tulip.")
The Continental Op (collection). Random House, 1974. (Not to be
    confused with the 1945 paperback collection of the same title.)

Creeps By Night (anthology, edited by DH). New York: Day, 1931
The Novels of Dashiell Hammett (reprints first five novels). Knopf, 1965
#*Secret Agent X-9* (collection of the DH/Alex Raymond newspaper
    comic strips). New York: Nostalgia Press, 1976. (Includes three of
    the four X-9 stories written by DH.)

Regarding Hammett's popularity abroad, Richard Layman reported: "His novels and short stories were published in sixty-eight
separate translations, in various languages, between 1948 and 1961.
Between 1961 and 1975, one hundred and fifteen additional translations were published."

Hammett completed more than one hundred pieces of fiction, of
which eighty-one have been printed. Only two of these appeared as
complete novels (*The Maltese Falcon* and *The Thin Man*).
    Of his seventy-nine shorter pieces, fourteen (in revised form)
were incorporated into his other four novels. Fifty-four have been
reprinted in various Hammett collections. Eleven remain uncollected.
    In addition, another thirteen completed stories (unsold and un-
printed) exist in manuscript as part of the Hammett Papers (Lillian
Hellman Collection) at the University of Texas. These, along with
manuscripts in private collections, bring the total of completed
fiction pieces past one hundred.

A BIBLIOGRAPHY OF HAMMETT SOURCE MATERIAL

I have drawn upon a number of books and magazines for information on Dashiell Hammett. For an extensive listing of book, magazine, and newspaper items relating to Hammett (through 1967), I refer the reader to my *Dashiell Hammett: A Casebook* (Santa Barbara, Calif.: McNally & Loftin, 1969). I updated these listings in two pieces written for *The Armchair Detective:* "The Dashiell Hammett Checklist Revisited" (August 1973) and "Revisiting the Revisited Hammett Checklist" (October 1976).

Richard Layman compiled a full listing of Hammett's work, including nonfiction, in *Dashiell Hammett: A Descriptive Bibliography* (University of Pittsburgh Press, 1979), and Layman's biography, *Shadow Man: The Life of Dashiell Hammett* (New York: Harcourt Brace Jovanovich, 1981), reflects superb scholarship and research. Peter Wolfe has written a concise critical study of the novels and shorter fiction in *Beams Falling: The Art of Dashiell Hammett* (Bowling Green, Ohio: Bowling Green University Popular Press, 1980). These three books are essential and highly recommended.

I also recommend the following:

Adams, Donald K. (editor). *Mystery & Detection Annual.* Beverly Hills, Calif: Adams, 1972.

Alvarez, A. *Beyond All This Fiddle.* New York: Random House, 1969.

Bazelon, David T. (contributor). "Dashiell Hammett's Private Eye," *Scene Before You,* edited by C. Brossard. New York: Rinehart, 1955.

Blair, Walter (contributor). "Dashiell Hammett: Themes and Techniques," *Essays on American Literature in Honor of Jay B. Hubbell,* edited by C. Gohdes. Durham, N.C.: Duke University Press, 1967.

Cawelti, John G. *Adventure, Mystery and Romance.* Chicago: University of Chicago Press, 1976.

City of San Francisco (a magazine), November 4, 1975. Edited by David Fechheimer. (Special DH issue. Contains the only printing of the original 1930 unfinished version of *The Thin Man.*)

Eames, Hugh. *Sleuths, Inc.* Philadelphia and New York: J. B. Lippincott, 1978.

Falk, Doris V. *Lillian Hellman.* New York: Frederick Ungar, 1978.

Gores, Joe. *Hammett* (a novel). New York: G. P. Putnam, 1975.

Grella, George (contributor). "The Wings of the Falcon and the Maltese Dove," *A Question of Quality,* edited by L. Filler. Bowling Green, Ohio: Bowling Green University Popular Press, 1976.

Hagemann, E. R. *A Comprehensive Index to Black Mask, 1920–1951.* Bowling Green, Ohio: Bowling Green University Popular Press, 1982.

Haycraft, Howard. *Murder for Pleasure.* New York: Appleton-Century, 1941.

Hellman, Lillian (editor). *The Big Knockover.* New York: Random House, 1966.

———. *An Unfinished Woman.* Boston: Little, Brown, 1969.

———. *Pentimento.* Boston: Little, Brown, 1973.

———. *Scoundrel Time.* Boston: Little, Brown, 1976.

Herron, Don. *Dashiell Hammett Tour.* San Francisco: Dawn Heron Press, 1982. (Contains photos and full descriptions of all DH San Francisco locations from his life and fiction.)

Hirsch, Foster. *The Dark Side of the Screen: Film Noir.* Cranbury, N.J.: A. S. Barnes, 1981.

Macdonald, Ross (Kenneth Millar). *Self-Portrait: Ceaselessly into the Past.* Santa Barbara, Calif.: Capra Press, 1981.

Madden, David (editor). *Tough Guy Writers of the Thirties.* Carbondale, Ill.: Southern Illinois University Press, 1968.

Marcus, Steven (editor). *The Continental Op* by DH. New York: Random House, 1974.

Margolies, Edward. *Which Way Did He Go?* New York: Holmes & Meier, 1982.

Moody, Richard. *Lillian Hellman Playwright.* New York: Pegasus, 1972.

Reilly, John M. (editor). *Twentieth-Century Crime and Mystery Writers.* New York: St. Martin's Press, 1980.

Ruehlmann, William. *Saint with a Gun.* New York: New York University Press, 1974.

Ruhm, Herbert (editor). *The Hard-Boiled Detective.* New York: Vintage, 1977. (Contains the only book printing of DH's first *Black Mask* story, "The Road Home," from the December 1922 issue.)

Shaw, Joseph T. (editor). *The Hard-Boiled Omnibus.* New York: Simon and Schuster, 1946.

Steinbrunner, Chris, and Otto Penzler (editors). *Encyclopedia of Mystery and Detection.* New York: McGraw-Hill, 1976.

Symons, Julian (contributor). "Dashiell Hammett: The Onlie Begetter," *Crime Writers* (England), edited by H. R. F. Keating. London: British Broadcasting Corporation, 1978.

Thompson, George J. "The Problem of Moral Vision in Dashiell Hammett's Detective Novels" (a seven-part thesis). *The Armchair Detective* (a magazine), May, August, November 1973; May, August, November 1974; February 1975.

Tuska, Jon. *The Detective in Hollywood.* New York: Doubleday, 1978.

ACKNOWLEDGMENTS

During my fifteen years of research for this book, I have drawn on the knowledge of many. My thanks are due each of these Hammett researchers and writers with whom I have been in contact:

Howard Benedict—for sharing memories of his long association with DH in Hollywood.

William Blackbeard—for data on the DH newspaper strip, *Secret Agent X-9.*

Betty Buchanan—for her generosity in allowing me to quote material from her unpublished memoir, "An Evening with Dashiell Hammett."

Hugh Eames—for his excellent research into Pinkerton's.

David Fechheimer—for sharing his carefully gathered research relating to DH's childhood in Maryland.

William Godshalk—for generously providing me with copies of his extensive notes on the Hammett Papers at the University of Texas.

Joe Gores—for insights into DH's early life.

Ron Goulart—for newspaper and pulp-magazine data on DH.

Will Gould—for recollections of his association with DH at King Features in New York.

Ned Guymon—for permission to copy DH's original *Thin Man* manuscript.

E. R. Hagemann—for biographical data on Raoul Whitfield.

Nils Hardin—for sharing Joseph T. Shaw's valuable *Black Mask* scrapbook.

Don Herron—for specialized data on California crime
fiction.

Al Hubin—for providing me with a variety of information
on DH via the pages of his *Armchair Detective.*

Inna Kaplan—for special research into DH in San Francisco.

Gus and Sydna Konstin—for the establishment of the Maltese Falcon Room at John's Grill in San Francisco, headquarters for the Dashiell Hammett Society.

Richard Layman—for sharing important biographical data,
gained through his own extensive research on DH's life
and career.

Rouben Mamoulian—for his help in recalling the origins
of *City Streets.*

Cliff McCarty—for special research into DH's film work.

Ken Millar (Ross Macdonald)—for critical guidance on my
original *Casebook* manuscript.

Ray Stanich—for research on DH radio dramatizations.

Ruth and Al Windfeldt—for promoting Hammett activities
through their Scene of the Crime Bookshop.

Peter Wolfe—for critical insights into the fiction of DH.

Additionally, I owe thanks to Donald K. Adams, Sanora Babb,
David Bazelon, Christopher Bentley, Joseph Blotner, Herb Caen,
John G. Cawelti, Alistair Cooke, James Cooper, John Dunning,
Doris Falk, Frederic Forrest, William C. Glackin, Mary Jane Ham-
mett, Richard T. Hammett, Phil Haultain, Lillian Hellman, Tim
Hunter, John Huston, Bernard Kalb, Jack Kofoed, David Madden,
Steven Marcus, Jack Matcha, William J. McNally, Richard Moody,
Dennis O'Flaherty, Robert B. Parker, Otto Penzler, Allen Rivkin,
William Ruehlmann, Herbert Ruhm, E. E. Spitzer, John Stanley,
Chris Steinbrunner, Julian Symons, Kevin Thomas, George J.
Thompson, Jon Tuska, William White, Garry Wills, Fred Wordon—
and to the staff members of the research library UCLA Special
Collections in Los Angeles; New York Public Library; Occidental
College; Library of Congress; Popular Publications; San Francisco
Chronicle; Pinkerton's Inc.; and the library of the Academy of Motion
Picture Arts and Sciences. I also wish to express sincere thanks to
my editor at Congdon & Weed, Thomas Congdon, and to his help-
ful publishing staff. Their work on this book is much appreciated.

Finally, I wish to honor the memory of others who also helped me in the formation of this book: Anthony Boucher, W. T. Ballard, William J. Clark, Frederic Dannay, Philip Durham, Erle Stanley Gardner, Frank Gruber, Josephine Dolan Hammett, Jack Kaplan, Frederick Nebel, Luther Norris, S. J. Perelman, William Sloane, and Albert B. Samuels.

W.F.N.
Agoura, California

PHOTO CREDITS

CHAPTER 2   *Hammett in the mid-1920s:* Author's collection. *620 Eddy Street; Flood Building; Jose:* Edmund Shea.

CHAPTER 5   *H. L. Mencken and George Jean Nathan:* The Granger Collection.   *20 Monroe Street; 891 Post Street; Samuels Jewelers:* Edmund Shea.   *First Hammett by-line:* Author's collection.

CHAPTER 8   The Cleansing of Poisonville *and* The Maltese Falcon *in* Black Mask: Author's collection.   *John's Grill; Miles Archer plaque:* Edmund Shea.

CHAPTER 9   The Glass Key *in* Black Mask; *manuscript page of* The Thin Man: Author's collection.   *1155 Leavenworth:* Edmund Shea.   *Hammett:* The Granger Collection.

CHAPTER 11   *Hammett:* The Granger Collection.   *James Thurber; Dorothy Parker; William Faulkner; Alfred and Blanche Knopf; Ben Hecht and Charles MacArthur; Hellman:* Culver Pictures.

CHAPTER 17   *William Powell and Myrna Loy:* Culver Pictures. *Still from* The Maltese Falcon: Collection of Otto Penzler. *Hellman:* The Granger Collection.   Black Mask *dinner:* Courtesy the Raymond Chandler Collection, the University of California Library at Los Angeles.

CHAPTER 22   *Hammett and staff on Adak:* Collection of Richard Layman.   *Hammett and Hellman at the 21 Club:* George Karger, LIFE Magazine, © 1973 Time Inc.   *Hammett before Subcommittee:* Hank Walker, LIFE Magazine, © 1976 Time Inc.

INDEX